CHINA AND CHRISTIANITY
HISTORICAL AND FUTURE ENCOUNTERS

CHINA AND CHRISTIANITY

HISTORICAL AND FUTURE ENCOUNTERS

James D. Whitehead
Yu-ming Shaw, N. J. Girardot
Editors

THE CENTER FOR PASTORAL AND SOCIAL MINISTRY
THE UNIVERSITY OF NOTRE DAME

Copyright (c) 1979 by

THE CENTER FOR PASTORAL AND SOCIAL MINISTRY

The University of Notre Dame

27 5.1 W

C 441

820 4 2822

International Standard Book Number: 0-268-00730-6
Library of Congress Catalog Number: LC-79-52165

Distributed by

The University of Notre Dame Press

Notre Dame, Indiana   46556

PRINTED IN THE UNITED STATES OF AMERICA

CONTENTS

THIS VOLUME IS DEDICATED TO
JOSEPH J. SPAE
SCHOLAR, MISSIONARY, CHURCHMAN
AND FRIEND OF CHINA

FOREWORD

In the summer of 1977 a conference was convened at the
University of Notre Dame on "China: The Religious Dimension." This conference, an ecumenical gathering of
theologians, historians, mission experts and social
scientists, belongs to the third stage of the long historical relationship between Christianity and the Chinese
culture.

The first stage was the four hundred years--mid-sixteenth
century to mid-twentieth century--of enthusiastic if confused evangelization. European Catholic missionaries
dominated the early part of this stage until American
Protestant missioners came to China in great numbers in
the nineteenth and early twentieth centuries.

A second, painful stage spanned the two-and-a-half decades
after the expulsion of Christian missionaries with the
triumph of Communism in China. This stage saw a movement
from frustration to anxiety as reflective Western Christians became increasingly aware of the cultural myopia and
arrogance that had infected centuries of missionary efforts.
Self-doubt during this period extended beyond questions of
missionary strategy to include hesitance about the role of
Christianity itself in a radically secularized world.

The two conferences on China and Christianity in Europe in 1974--at Bastad, Sweden in February and at Louvain, Belgium in September--marked the initiation of the third stage of this complex relationship. This stage found Christians in a quite different posture; decidedly chastened by history, Western Christians showed a new interest in learning about China, both its complex and partly hidden contemporary events and its rich religious history. Complementing a desire to have the Good News heard in China was an ambition to attend to the workings of God and man in the new China.

The Notre Dame conference represents the effort of American Catholic scholars to join the ecumenical reflection on the more-than-missionary question of the religious future of China. As an interdisciplinary and ecumenical enterprise, the conference sought to examine China's religious past and confusing present.

The three-day conference (June 29-July 2, 1977) began with Professor Langdon Gilkey's exploration of the possibility of Christianity fashioning a covenant with the Chinese in a manner analogous to Christianity's early covenant with Hellenism and more recent covenant, still unfinished, with the modern West. The first day had an historical focus, addressing "the spiritual roots of the Chinese tradition." Attention turned during the second day to an explicit reflection on Christianity's presence in China. On the final day of the conference the participants formed subgroups to review and isolate unresolved questions. These groups addressed (1) the theological implications of Christianity's encounter with China; (2) the need for more and better information about contemporary China; and (3) next steps to follow up this conference. The results of these final reflections can best be expressed by recalling the two major challenges that surfaced during the conference.

The first of these, not surprisingly, concerned the relationship of the Christian Church to cultures and to the world. This challenge was confronted on the first evening of the conference in Langdon Gilkey's theme of covenant and also recalled Julia Ching's call at the Bastad conference for the development of non-Western forms of Christian theology. The theological task hidden in much of the discussion during the conference was the disengagement of a theology of the Kingdom from a theology of the Church. This is necessarily a slow and painful process for scholars of a universal religion as they seek to understand how God

can be active where the Church apparently is not. Examples
of theological areas needing exploration which arose in the
final session of the conference were the different meanings
of transcendence in a Chinese context; the meanings of
selflessness in Taoism, Buddhism, Christianity and Maoism;
and the Christian theology of revelation and providence.

The second challenge concerned the ideology and exercise of
Maoism in contemporary China. Debate about what is actually
happening in China illustrated the continuing ignorance of
details about life on the Mainland today. Many at the
conference no longer saw demonic forces at work in Maoism,
arguing that the widespread defeat of poverty and sickness
indicated a human liberation that Christianity could
acclaim. This debate about the merits of Maoism will
necessarily continue beyond this and future conferences,
due to lack of data, changing conditions in China, and to
differing theological convictions in the Christian community.

The Chinese participants presented a memo to the conference
in which they shared four central concerns which they saw
arising from the Notre Dame meeting. The importance of
these concerns demands that they be presented at the outset of this volume.

A Memo to the Conference.

    1. As Christians, we consider it of primary impor-
    tance to ascertain our Christian beliefs, distin-
    guishing the essentials from the nonessentials.
    This should come before the making of theological
    reflections on China.

    2. We consider an urgent priority the need of
    thinking out theology in Chinese terms, in the
    context of the whole Chinese experience, past and
    present. This requires an in-depth knowledge of
    the spiritual roots of Chinese culture, as well
    as a continual effort to understand the implica-
    tions of the Chinese revolution.

    3. Many of us note a tendency among some partici-
    pants to project a certain image of China, and use
    it for their own purposes, whether theological,
    social, or otherwise. We urge here the importance
    of making better use of available resoures, to

assure a more informed knowledge of China, and not
be satisfied with "myths."

4. We regard it important to face facts squarely--
to accept the realities of the situation of Christianity in China today (however disappointing that
may be) and to balance the sense of failure with
that of positive contributions made by Christian
efforts. We urge against taking consolation in
projections, such as that of regarding the entire
Chinese society as a secular "kingdom of God"
already realized.

Finally, the dominant posture of the conference is worth
recalling. There was evident neither a naive confidence
in "converting" the Chinese people, nor a defensiveness
about having nothing to say. Instead, a posture of
attentiveness was much in evidence--an attentiveness not
at all passive, but alert and respectful. Not infre-
quently in presentations and discussions the plea was
heard for silence during this period of confusion. By
this was meant not a defeated or passive silence, but one
which allowed an active listening and discerning--a
listening to be directed to our own self-understanding
as Christians, to the rich Chinese religious heritage,
and finally, to the possible workings of the Spirit in
Maoist China. Such attending is a requisite first step
of a longer theological reflection being attempted in
regard to China.

Although it was little discussed at the conference, it
seemed widely recognized that the form of discipline or
asceticism required for such effective listening was
emptiness (whether that be Christian kenosis, Buddhist
k'ung, or Taoist hsü). This would be an emptying of our
missionary agenda and theological presuppositions. In
such self-emptying we might come to hear the word spoken
in history. Out of such disciplined hearing will come
the selfless witness of the Gospel, be it in China or
elsewhere.

ACKNOWLEDGMENTS

The idea of an interdisciplinary, ecumenical conference on
"China: The Religious Dimension," once conceived by Father
Joseph J. Spae and taken up by Professor Norman J. Girardot,
received an enthusiastic response from its sponsors: the
Center for Pastoral and Social Ministry at the University
of Notre Dame; the China Program of the Committee for East
Asia and the Pacific, National Council of the Churches of
Christ in the United States; the Midwest China Study and
Resource Center; and the American Lutheran Church Division
for World Mission and Inter-Church Cooperation.

Special gratitude is extended to Monsignor John Egan of the
Notre Dame Center, Dr. Franklin Woo of the National Council
of Churches, Dr. Donald E. MacInnis of the Midwest Center,
and Father Joseph J. Spae of Pro Mundi Vita, Brussels.

Due to financial limitations, some of the papers and all of
the responses presented at the conference could not be included in the present volume.   Happily, Professor Ellen
Marie Chen's paper on "The Unitive Way--Taoism--Ch'an and
Christianity" has since been published in China Notes
(summer, 1977).   The editors are both grateful and apolo-
getic to the following responders: Edward T. Ch'ien,
Theresa Chu, Donald E. MacInnis, Richard Madsen, Peter

Moody, Richard Sorich, Donald W. Treadgold and Paul A. Varg.

We here acknowledge permission received to publish those papers which, since the conference, have been published elsewhere: Julia Ching's "Confucianism: A Philosophy of Man," published in expanded form as chapter three, "The Problem of Man," in Confucianism and Christianity: A Comparative Study (Tokyo: Kodansha, 1977); Langdon Gilkey's "The Covenant With The Chinese," published in China Notes, volume 15, Number 3 (Summer, 1977), pages 1-6, and in Dialog, Volume 17, Number 3 (Summer, 1978), pages 181-187; Raymond L. Whitehead's "Christ, Salvation and Maoism," published in China Notes, Volume 15, Number 4 (Fall, 1977), pages 1-7. We are also grateful to China Notes and to Professor Charles West for permission to reprint his "Theological Reflection on China--II," which first appeared in China Notes, Volume 15, Number 2 (Spring, 1977), pages 16-18.

The editors are thankful to Mrs. Hildegarde Cox who typed the final manuscript, and are most grateful for the extraordinary assistance and editorial guidance of Ms. Peggy Roach of the Center for Pastoral and Social Ministry, University of Notre Dame.

PART ONE

SPIRITUAL ROOTS
OF THE CHINESE TRADITION

INTRODUCTION

N. J. Girardot

In trying to understand the contemporary China of the 17th century, Gottfried Wilhelm Leibniz knew that it "would be highly foolish and presumptuous" to evaluate Chinese tradition and religion without an historical context of inquiry: "there is in China...an admirable public morality conjoined to a philosophical doctrine, or rather doctrine of natural theology, venerable by its antiquity, established and authorized for about 3000 years.... Furthermore, it is highly unlikely that one could destroy this doctrine without great upheaval."[1]

It may well be argued that the Chinese Communist revolution constitutes just such a "great upheaval" and break with traditional China. Such an evaluation is even strengthened with respect to continuities with the Chinese religious heritage because contemporary China, as avowedly Marxist and atheistic in doctrine, has consciously tried to sever its connections with the "superstitious" and "feudal" past. The significance and validity of this radical evaluation can only be known, however, through the comparative judgements of a historical perspective--a principle that the Chinese communists themselves have recognized in their constant and changing reappraisal of China's cultural legacy. Indeed, the spirit of Chinese tradition teaches us the need for

extreme caution in judging the dialectical cycles of history.
As the Romance of the Three Kingdoms states in its opening
lines: "Empires wax and wane; states cleave asunder and
coalesce."

In other words, there is nothing really ever "new" within
the way or Tao of Chinese history; or, as the Taoists would
have put it, every transmutation in the life of man, society,
state, or universe represents a "return to the root."
Therefore, to evaluate and assess properly the implications
of contemporary China in relation to religion, and with
respect to the encounter with Christianity, it is both an
historiographically necessary, and traditionally attested,
method to examine the intellectual and spiritual "roots" of
China.

Such a rationale goes further, however, in that it was the
express intention of the Notre Dame conference to reassert
some of the pioneering ecumenical attitude of Matteo Ricci
who recognized that any encounter with another cultural and
religious tradition implies an exercise in self-reflection
on the meaning and nature of Western and Christian culture.
Contemporary China, along with the historical traditions of
Chinese humanism and religion, suggests, in the words of
Franklin Woo, one of the sponsors of the conference, that
Christian "theology as we currently have it, is woefully
inadequate." Understanding China, both in its current and
past manifestations, and in relation to the understanding
of other traditional and non-Christian traditions, calls
for a reassessment of our most basic beliefs. Such a reassessment of beliefs should not be simply directed, again
in the words of Dr. Woo, at a new missionary "strategy for
expressing these beliefs more accurately, but rather
towards a deeper self-understanding."

This spirit of a reflective and reflexive self-understanding is in concert with the best sense of Western
intellectual and humanistic study. Moreover, such a
concern demands an ecumenical theology or pluralistic
"theology of religions and cultures" that is grounded in
an interdisciplinary and comparative context of inquiry.[2]
With these general considerations in mind, the following
collection of papers attempts, in a selective and synthetic way, to set out some of the traditional and contemporary issues of religious meaning coloring the Western
and Christian appraisal of China. In this way the papers
are intended as more than just background documents and
should be seen as relevant to any fully balanced evaluation

of modern China. It is obvious that not even a partially
complete treatment of the richly complex history of Chinese
religion is possible. At the very least, however, the
various scholarly perspectives represented here touch
significantly on two important issues--i.e., the comparative meaning and significance of traditional Chinese
religion for both Christianity and Chinese communism and,
secondly, the nature and extent of "religious" elements
in Maoism.

The first of these issues is especially reflected in the
papers of Julia Ching and Laurence Thompson. Professor
Ching's contribution is particularly valuable for its
comparative and dialogical focus on the religious and
philosophical relationship between Chinese and Christian
humanism. In the light of her remarks, it may be worthwhile to observe that, despite the recent vagaries of the
so-called anti-Confucian campaign, Confucian humanism may
not yet be dead and buried in China. Professor Thompson's
paper attempts the difficult task of setting out a general
definition of the nature of the Chinese religious vision;
as such this chapter provides further documentation and
insight into those crucial normative issues of existential
involvement, ultimate meaning, and salvational purpose
brought out by Ching.

Richard Bush's paper, "A Religious Dimension in Chinese
Communist Thought," addresses the second issue of this part
of the book, the "religiousness" of Maoism. While this is
a topic plagued with methodological, theological and philosophical problems, Professor Bush makes a persuasive case
for a "process" type of metaphysics at the heart of Maoism.
As Joseph Needham has so brilliantly shown in his Science
and Civilisation in China,[3] this kind of organismic philosophy represents one of the most traditional and fundamental elements of the Chinese intellectual heritage. The
final chapter, Norman Girardot's "Chinese Religion and
Western Scholarship," analyzes the various misinterpreta-
tions visited on Chinese culture by Western observers over
the past four centuries.

Taken together, these papers demonstrate the need for a continuing discussion of the religious meaning and significance
of contemporary China that is not isolated from comparative,
historical and philosophical considerations. China has been,
and to a large extent, remains a theater for the shifting
shadow-play of the Western imagination. Thus, in the 18th
century we witness the enlightenment vision of a perfect

religionless government of Confucian <u>philosophes</u> and in the
19th century the stentorian missionary condemnation of the
"heathen Chinese." For the modern age, equally affected by
various cultural and political prejudices, there is either
the specter of the yellow peril or the image of Maoist
China as a veritable socialistic paradise on earth. With
such different and contradictory images to contend with, it
is not surprising that China remains an enigma. "China
obscures," as Pascal reminds us, "but there is light to be
found. Look for it."[4]

6

NOTES

1. Gottfried Wilhelm Leibniz, Discourse on the Natural
Theology of the Chinese, trans. by Henry Rosemont, Jr. and
Daniel J. Cook, monograph No. 4 of the Society for Asian and
Comparative Philosophy (University of Hawaii Press, 1977): 59.

2. See, for example, Wolfhart Pannenberg, Theology and
the Philosophy of Science, trans. by F. McDonagh (Philadelphia: Westminster Press, 1976).

3. Joseph Needham, Science and Civilisation in China
(Cambridge: Cambridge University Press, 1956), Vol. 2.

4. Blaise Pascal, Pensées, 397 (159), Oeuvres Complétes,
1960 (quoted by Francois Geoffroy-Dechaume in China Looks
At The World (New York: Pantheon, 1967), p. 9).

I – CONFUCIANISM:
A PHILOSOPHY OF MAN
Julia Ching

What is man, and wherein lies his worth? This question has
been asked probably as long as man has existed--and by himself. For man has always been fascinated with himself, with
his limitations as well as his potentiality for greatness.
And man has also been fascinated with this question about
himself as human being--because it can never be fully
answered.[1]

Both the Old and New Testaments represent the human being
first and foremost as a creature and child of God. His
worth lies in his relationship to God, from whom he has
received everything. Man is, because God is. And Man can
become God-like: Eritis sicut Deus (Gen. 3:5)--but in the
good sense of the words also, since he has always borne in
himself the image and likeness of God (Gen. 1:27, 5:1,
1 John 3:1-3).

Besides, the human being is usually considered by the Scriptures as a "whole person." His "heart" is the seat of
understanding, volition, and emotions. He does not "have"
a soul and a body; he is soul and body, related to God as
Lord of history and partner of a sacred Covenant, and committed also to other men in family, tribal and other

relationships. Such words as <u>soma</u> (body) and <u>pneuma</u> (spirit) are employed, even in St. Paul, usually as signifying each a "part" of man which stands for the <u>whole</u> person (Rom. 12:1, 1 Cor. 6:20, 1 Cor. 2:11, 13:3, 7:4, 7:34), who, in turn, is a living "I," and not a metaphysical principle.

But there are also dualistic overtones in the concept of man, especially in certain passages of St. Paul, where the notion of sin introduces a note of tension in the human being (Rom. 7:15-25, 8:10-13).[2] These passages point to some important differences between the Christian concept of man and the Confucian. For whereas man's propensity for evil as well as for good has never been denied in Confucianism, the dualism that this implies has also been minimized in a tradition preoccupied with man's natural perfectibility.

The Confucian Classics do not deny Man's creatureship or sonship in relation to God. On the contrary, there are several explicit references.[3] But the Confucian Classics make this affirmation, not by appeal to creation myths, but by emphasizing the common human nature which all have received from Heaven. This is inherent in the very term "human nature," the Chinese word <u>hsing</u> (忄生), a compound including the term for mind or heart (<u>hsin</u> 心), and life or offspring (<u>sheng</u> 生). Philological scholarship demonstrates the association between its etymology and early religious worship. Man is he--or she--who has received the gift of life and all the innate endowments of human nature from Heaven.[4]

Man acquires self-knowledge by differentiating himself from other animals, and by identifying himself with other humans. Like all animals, it is "the nature of Man that when he is hungry he will desire satisfaction, when he is cold, he will desire warmth, and when he is weary he will desire rest."[5] These are the words of Hsün-tzu (298-238 B.C.), who adds that man is born <u>evil</u>, but is able to act <u>against</u> his natural inclinations. For, unlike other animals, Man has a unique ability for social and moral behavior: "Fire and water possess energy but are without life. Grass and trees have life but no intelligence. Birds and beasts have intelligence but no sense of duty. Therefore (Man) is the noblest being on earth."[6] To be "human," after all, is to be able to acquire the perfect virtue of benevolence, of "humanness" (<u>jen</u>). As <u>the Doctrine of the Mean</u> puts it, "The meaning of <u>jen</u> (virtue) is humanness."[7]

The Confucian focus on a common human nature has led to another emphasis: the <u>natural equality</u> of all men. For

Christians, this doctrine would flow more directly from mankind's common origin as creatures and children of God. For Confucians, the importance is placed in a common, moral nature, and an ability to discern good from evil, which is rooted in a common mind or heart. Indeed, this natural equality exists in spite of social hierarchy, and even in spite of any distinction between the "civilized"--the Chinese--and the "barbarians."[8] Confucius has said: "Within the Four Seas all men are brothers" (Analects 12:5). And Mencius (371-289 B.C.?) has added, that every human being can become a sage-king (6B:2). If certain Chinese terms for "barbarians" often possess "dog" or "reptile" radicals, suggesting a human contempt for the "subhuman," there never was any doubt that the "barbarian" could become fully human by acculturation. After all, even certain sage-kings are considered to have had "barbarian" origins.[9]

The Problem of Sagehood

The Confucian preoccupation with ideals of sagehood illustrates a certain tendency to emphasize the potentialities in human nature for good rather than for evil.[10] Traditional Confucian thought, going back to Mencius, usually upheld the basic goodness of human nature, explaining evil as a deflection from the good, a perversion of the natural. This was accepted by Matteo Ricci, who declared in his famous Catechism (The True Idea of God) that human nature is essentially good although it is capable of both good and evil, the latter arising on account of the presence of concupiscence.[11] But later catechisms stressed man's evil inclinations--the results of original sin--in such a way that the impression arose that while Mencius taught the essential goodness of man, Christianity asserts the contrary. Moreover, when one examines the writings of Chinese philosophers, one cannot help but be impressed by their general optimism in human nature, and by their concern with achieving moral perfection and sagehood. The Chinese equivalent to the English word holiness is sheng, sageliness. It does not contain a cultic meaning as does the Greek. It occurs in the Book of Documents,[12] in a description of the legendary Shun, an ancient sage-king, wise minister, ruler, and filial son. There, the quality ascribed to him is especially that of the natural (tzŭ-jan). Shun is especially he, whose virtue proceeds from "the natural." Another and more frequent attribute is that of "penetration" (t'ung). According especially to the Han dictionary, Shuo-wen chieh-tzu (ca. A.D. 100),[13] a sage is a man who possesses a penetrating intelligence regarding all affairs. This is echoed in the other Han work, Po-hu-t'ung (ca. A.D. 80) which describes him as "possessing a Way which penetrates everywhere, a brilliance which radiates everywhere," and as one who "is in union with Heaven and Earth in his virtue, with the sun and the moon in his brilliance, with the four seasons in his regularity, and with ghosts and spirits in his (gift) to divining fortunes and misfortunes."[14] The ritual texts confirm this concept of "penetration." Tai the Elder defines the sage as a man "whose wisdom penetrates the great Way, who responds to (endless) changes without becoming exhausted and who perceives the inner essences of the myriad things."[15] To this, the canonical Book of Rites adds the idea of giving life. The sage is thus presented as he "who gives birth to the myriad things."[16]

And what about the great sages themselves? What did Confucius say about sagehood? What did Mencius say after him?

In the Confucian Analects, we find little talk of the attributes of sagehood. We find, indeed, a certain reluctance to discuss this question. Confucius did not consider himself worthy to be called a sage. He was content in being a transmitter of the sagely Way. And this Way belonged to three kinds of sages: kings, ministers or hermits--that is, men who chose retirement for noble reasons, not for escape from social responsibilities. And Confucius referred to himself as their admirer and follower. He was a "student," a man who desired sagehood, and made efforts to achieve it.[17]

Confucius' high regard for sagehood is expressed more by his silence than by his words. His modesty is partly motivated by his high esteem of this state. As he put it, "I do not expect ever to see a sage, and shall be content with seeing a gentleman (chün-tzu). I do not expect ever to see a good man (shan-jen), and shall be content with seeing a persevering man."[18] He therefore leaves the floor open for future debates regarding whether sagehood is a state into which one is born, or whether it is attainable by human effort and learning.

The word sheng (聖) occurs more frequently in the Book of Mencius. Here, sages appear as men who manifest perfectly the virtues which govern human relationships, and Mencius gives, like Confucius before him, such examples as those of

the former kings Yao and Shun, the ancient ministers, the
Duke of Chou and others, and the hermits, Po-yi and Liu-hsia
Hui, who exemplified political loyalty even in retirement.[19]
For Mencius, the sage is a teacher, if not by word, then
certainly by example. But where an ordinary man exerts his
influence through education over a limited circle of persons,
the sage is "a teacher of a hundred generations."[20] He
adds to this a polemical orientation: the sage is a man
who combats false teachings, like those of Yang Chu and
Mo Ti. In this respect, he also declares his own determination: "I also desire to rectify men's hearts, stop per-
verse teachings, oppose one-sided actions and banish
licentious actions."[21] And then, in a passage describing
directly the meaning of sagehood itself, Mencius proposes
it as the common object of men's hearts. For just as "men's
mouths accord in enjoying the same delicacies, men's ears
accord in taking pleasure in the same sounds, and men's
eyes accord in delighting in the same beauty," so too, their
hearts find rest in a common object, that which they all
approve of: the moral principles of human nature, which
the sages, before us, also apprehended."[22]

Where Confucius declined to call himself a sage, later
generations did not share the same scruple. They were
particularly quick in recognizing him as a sage, and even
as the sage par excellence. This is hinted at in the
Doctrine of the Mean, which describes him as a man who
traces himself back to Yao and Shun as his "(spiritual)
ancestors," and who models his life upon those of the Kings
Wen and Wu:

> He harmonizes above with the heavenly seasons, and
> below with (the elements of) water and land. He
> may be compared to Heaven and Earth which contain
> and support...all things, to the four seasons in
> their cyclical progress, and to the sun and moon
> on their alternating task of giving light.[23]

It is the same metaphysical language of the Po-hu-t'ung and
of the Great Appendix of the Book of Changes.

The Confucian doctrine of sagehood, and the agreement of
Mencius and Hsün-tzu regarding man's ability to transcend
himself--whether through an innate gift or through the
malleable influence of education--did not thereby make
sages more abundant. Later scholars purported to see
passages in the Classics susceptible to a different interpretation. Are sages born or made? If they are born, are

they not superhuman? Would they have "emotions?"[24] If they
are made--self-made--why are they so few? Why did they only
exist in the remote or historical antiquity? These questions preoccupied many thinkers, some of whom preferred to
exalt the concept of sagehood into a Neo-Taoist impersonal
ideal, inaccessible to human realization. Such discussions
ran parallel to Buddhist debates regarding the universal
presence and accessibility of Buddhahood.[25] Theories of
"human predestination" generally prevailed in the more
aristocratic ages, in a hierarchically organized society,
as during the Wei-Chin periods (A.D. 220-420), when a
"grade theory" of human nature corresponded with the practice of civil recruitment through a "nine-grade ranking
system" which gave preferment to scions of important families.[26] The Buddhist reaction came especially in the
assertions of Tao-sheng (d.434) of the presence of Buddhahood in all sentient beings, and the possibility of
acquiring "Sudden Enlightenment."[27] The Neo-Confucian
movement, associated first with Han Yu (768-824) and then
with Ch'eng Yi (1033-1108) and Chu Hsi (1130-1200), also
announced itself in favor of the universal possibility of
sagehood--in the name of a return to Confucius and Mencius.

The Confucian Conscience

The word "conscience" (Latin: conscientia; Greek:
syneidesis) refers, according to the Stoics, to knowledge
about the good and one's relationship to the good. Ovid
calls it "deus in nobis" and Seneca, the indwelling holy
spirit, observer of our good and bad deeds. In the Book
of Wisdom (17:10 ff), syneidesis is given a pejorative
meaning, as the "bad" conscience, while the good conscience
is the spirit, the soul, the heart, which admonishes man
within himself, crying out to God, who alone searches the
heart and the reins. In the New Testament, the word receives once more a positive meaning, especially when it is
ennobled by faith in Christ. It is spoken of as a spiritual disposition, a power to act as well as the act
itself.[28]

Confucian teaching has always acknowledged man's possession
of an inner faculty of moral discernment--his conscience.[29]
Mencius says that the sense of right and wrong is common to
all men (2A:6). It is, indeed, that which distinguishes
the human being from the beast, that which assures a natural
equality to all human beings. Mencius also speaks of a
knowledge of the good (liang-chih) and an ability to do good

(liang-neng) that man has without need of learning (7A:15).
The philosopher, Wang Yang-ming (1472-1529) made of this the
basis of his entire philosophy--metaphysics as well as
ethics. Yang-ming speaks of liang-chih as an ability to
discern between good and evil--as well as the application
of such discernment to particular situations, in view of
practical behavior. It refers, however, not merely to
man's moral sense and intuition, but also to the ground of
the moral faculty itself, and of human existence.[30]

The difference between the Confucian teaching of conscience
and the Christian lies especially in the Christian's emphasis
on God, the giver of moral law and the judge of human conscience. Confucian teaching implies that conscience is a
gift. It is that which comes with life. But Confucian
philosophy does not dwell on God's role as supreme lawgiver
and judge. It prefers to analyze the meanings of conscience
itself.

It is interesting to note here the great resemblance between
Confucian teaching and the traditional Catholic doctrine of
a natural moral law--that which is based on human nature
itself, the law written in men's hearts.[31] Specialists of
comparative law often have a negative opinion of the Confucian understanding of natural law.[32] They point to the
Confucian disparagement of positive law (fa) as evidence
that it has only a penal character. Certainly, the Confucian tradition places much more emphasis upon the moral
personality of the ruler than upon the laws governing the
country. But this does not mean Confucian philosophy would
not agree to the self-evident principle--attributed to
natural law--that man knows as though by moral instinct to
do good and avoid evil, even if this same instinct does not
enlighten him as to what is good and what evil. However,
the Confucian tradition has not given the name of "law" to
this basic human ability of discernment--the very ground
indeed of man's possibility of self-transcendence. In the
Confucian consciousness, law is always something imposed
from outside--whereas man's ability to do good--according
to the school of Mencius--is considered as an innate endowment, even if in need of education and development. Thus,
the Confucian theory of conscience emphasizes the immanence
of such a moral law, without denying its openness to transcendence. To make use of the soteriological terms of
Japanese Buddhism, one may say, in this regard, that the
Catholic teaching joins the Confucian theory here in showing
more sense of self-reliance (jiriki), where Protestant
theology, with its preference for Scriptural law, insists

upon faith alone and exclusive dependence on God's power (tariki).

"The Heart of Man"

If conscience is man's moral faculty, it is also more than that. The word can refer also to a deeper reality--to the seat of the moral faculty itself, the innermost center of the soul, its apex, the locus for man's meeting with God, the source and principle of human freedom and human responsibility.

Already in the Old Testament, we find the constant reiteration that God looks less at our exterior actions than at our "heart." "I will give them a (new) heart, and...a new spirit..." (Ezech. 11:19). In the Sermon on the Mount, Jesus also lays emphasis on the importance of having the right inner dispositions: "Blessed are the pure of heart" (Matt. 5:8). St. Paul speaks of the "circumcised heart" (Rom. 2:5, 29). "Have this mind in you which was also in Christ Jesus" (Phil. 2:5). To repent, and turn to God is to have a change of heart, metanoia.[33]

The Chinese word for mind-and-heart, hsin, derived originally from an image of fire. It referred to intentions, feelings, as well as the activity of knowing and judging. The mind-and-heart is that which discerns between right and wrong, as well as that which commands conformance with its judgements.[34] The Neo-Confucian philosophers speak of hsin as that which controls both nature (hsing) and emotions (ch'ing). It is also the locus of man's meeting with Heaven. "He who gives full realization to his heart (hsin) understands his own nature, and he who understands his own nature knows Heaven" (Mencius 7A:1). And Wang Yang-ming has said:

> The heart (hsin) is the Way (Tao), and the Way is Heaven.
> If one knows (his own) heart, he would also know the Way
> and Heaven.[35]

The heart comes to us from Heaven (Mencius 6A:15). It also leads us back to Heaven. It represents both the symbol and reality of man's oneness with Heaven. Even more than Christianity, Confucianism has made explicit the continuum between the various levels of conscience, and between conscience as moral faculty and as the ground of such faculty, as mind-and heart.

The heart is also the reason for man's oneness with himself.
The Confucian man is not a dualist, a man at war with himself. The Confucian man knows himself to be one, in his
heart. He seeks to keep to his heart, to be true to his
heart. "Seek, and you will get it; let go and you will lose
it. If this is the case, then seeking is of use to getting
and what is sought is within yourself" (Mencius 7A.3).

The Confucian honors Heaven as the giver of life and humanity, from whom he has received everything, sense organs, as
well as a human heart. The Confucian treasures Heaven's
gifts, and seeks to develop them to the full. The Confucian,
however, speculates little over such questions as spiritual
immortality, a preoccupation which is also more Greek than
Semitic.

Much less important than the word hsin are the words "spiritual soul" (hun) and "sentient soul" (p'o). They are not
to be found in any of the Four Books. In the Annals of
Tso--A Confucian Classic--the word hun refers to all conscious activity, the word p'o to bodily form. The common
element of the two ideograms originally depicted a person
wearing a mask: the "impersonator" at the ceremony wore the
mask, and the dead man's spirit took up residence in it. The
words, therefore, were early associated with ritual practices of honoring the dead. In popular belief, the higher
soul, hun, ascends to heaven, and the lower soul, p'o, joins
the earth. With the development of a Confucian metaphysics,
hun became related to vital force (ch'i) and p'o bodily
form itself. In the Book of Rites, it is said that "the
spiritual soul (hun) and the vital force (ch'i) return to
Heaven (after death); the body and the sentient soul (p'o)
return to earth."36 It seems usually assumed that the sentient soul becomes eventually a part of the earth itself.
But how about the spiritual soul? Its final fate is left
unclear. We read in Wang Ch'ung's Lun-heng arguments against
believing in dead persons surviving as spiritual beings or
ghosts, which shows that disagreement on this question--a
question Confucius refused to answer--existed. But the
question only became prominent with the coming of Buddhism
into China, and the ensuing debate between Taoists and
Buddhists. Interestingly, the Taoists claimed especially
that the Confucian sages, including the Master himself,
became immortals, while the Buddhists denied the possibility
of personal immortality.

The Confucian position may be summed up this way: The age-
old custom of venerating the dead, the passages in the

Classics about sage-kings enjoying an intimacy with the Lord-on-High or Heaven, point to an early belief in some form of personal immortality. But Confucius himself kept silence on this question, while participating actively in the rituals honoring the dead (Analects 11:11, 3:12). The passage in the Annals of Tso relating the discussion of survival after death is interesting, but continues to emphasize the immortality of virtue, personal accomplishments and words.[37]

The Universal Virtue

The Confucian man is one--in his life and in his heart. The Confucian man need practice only one virtue: that which makes him fully and perfectly human, that which embraces all other virtues. It is the universal virtue, jen.

The Confucian jen offers certain parallels to the Christian virtue of love or charity (agape). It has been translated as human-hearted-ness, benevolence, love. The Christian teaching of charity has its raison-d'etre in God's love for man, which is revealed in Jesus Christ.[38] The Confucian teaching of jen, on the other hand, does not offer explicitly Heaven's love for man as a reason and model for imitation. According to the Classics, Heaven is the source of life, the protector of man and the provider of needs. But the virtue of jen is rather based on human nature itself. Man is able to practice jen. He is not truly human unless he does so.

Charity is a universal virtue. It is the "bond of perfection" (Col. 3:14), the inner principle of dynamism which imparts to the whole life of virtue its warmth, value and firmness. It embraces and animates all other virtues. This is true also of jen. Before the time of Confucius, jen was regarded as an aristocratic virtue, as the kindness shown by a superior to an inferior. But the teachings of Confucius transformed it into a universal virtue, that which can be practiced by all.[39]

And what is the meaning of jen? Asked this question many times, Confucius has given a number of different answers. To the disciple Fan Ch'ih, he says it means to "love men" (Analects 12:21). To Yen Hui, he speaks of jen in terms of subduing oneself and returning to propriety (Analects 12:1). To still another, he offers the famous Golden Rule: "What you do not wish others do unto you, do not do unto them" (Analects 12:2, 15:23).

Jen is perfect virtue; he who has jen is already perfect, a
sage. For this reason, Confucius shows a certain caution in
speaking of jen. He says:

> I have never seen one who really loved jen, nor
> hated what was not jen. He who loved jen would
> esteem nothing above it, and he who hated what
> was not jen would practice jen and would allow
> nothing that was not jen to affect him. Is there
> anyone who for a single day is able to employ all
> his strength for jen? I have never seen one with
> insufficient strength. There may be such a person,
> but I have not seen him (4:6).[40]

According to Confucius, jen should come before any other consideration (4:6). The gentleman never abandons it even for
a moment (4:5). It comes only after one has done what is
difficult (6:20). One may have to give one's life for jen
(15:8). And yet, jen is not a distant, far-off entity. "I
desire jen, and jen is close at hand" (7:29).

In its etymology as well as in the interpretation given it by
Confucius, jen is always concerned with the relationship between man and man. It is associated with loyalty (chung)--
loyalty to one's own heart and conscience--and reciprocity
(shu)--respect of, and consideration for others (Analects
4:15). Jen is also related to li (propriety; ritual). The
latter refers more to ritual and social behavior, the former,
to the inner orientation of the person.[41]

Jen is rooted in human sentiment as well as in a fundamental
orientation of life. Jen means affection and love. "The
man of jen loves others" (Mencius 4B:28). Indeed, he loves
all and everyone (7A:46). He "extends his love from those
he loves to those he does not love" (Mencius 7B:1). Hsün-tzu
concurs with this definition of jen as love. The Book of
Rites describes jen also as love. The Han Confucian Tung
Chung-shu (176-104 B.C.) defines jen as the love of mankind,
while Yang Hsiung (53 B.C.-A.D. 18) calls it "universal
love." The early lexicon Shuo-wen (C.A.D. 100) equates love
with affection (ch'in).[42]

The Confucian interpretation of jen as universal love, however, differs from that of some other early schools of
thought, especially the Mohist, that founded by Mo-tzu.
Mo-tzu advocated a love of all without distinction. The
followers of Confucius emphasized the need of discernment,
even of distinction. "Charity begins at home." So too

does jen. The roots of jen are filial piety and brotherly respect (Analects 1:20). The Confucian man reserves for his parents and kin a special love (Doctrine of the Mean 20). And Mencius has said:

> The gentleman is careful (and sparing) with things, but shows them no jen. He shows jen to the people, but is not (sentimentally) attached to them. He is (affectionately) attached to his parents while showing jen to the people. He has jen for the people and is considerate of things (7A:45).[43]

The Confucian interpretation of jen is sometimes called a "graded love." But it is not a calculating kind of love. It is rooted in human feeling, and in a sense of responsibility. It is sentiment, virtue, and commitment. It is the noblest quality a human being can possess.

The understanding of jen as a universal virtue--transcending the particular virtues--continued after the death of Confucius. With the emergence of the Sung philosophers, it also assumed an added meaning: that of creativity, of life and consciousness, and also of ultimate reality.[44] According to Ch'eng Hao, the man of jen forms "one body" with all things, and the virtue of righteousness, propriety, wisdom and truthfulness are all expressions of jen. He recommends the student to understand jen-t'i (jen-in-itself) and to strive to make it part of himself, and then to "nourish" it with the practice of virtues. Chu Hsi teaches the life-giving power of jen. It is that through which Heaven and Earth give life to men and things. Chang Tsai speaks of jen as the work of the sage, the man who is

> ...to give heart to Heaven and Earth, to establish the Way for living peoples, to continue the interrupted teachings of the former sages, and to open a new era of peace for coming generations.[45]

Except for the absence of an explicit mention of God, this expression of a mystical love of men and the cosmos should recall to mind the words of John and Paul, of Henry Suso, and closer to our days, of Teilhard de Chardin. The life-giving movement it describes as flowing down from Heaven and Earth to Man and then back to Heaven and Earth is a good analogy for an understanding of charity as the life-giving grace in Christian theology.

It is with this understanding of jen and of the Man of jen

that we may be led to an understanding of "the oneness of
Heaven and Man" (T'ien-jen ho-yi). For if the ideal of
sagehood implies the unity between Man and Heaven, then the
heart (or the mind), which is at the center of Man's being,
is the locus for this communion. This concept of the Man
who communes with the Absolute in his inner being is very
close to the ideal of Christian mysticism--defined, theologically, as the flowering of charity.

The Confucian Community

The Confucian man is no dualist. He is not divided against
himself, and his love of others is not strained. He loves
most those who, by Heaven's ordinance, are most closely related to himself. And he extends this love to others--to
friends first, and then to all in society and the world.
He has a deep sense of community, of responsibility toward
others.

The Five Relationships

The Confucian regards human society in terms of personal
relationships and ethical responsibilities resulting from
such relationships. The well-known "Five Relationships"
include the ruler-subject, father-son, husband-wife, elder
and younger brother, and friend and friend. Three of these
are family relationships, while the other two are usually
conceived in terms of the family models.[46] For example,
the ruler-subject relationship resembles the father-son,
while friendship resembles brotherliness. For this reason,
the Confucian society regards itself as a large family:
"Within the four seas all men are brothers" (Analects 12:5).

The responsibilities ensuing from these relationships are
mutual and reciprocal. A subject owes loyalty to his sovereign, and a child filial affection to his parent. But the
sovereign is also expected to care for his subjects, and
the parent for his child. Indeed, Mencius so interpreted
the Confucian doctrine of "Rectification of Names"--that a
sovereign be a (good) sovereign, a subject a (good) subject,
a father a (good) father, and a son a (good) son--as to
infer that a wicked ruler might forfeit the rights of his
position, becoming a mere "tyrant" whom his subjects could
depose (1B:8). But he never extended this inference to
cover the natural relationships of human kin. Sons, for
example, are encouraged to protect their parents' good name,

in spite of the knowledge of their wrongdoings.

The system of Five Relationships, all the same, emphasizes a
basic sense of hierarchy. The only truly horizontal relationship is that between friends, and even here, seniority
of age demands a certain respect, as also with brothers. The
husband-wife relationship bears more natural resemblance to
that between elder and younger brothers, but is more usually
compared to the ruler-subject relationship. And the duty of
filial piety, the need of procuring progeny for the sake of
assuring the continuance of the ancestral cult, has been for
centuries the ethical justification for polygamy.

The family has always been the center of Confucian life and
ethics, and family life itself has demonstrated the nature
of Confucianism itself, not only as a system of ethics, but
also as a philosophy of religion. In many Chinese houses in
Hongkong, Taiwan and Southeast Asia--as well as in Korea and
Japan--the ancestral altar is still maintained. Here, a
number of tablets is kept, each representing a dead ancestor.
They are traditionally made of wood, although a sociologist
has noticed how paper tablets have replaced wooden ones in
certain Hongkong families today,[47] those who have left behind their older tablets on the mainland. In front of these
tablets burns a dim lamp, near which are placed incense and
candles. All this is evidence of the religious significance
of the Confucian family, a community of the living and the
dead.

Filial piety is the first of all Confucian virtues, that
which comes before loyalty to the sovereign, conjugal affection, and everything else. The ancestral cult has continued
throughout the centuries from time immemorial to strengthen
these sentiments of filial piety and familial loyalty. It
has always exercised an integrating and stabilizing influence, pulling together, not merely the large, patriarchal
family, but also the whole clan, all the descendants of the
same ancestors, and the entire Chinese kinship system.
Births and marriages are related to the ancestral cult and
the duty of filial piety, since every birth increases the
number of descendants, and since marriage is intended as a
means for continuing the family lineage and the ancestral
cult itself. Filial piety has usually assured for aged
parents the support of their mature children, while the
strong sentiment of family and kid has promoted mutual help
among family relatives, and even beyond the family circles,
among persons coming from the same ancestral town, albeit
not related by blood or marriage, as well as among persons

bearing the same surnames, and so, allegedly or possibly, of the same ancestors.[48]

Familial relations provide a model for social behavior. Respect your own elders, as well as others' elders; be kind to your own juniors and children, as well as others' juniors and children. These are the words of Mencius (1A.7). They have provided inspiration for generations of Confucians. They have been the reason for the strong sense of solidarity not only in the Chinese family, but also in Confucian social organizations, and even among overseas Chinese communities today. If Confucianism remains alive today, if Confucianism is to remain alive for many generations to come, the credit belongs to this strong sense of human solidarity, based fundamentally on familial sentiments by implying a belief in a universal brotherhood.

The hierarchical orientation in Confucianism has been strengthened in later developments, with its establishment as the state philosophy in the Han dynasty, the incorporation of yin-yang metaphysics and of Legalist notions of authority and obedience into this state orthodoxy. In the words of the Han thinker, Tung Chung-shu:

> In all things there must be correlates. Thus if there is the upper, there must be the lower...The yin is the correlate of the yang, the wife of the husband, the subject of the sovereign...[49]

From the five relationships, Tung selects the three: ruler-subject, husband-wife and father-son. He calls them the "Three Bonds." According to his reinterpretation, the sovereign is the master of the subject, the husband of the wife, and the father of the son. The relationships continue to require reciprocal duties and responsibilities. But the superior partners have more rights, and the inferior more duties.[50]

The incorporation of yin-yang metaphysics into Confucian social ethics has, however, underlined another dimension of the Confucian humanism: its openness to the divine, the transcendent. Tung Chung-shu has especially articulated the doctrine of the oneness of Heaven and Man, in terms of the "triad:" Heaven, Earth and Man. According to him, man is a replica of Heaven, the microcosm of the macrocosm, both in spirit and in body. He is far superior to all other creatures. "Heaven, Earth and Man are at the origins of all things: "Heaven gives them birth, Earth gives them nourishment, and Man gives them perfection."

These three are related to each other like the hands
and feet; united they give the finished physical
form, so that no one of them may be dispensed with.[51]

Tung Chung-shu has especially exalted the notion of kingship.
The ideal king is the perfect man, the human paradigm, the
co-equal of Heaven, the mediator between the ways of Heaven
and Earth, and the ways of human society.

Heaven's will is constantly to love and benefit,
its business to nourish and bring to age...The
will of the king likewise is to love and benefit
the world, and his business to bring peace and
joy to his time...If the ruler of men exercises
his love and hate, his joy and anger, in accordance with righteousness, then the age will be
well governed, but if unrighteously, then the
age will be in confusion...So we see that the
principles of mankind correspond to the way of
Heaven.[52]

Of course, not every man is a king. But Confucian philosophy has always emphasized every man's duty to participate in
government, to assist the king in assuring good government.
Every official, for example, is exhorted to become the
father-and-mother of his people. And Confucian sage-models
include not only sage-kings, but also sage-ministers. Indeed, a Confucian is expected to serve the state unless
other responsibilities, such as toward his parents, prevent
him from doing so, or unless the times are such that service would compromise his principles.

Besides, Confucian philosophy has always spoken in universal
terms. Just as there is Heaven above, so too there is the
world below: all under Heaven. Confucius was no particu-
larist, no nationalist. He traveled from state to state,
seeking a ruler who would use his services, for the good of
the whole world. He envisages good government always in
terms of the world. So too his later followers, throughout
the centuries when China remained the center of a known
world, a known universe. The Confucian community is a world
community, a human community.

The Confucian man must, of course, prepare himself for this
task. And he is exhorted to do so, by remaining faithful to
this integrated view of man and of life, a view which

transcends the differences between subject and object, self
and world. The Confucian book, the Great Learning, offers a
good illustration of this organic unity between self-
perfection and the ordering of family, country and world.
Differentiations between various levels are overcome by an
all-comprehensive, circular process:

> Things have roots and branches, and affairs have
> beginning and ends. To know the order of priority
> is to be near the Way (Tao). The ancients who
> wished to make manifest the principle of virtue
> in the world, first made sure that their own states
> were well governed. To assure the good government
> of their states, they first cultivated their per-
> sons. To assure this personal cultivation, they
> first made sure that their minds and hearts were
> upright. To assure that their minds and hearts
> were upright, they first made sure that their in-
> tentions were sincere. It is not possible to
> neglect the roots and order well the branches.
> It is not possible to neglect the essential, and
> order well the details.[53]

A Community of Culture

The Christian Community, the Church (Ecclesia), considers itself an assembly called forth by God, a community of believers.[54] It is, of course, an assembly of communities, of
local churches. But it remains an assembly, a community in
itself, because of the common bond of faith uniting all its
members, in spite of differences of time, place and culture,
in spite, also, of differences of political ideology and
social organization. And it is a community because the bond
of faith, which joins man to God, and believer to believer,
is much more important than its own social organization or
juridical statutes. Faith is the very life of the Christian
community.

The Confucian society also has its rulers, laws and statutes.
But it is more than a society. It is also a community of
personal relationships. It is joined together, not by religious belief--although such is also present--but by the
acceptance of a common culture, a culture which esteems the
person above the law, and human relationships above the
state. Culture is the life of the Confucian community. In
traditional China, when the Confucian state allegedly
embraced the then known world, Confucian culture was also

regarded as <u>human</u> culture--that which distinguished the civilized from the barbarian.

Confucian culture was at the same time religious and secular. It did not distinguish between these two realms. Its basic faith--the oneness of Heaven and Man--inspired a great optimism in human nature and its perfectibility, a faith which impelled the quest for a universal way of life and a universal order on earth. The Confucian Man regarded Heaven as the source of his life and being, and looked to it for protection and the satisfaction of his needs. He considered Earth as his dwelling place, in life and death, a storehouse of resources as well as a living garden, nourished, like himself, by gifts from Heaven. He regarded himself as participating in the life and being of both Heaven and Earth, and related to other men through this common participation, and a common origin from Heaven.

Confucianism has never known an organized, ecclesiastical priesthood. The emperor was the mediator between Heaven and the people, by virtue of his position as political ruler. He was assisted by his ministers--an educated bureaucracy of men versed in rituals and ethics. Together, they represented a kind of lay priesthood, although their dignity and mission flowed more from their education and merit than from any personal <u>charisma</u>.[55] They constituted a special class in society, representing a commitment to service of state and society, in the name of the common good.[56] They were sometimes called "gentlemen" (chün-tzu).[57] Time and again, from among these ranks, a "prophet" would emerge who raised his voice of protest against misrule, directing his complaints to the "kings" as did his Hebrew counterparts. Such a man would be a true follower of Confucius and Mencius. Such a man would speak in the name of the Classics, the sages, and of Heaven.

It is interesting to note here that the Confucian Man has always been regarded as "king"--real or potential, with the duty to govern or to assist in government. The teaching of the <u>Great Learning</u> is addressed to all: to manifest the principle of virtue (by personal cultivation), <u>to love the people</u> (ordering well family and state), and to rest in the highest good (including giving peace to the entire world). "From the Son of Heaven down to the commoners, it is the same: all must regard personal cultivation as the root (and foundation)" (Chapter one).

Conclusion

In the course of this study, we seem to have discovered
more similarities than differences between Confucian and
Christian notions of man. But we must not overlook the
differences, especially where these lie in varying emphases
of the two traditions. For example, Confucian teachings
have focused more upon human perfectibility where Christianity has tended to stress human fallibility. Thus,
Confucianism projects the image of a man in harmony with
society and the universe, where Christianity appears to
support the idea of a man at war with himself and his sinful nature, struggling to overcome a world estranged from
God. This difference has also been formulated in terms of
complacency and dynamism. The harmony-loving Confucian has
been depicted as resistant to change, where the militant
Christian is allegedly changing the face of the earth. But
there is yet another side to the picture. Estrangement and
alienation have also been responsible for outrageous vio-
lence against man and nature.

And so what about the strengths and weaknesses of the two
humanisms?

The admirers of Confucianism have emphasized that Confucianism is a humanism, that the heart of its teachings is man's
self-realization and self-fulfillment, described in terms
of acquiring wisdom and sageliness. The critics, however,
have pointed out de-humanizing tendencies, in particular,
its hierarchical orientations, which have so evolved as
to grant only obligations and no rights, to the inferior
partner of each of the "Five Relationships." The admirers
of Christianity likewise indicate how divine revelation has
made known the real possibilities of human greatness, while
its critics regard it as the enemy of humanism, on account
of its preoccupation with the next life and with God.

It appears that Confucian and Christian humanisms must each
preserve a delicate balance of inner tensions, in order to
remain authentic expressions of human aspirations. Confucianism has need of a more articulate theory of human
fallibility, and even more, of human suffering and its
meaning in the order of values. Christianity, on the other
hand, has need of a more profound inquiry into the question
of human goodness, even outside the framework of a doctrine
of redeeming grace. Here, I believe that it can yet learn
from the Confucian pedagogy, insofar as the varying emphases on human fallibility or perfectibility can themselves

promote the consciousness of guilt and frustration, or that
of strength and commitment. It is, for example, quite impossible for the Confucian tradition to produce a novel of
human wickedness as Anthony Burgess' A Clockwork Orange[58]
which represents another step in the increasing fascination
of fiction and society with the analysis of sin--and perhaps without adequate acceptance of freedom and responsibility.

The history of the unfolding of Confucian culture has witnessed many vicissitudes, of human greatness as well as of
foibles, of institutional fossilization as well as rebirth.
When judging Confucianism against its records of ups and
downs, one must have the caution to ask: is it Confucianism that failed, or is it something else? Did not Confucianism become subjugated to state authority, as a
system of state orthodoxy? Has it not led to the intrusion of Legalist ideas of authority and obedience, which,
in turn, gave rigidity to the ethics of human relationships? But then, with all that, are there yet certain
ideals and values which remain vital and inspiring throughout the passage of time?

Certainly, contemporary man, whether in a socialist or open
society, sees many practices associated with the Five
Relationships as worthless, even inhuman. Why should youth
always yield to age, and woman to man? Why should the past
be exalted rather than the present--or the future? Has
not the backward-looking tendency of Confucian culture itself been responsible for the tragedies of China's recent
past, as she found herself helpless in front of the youth-
ful and dynamic "barbarians" of the West, who assaulted her
with weapons and technology--all that was formerly despised
by the Confucian gentleman and his culture of leisure?

There is much that is true of the criticisms leveled against
the Confucian culture. The debacles it has suffered are
themselves telling witnesses of the need for rejuvenation,
in a culture so ancient. But they are not reasons for
imagining that Confucian culture is already dead, and can
have no future.

Human cultures have their cycles of life and death. Confucian culture has witnessed many such cycles, with the
burning of books (213 B.C.), and with the later predominance
of Buddhism and Taoism, as well as with the recent challenges of Western secularism and Marxism. So far, every
time, Confucian culture has been able to resurrect itself,

frequently after having learned certain lessons, whether
for good or ill.

Any creative dialogue between two traditions must rest upon
their points of convergences, rather than their differences.
For the dialogue between Christianity and Confucianism, an
understanding of faith in man as openness to the transcendent remains the most promising starting point.[35] It is
this faith which has given Confucianism its dynamism,
which has also counteracted the abuses of Legalism--and so
many crimes attributed to Confucianism have emerged from
the infiltration of Legalist concepts into the Confucian
system. It is this faith which provides a starting point
for contemporary theology itself, and which also, for the
Christian, takes priority over law and precepts, being itself the only <u>rationale</u> for any authentic legal order.
And lastly, it <u>is this</u> faith, in each case, which makes
possible that creative exercise of freedom which brings
man nearer to his transcendent goal, the achievement of a
<u>radical</u> human-ity.

NOTES

1. On the subject of humanism, Christian and Confucian, see a Chinese work, T'ang Chun-i, Chung-kuo jen-wen ching-shen chih fa-chan (The Development of the Chinese Humanist Spirit) (Hongkong, 1958), in which the author, understandably, traces the origin of Western humanism to Greek and Roman philosophy. He mentions, however, the gradual fusion of Christian religious notions and the secular philosophical notions in the development of this humanism (see especially pp. 69-76), and concludes the book with a discussion of the value of religious belief and the problem of the future of Chinese culture (pp. 337-99), taking into consideration all the traditional forms of Chinese religion as well as Christianity. For Christian humanism itself, see also Roger L. Shinn, Man: the New Humanism (Philadelphia, 1968); E. Schillebeeckx, God and Man, translated by E. Fitzgerald (New York, 1969).

2. For the notion of man in the Christian scriptures, see W. Eichrodt, Man in the Old Testament, tr. by K. and R. Gregor Smith (Chicago, 1951), H. Conzelmann, An Outline of the Theology of the New Testament, tr. by J. Bowden (New York, 1969), pp. 173-80. See also Jurgen Moltmann, Mensch: Christliche Anthropologie in den Konflikten der Gegegwart (Stuttgart, 1971), English translation by John Stundy: Man: Christian Anthropology in the Conflicts of the Present (Philadelphia, 1974), ch. 1; Neues Glaubensbuch: Der gemeinsame christliche Glaube, ed. by J. Feiner and L. Vischer (Freiburg im B., 1973), English translation in The Common Catechism: A Book of Christian Faith (New York, 1975), pt. 3. Evangelischer Erwachsenen Katechismus, ed. by W. Jentsch et al. (1975), Part 5. See also Reinhold Niebuhr, The Nature and Destiny of Man (New York, 1941), vol. 1.

3. Book of Documents, Part 4, Book 2, in James Legge, tr. The Chinese Classics (Oxford, 1893), vol. 3, pp. 177-78; Book of Odes, Part 3, Book 3, in Legge, ibid., vol. 4, p. 64.

4. See Donald J. Munro, The Concept of Man in Early China (Stanford, 1969), pp. 65-67. See also his lengthy notes (n. 45-46) on pp. 214-15.

5. Hsün-tzu: Basic Writings, tr. by Burton Watson (New York, 1963), p. 159.

6. Ibid., p. 45.

7. Doctrine of the Mean 20.

8. Munro, op. cit., ch. 1.

9. Mencius 4B:1.

10. See Julia Ching, "The Problem of Evil and a Possible Dialogue Between Christianity and Neo-Confucianism," Contemporary Religions in Japan 9 (1968), pp. 161-93.

11. See Ricci's Catechism, T'ien-chu shih-yi (The True Idea of God), Part 7.

12. Book of Documents, "Counsels of Great Yu" and the "Great Plan," English translation in Legge, The Chinese Classics, vol. 5, pp. 54, 327.

13. Hsu Heng, Shuo-wen chieh-tzu (Lexicon, with explanations by Tuan Yu-ta'ai), (Taipei, 1955), p. 598.

14. Pan Ku, Po-hu-t'ung-yi (Taipei, 1968), pp. 276-81.

15. Ta-Tai Li-chi (Book of Rites by the Elder Tai), "Duke Ai's Questions on Five Meanings." See Benedict Grynpas, tr., Un Legs Confucen: Fragments du Ta Tai Li Ki (Brussels, n.d.), p. 50.

16. I refer here especially to the Doctrine of the Mean, which is also ch. 28 of the Book of Rites.

17. Analects 7:33.

18. Analects 7:25.

19. Book of Mencius 4A:2.

20. Book of Mencius 7B:15.

21. Book of Mencius 3B:9.

22. Book of Mencius 6A:7.

23. Doctrine of the Mean, ch. 30, in Legge, tr., The Chinese Classics, vol. 1, pp. 427-28.

24. For such discussions, see Fung Yu-lan, A History of

Chinese Philosophy, tr. by Derk Bodde (Princeton, 1953), vol. 2, pp. 187-89.

25. Ibid., pp. 274-84.

26. See Ching, "The Problem of Evil," p. 169.

27. Fung Yu-lan, vol. 2, pp. 274-84.

28. On conscience, see Bernard Häring, Das Gesetz Christi, English translation by Edwin G. Kaiser, The Law of Christ (Paramus, 1961), vol. 1, pp. 135-43, Neues Glaubensbuch, pp. 473-76.

29. See Cheng Chung-ying, "Conscience, Mind and Individual in Chinese Philosophy," Journal of Chinese Philosophy 2 (1974), pp. 6-25.

30. See Ching, To Acquire Wisdom, ch. 4-5; see also Cheng's article, pp. 24-25.

31. On the subject of natural law, see Bernard Häring, The Law of Christ, vol. 1, pp. 238-50. See also N. H. Soe, "Natural Law and Social Ethics," in John Bennett, ed., Christian Social Ethics in a Changing World (New York, 1966), pp. 289-91, for his critique of natural law.

32. Among others, John C. H. Wu, himself a jurist, has discussed positively the presence of "natural law" in Chinese philosophy. See "Chinese Legal and Political Philosophy," The Chinese Mind, ed. by Charles A. Moore (Honolulu, 1967), pp. 217-76. See also p. 235, n. 18 where Wu also gives a summary of Hu Shih's views on this subject, taken from Hu's article, "The Natural Law in the Chinese Tradition," Natural Law Institute Proceedings 5 (1951).

33. Bernard Häring, The Law of Christ, vol. 1, pp. 206-09.

34. Munro, op. cit., pp. 50-51.

35. This is quoted in Ching, To Acquire Wisdom, ch. 5.

36. Li-chi (Book of Rites), ch. 26 (On Sacrificial Victims), see also ch. 47 (Meaning of Sacrifices), Donald Munro, op. cit., p. 50 and p. 209, n.4.

37. Wang Ch'ung, Lun-heng, ch. 62 (On Death), English translation in W. T. Chan, A Source Book of Chinese Philosophy (Princeton, 1963), p. 300. On this whole question of immortality and its debates, see also these monographs: Hu Shih, "The Concept of Immortality in Chinese Thought," Harvard Divinity School Bulletin (1946), pp. 26-43; Walter Liebenthal, "The Immortality of the Soul in Chinese Thought," Monumenta Nipponica 8 (1952), pp. 327-97. The passage in the Annals of Tso referred to is taken from the seventh year of Duke Chao, see J. Legge, The Chinese Classics, v. 5, p. 613. In Matteo Ricci's Catechism (T'ien-chu shih-yi, 1603 ed., ch. 3), the Chinese scholar in the dialogue expresses the belief that the spiritual soul eventually disintegrates, while the Western scholar (Ricci's alter ego) seeks to prove, by the help of Scholastic philosophy, that it is immortal.

38. On the subject of Christian charity, see R. Schnackenburg, The Moral Teaching of the New Testament, tr. by J. Holland Smith and W. J. O'Hara (Freiburg, 1965), ch. 3.

39. See Wing-tsit Chan, "Chinese and Western Interpretations of Jen (Humanity)," in Journal of Chinese Philosophy 2 (1975), pp. 107-09.

40. English translation adapted from James Legge, The Chinese Classics, v. 1, p. 167.

41. Herbert Fingarette, Confucius--the Secular as Sacred (New York, 1972), pp. 37-38; Munro, op. cit., pp. 28-29, 208-09, 219.

42. The references are to Hsün-tzu, ch. 27, Book of Rites, ch. 19, Tung Chung-shu, Ch'un-ch'iu fan-lu, pp. 29-30.

43. English translation adapted from D. C. Lau, Mencius (Baltimore, 1970), p. 192.

44. Wing-tsit Chan, "Chinese and Western Interpretations of Jen," pp. 115-16.

45. Chang Tsai, quoted in Chu Hsi's Chin-ssu lu 2; English translation is my own.

46. Fung Yu-lan, A Short History of Chinese Philosophy, ed. by Derk Bodde (New York, 1948), p. 21.

47. That the ancestral cult is still alive is attested to by Arthur P. Wolf, in his study on "Gods, Ghosts and Ancestors," in Religion and Ritual in Chinese Society, ed. Arthur D. Wolf (Stanford, 1974), pp. 146, 155-62. He treats especially of Taiwan but refers also to the Chinese mainland and elsewhere.

48. C. K. Yang, Religion in Chinese Society (Berkeley, 1961), pp. 29-53.

49. Tung Chung-shu, Ch'un-ch'iu fan-lu, 53, quoted in Fung Yu-lan, A Short History, p. 196.

50. Fung Yu-lan, ibid., p. 197.

51. Tung Chung-shu, 19, quoted in Fung Yu-lan, ibid., pp. 194-95.

52. Tung Chung-shu, 43, quoted and translated in W. T. deBary, ed., Sources of Chinese Tradition (New York, 1960), p. 163.

53. Great Learning, taken from the text attributed to Confucius. English translation adapted from James Legge, The Chinese Classics, I, 356. This passage is referred to by Bernard Häring, in Christian Renewal in a Changing World, tr. by Sr. M. Lucidia Häring (New York, 1968), p. 95. Häring comments on the closeness of the spirit of this text with that of the Gospels.

54. Hans Küng, Die Kirche (Freiburg, 1967), pp. 99-107.

55. I have in mind especially Max Weber's The Religion of China, English translation by Hans H. Gerth (New York, 1964). Weber sees the Confucian literati as performing a sort of priestly role, but denies that China has ever had any experience of "ethical prophecy of a supramundane God who raised ethical demands." See pp. 229-30.

56. The "universalist" orientation of Confucian life and education has certainly caused a neglect of special- ization, particularly in science and technology. And yet, such an orientation is the very life of a humanism true to the whole man, even if it may inspire curiosity and an urge to discover and dominate the world around us. The problem with Confucianism was the positive prohibition against technological specialization, deemed to be below the ethical attention of the gentleman.

57. For the meaning of chün-tzu in Confucian ethics,
see Antonio S. Cua, "The Concept of the Paradigmatic Individual in the Ethics of Confucius," Inquiry 14 (1971),
pp. 41-55.

58. This was published in London in 1962. Of his own
religious views, the novelist, whose full name is John
Anthony Burgess Wilson, says: "I was brought up a Catholic, became an agnostic, flirted with Islam, and now hold
a position which may be termed Manichee--I believe the
wrong god is temporarily ruling the world and that the
true god has gone under." (This is quoted in A. A.
DeVitis, Anthony Burgess, New York, 1972.)

59. See "A Manifesto for a Reappraisal of Sinology and
Reconstruction of Chinese Culture" (1958), signed by Carsun
Chang, T'ang Chun-i, Mou Tsung-san and Hsu Fu-kuan, and
given in English in Carsun Chang, The Development of Neo-
Confucian Thought (New York, 1962), vol. 1, pp. 462-64.
See also Robert P. Kramers, "Some Aspects of Confucianism
in its Adaptation to the Modern World," Proceedings of the
IXth International Congress for the History of Religions
(Tokyo and Kyoto), 1958 (Tokyo, 1960), pp. 332-33. (T'ang
Chun-i's ideas can be further pursued in Chung-kuo wen-hua
chih ching-shen chia-chih (The Spiritual Values of Chinese
Culture), Taipei, 1960, pp. 326-44.)

II – THE SCRUTABLE CHINESE RELIGION

Laurence G. Thompson

It was suggested that I should take as my assignment to bring before this conference some important problems in Western understanding of Chinese religion. Several assumptions are implicit in such an assignment. First, that there is an identifiable something we may call "Chinese religion" as opposed, perhaps, to "religions of China." Second, that this Chinese religion is still relevant to understanding China today. Third, that there are difficulties in the way of Westerners who, recognizing this relevance, seek to understand the posited Chinese religion.

While I would accept all of these assumptions as true, there is one more assumption which causes me some uneasiness. I assume, that is, that one would go about the task of analyzing problems in Western understanding by analyzing Westerners. It seems evident that the real difficulties in understanding anything lie not so much in the thing we study as in ourselves. Such difficulties are not hard to name: we are blind, we are biased, and we fail to ask the right questions.

But because analyzing Western failings is a task that is much less congenial to me than analyzing Chinese religion, I propose to undertake the latter rather than the former.

I do not underestimate the value of confessions of shortcomings, and I particularly do not disregard the benefit that
would be gained by a historical survey of Western interactions with Chinese culture. As it happens, we have among
the participants in this conference several scholars who are
exceptionally well qualified in the latter subject, which
may serve as one good reason for me not to dabble in it. I
trust that in talking about Chinese religion rather than
Western difficulties I may make some positive contribution
to our common cause of inter-cultural understanding. Should
this procedure sharpen our perception of Western misappre-
hensions, that would not be merely serendipitous.

One further preliminary observation should be made. Because
of the nature of this presentation as a public address, I
should not presume any special knowledge of the subject
among the audience. On the other hand, the active participants in this conference are all specialists in one or more
aspects of religious studies or sinology. To them, therefore, I offer a prefatory apology for any lack of "scholarly
tone" in what is to follow.

i

It is always helpful in a discussion to know what the subject is. Unfortunately religion is in worse case than the
weather: everybody talks about it but nobody really knows
what it is. Not for lack of trying; on the contrary,
definitions have been framed in every conceivable way,
some so as practically to exclude all but the proposer's
own religion, and some so liberal as to include practically
every dimension of human life. Some definitions are dis-
cipline-bound, and even more are culture-bound. The difficulty is, of course, that religion is not something "out
there," like a physical object that can be touched, measured,
photographed. One can objectively deal only with the
effects of religion, and not with religion itself.

All of which does not prevent most people from feeling that
they know what religion is in some general sense. This is
because religion is found in every society and affects
everyone. It is somehow familiar, and it is also, as we
are only too well aware, one of the commonest sources of
strong opinions and emotions. Not only are people highly
judgmental about religion, but they take it so seriously

that they have often killed and been killed in its name.

When a subject is so basic and so sensitive for so many
people, it is no wonder that its study has seldom been pursued with truly scientific impartiality. Those who have
most profound interest in it are apt to be the same people
who have most personal stake in the "triumph" of some particular religion, which goes far to explain why so much of
what used to be called "comparative religion" turned out
to be Christian apologetics. If the academic study of religion in the broad sense has by now attained a certain
respectability, it is due to the determined efforts of
anthropologists, phenomenologists, historians and other
scholars to transcend private commitments and prejudices.
In our consideration of Chinese religion I must assume that
you join me in such a spirit of scientific objectivity.

Inasmuch as I started out by raising the question of what
religion is, you will already be anticipating that I have
my own answer. In front of an audience that numbers so many
experts, I should be foolish indeed to venture an amateur
definition. But for purposes of this discussion I shall at
least have to tell you what it is I think I am talking about.
Although I am side-stepping definitions, like everyone else
I have a fairly positive idea about what religion works at.
It seems to me that like all human activities, religion is
some sorts of responses to stimuli, or as Toynbee would put
it, challenges. In other words, it is one of man's ways of
adapting to his circumstances. It does something to serve
his needs. Now, many scholars have devoted careful attention to showing how religion functions in societies to
promote nonreligious ends, and although my statement may
have triggered the word functionalism in your minds, I
should immediately make clear that this is not what I have
in mind.[1] My intention is in fact to invert the social
scientific version of functionalism. I suggest that, in
trying to understand what religion is, we should look for
what the socially functional manifestations of religion
reveal of religious significance, rather than for significant ways in which religion functions in society. As Eliade
has taught us, and so brilliantly exemplified in his many
works, "a religious phenomenon will only be recognized as
such if it is studied as something religious."[2]

What are the stimuli or challenges to which man makes what
we call "religious" responses? The neatest (if slightly
sophistical) answer is that they include all that man cannot
adequately respond to otherwise. Always and everywhere man

attempts to cope with physical, psychological, and social
problems, and while much of his coping is in the form of
practical action--whether technologically simple or compli-
cated--there are problems that are not amenable to practical
action. Because always and everywhere such problems fall
within a certain limited range, so likewise do the ways of
conceptualizing and handling them. It is in this sense
that Lévi-Strauss once made the outrageous comment that
"the poverty of religious thought can never be overesti-
mated."[3] For though particulars will differ, these problems
are universal and easily enumerated: one thinks, for instance, of suffering, the unpredictable quirks of Fate or
what in the West are commonly called Acts of God, human
inadequacy in vital tasks, the meaninglessness of life,
authority and submission, the omnipresence of evil, and of
course death. Man is driven by circumstances to seek an
end to suffering, courage to meet his unavoidable trials,
superhuman help in his most urgent responsibilities,
assurances that existence is meaningful, ultimate sanctions
for conditions of power and subservience in his society,
comfort in the thought that eventually good will triumph
despite the flourishing of evil today, and at the last,
salvation or the victory of self--even whatever self it may
be that undergoes rebirth in Theravada Buddhism--over piti-
less Time.[4]

The problems being universal, "religious" modes of reacting
are likewise similar in structure, if endlessly various in
outward mode. In most societies religion remained such an
integral part of everyday coping that it developed no
unique personality. But occasionally, when there was a
conjunction of historical readiness and individual genius,[5]
"religion" has become "a religion."

Just as the hallmark of science is verification through
mathematics and experimentation, so the hallmark of religion
is verification through faith. Faith is not, of course,
foreign to science, whose hypotheses must survive by it
until proved or disproved. But religious faith, while not
subject to mathematical or experimental proof, can yet produce objectively verifiable results, as for instance in
seemingly miraculous healing. It is likewise a kind of
"reverse faith" which produces "psychosomatic illness," or
even more dramatically in certain cultures the "psychosomatic death" brought on by the sorcerer's spell.[6]

Please note that in these thoughts of what religion is about
I have made no attempt to extrapolate hypothetical origins

from later developments, a procedure which has for the most
part been abandoned as hopelessly speculative by scholars
in the field.[7] Please notice also that in speaking of religion as a means of coping with problems, I have carefully
avoided defining any specific problems, but have tried to
phrase the matter in the most general terms, as man's existential situation. Finally, I draw your attention to a
clearcut distinction in this formulation between religion
and philosophy: in the view of religion taken here, <u>action</u>
is essential. To be sure, we can never actually separate
action from rationalization, but rationalization that has
no issue in action we take to be philosophy and not religion.

ii

The word "scrutable" in the title of this essay may now be
understood to refer to the conception of religion outlined
in the foregoing discussion. We suggest that Chinese religion may be understood at its basic level as a set of
responses to challenges inherent in the existential situation. We think it can be understood with least difficulty
as a process of coping with otherwise insoluble problems.
We want to avoid the misunderstandings that arise from
applying any preconceived categories whatever, aside from
the universal plight of man. We address ourself to the
essential circumstances, and disregard historical or social
factors. "Scrutability," in this sense, means recognizing
the modes whereby Chinese expressed "religious" adaptation
to these circumstances, and which we therefore consider to
be "the Chinese religion." Our analysis will necessarily
be brief and incomplete, but we hope adequate to expose the
main outlines of this Chinese religion. We shall proceed
by taking up in turn each of the general types of human
problems mentioned in the preliminary discussion.

Suffering

. . . "Oh! suffering world,
Oh! known and unknown of my common flesh,
Caught in this common net of death and woe,
And life which binds to both! I see, I feel
The vastness of the agony of earth,
The vainness of its joys, the mockery

Of all its best, the anguish of its worst;
Since pleasures end in pain, and youth in age,
And love in loss, and life in hateful death,
And death in unknown lives, which will but yoke
Men to their wheel again to whirl the round
Of false delights and woes that are not false . . ."[8]

Thus, the future Buddha, as Sir Edwin Arnold imagines him to cry out when he has felt the full import of the Four Signs.[9] To Buddhism, indeed, suffering is simply a synonym for existing. The first of the Four Noble Truths in the formulaic summary of the Buddhist thesis is duḥkha-āryā-satyam (k'u sheng ti in Chinese) which may be interpreted: to exist is to suffer. Of course the Chinese knew about suffering before Buddhism arrived (at about the beginning of the Common Era). But to judge from the record, it is surely Buddhism that has impressed the omnipresence and inescapability of suffering upon Chinese minds.

Likewise, certain of the Chinese responses to suffering were imported with the Indian religion. These most obviously include the whole monastic system of the Sangha, or Community of monks and nuns, whereby release from suffering may be sought systematically under the most favorable conditions. The Buddhist monk or nun severs worldly ties, is freed from social responsibility, has a minimum of economic distraction. He or she ideally lives far from population centers, amidst quiet and beautiful mountain scenery, in company only with like-minded companions. The setting and the routines of the monastery are designed exclusively to serve the single end of terminating suffering. Insofar as it is possible to design a way of life that will serve this end, Buddhist monasticism is a highly functional institution.

The final solution to suffering in Buddhist theory is the most radical of all religions: to end suffering we must end existence. For non-Buddhists this may seem like the old joke about the operation being successful although the patient died. Seen from the viewpoint of Indian thought, however, it is reasonable. In this Indian tradition the present life was considered only one in an endless succession of existences. Given that life is mostly suffering, this means enduring literally endless suffering. Clearly, with such an assumption, the problem is to put a stop to the whole wretched process. Buddhist thought posited that rebirths were due to a vital force accumulated from a person's every thought and deed, called karma (or karman). Karma was a concept something like the law of conservation of energy:

the energy built up through our mental and physical actions
has to be released in a new birth. The vital energy of
karma accumulates from the passions, identified most particularly as grasping, craving, attachment, desire. Knowing
that desires build karmic force which will propel one into
still another existence in which to suffer, the victim has
only one way out, which is to cease victimizing himself, or,
in other words, to reduce and ultimately eliminate these
desires, graspings, cravings, and attachments. Basic
Buddhist theory thus requires no outside agency to account
for human sufferings, and knows no supernatural assistance
in their cure. The motto might be: Sufferer, cure thyself!

So now the problem is, how to accomplish the eradication of
desire. The method prescribed is easy to formulate, but
supremely difficult to perfect. It consisted of working
toward enlightenment as to the nonexistence of self, relying
upon the doctrine of "co-dependent origination," which is
the Buddha's discovery of causality. According to this
doctrine, analysis shows us that there is no self-sufficient
entity whatsoever. All things come into being through
causes, and disappear with the vanishing of their causes:
"This being so, that comes to be; this ceasing to be so,
that likewise ceases to be." The doctrine applies most
pertinently to the self or soul. By "nonexistence" is
meant that ego has no existence in and of itself, no permanent existence. To grasp this truth is so crucial to
stopping the desires which lead to rebirth and more
suffering as to be called "enlightenment." If one really
becomes clear about the contingency and impermanence of
the "self," one will cease to love that self and to pander
to it.

No matter how far later developments seem to take the religion of Buddhism away from this simple gospel, it is
always central and final. All the schools of Buddhism in
China as elsewhere are merely interpretations and techniques. As interpretations, they are attempts to grasp
the meaning of the phrase "to exist"; as techniques, they
attempt to supply specific means by which to "end existence." The problem of existence was the theoretical
aspect, and the problem of ending existence the practical
aspect of Buddhism. The problem of existence evolved into
Buddhist philosophy, while the problem of ending existence
led to the various forms of Buddhist religion.

It goes without saying that the vast majority of Buddhists
down through the ages have not been philosophers, but were

satisfied to accept what they understood of the theories on
faith. To such ordinary people, it was not the problem of
existence that mattered, and not even the problem of ending
existence. Ordinary people were concerned with <u>ending</u>
<u>suffering</u>--and they could hardly comprehend the exact con-
gruence of the two terms, "to end existence," and "to end
suffering." To the mind of the ordinary person such an
identity would not only be difficult to understand, but
would in fact be too terrifying to accept. No training in
psychology or psychiatry is needed to convince us that the
individual's ego is the central, basic fact, and that destruction of that ego is intolerable to contemplate. This
is of course why religions other than Buddhism have assumed
and cherished the notion of the soul, the individuality
which death shall not terminate. It is also why even in
Buddhism itself allowance has been made for this human
frailty, just as so much else that seems utterly incom-
patible with the clear and simple doctrine of the Buddha
can not only be accepted, but approved, by Buddhism. Such
tolerance derived from the view that every person could
only be led from where he was at this given lifetime by
teachings that were adapted to his particular level of
understanding. The Buddhist <u>Dharma</u>, or Law, was not an
inflexible orthodoxy but a compassionate way of salvation
in which <u>upāya</u>, or expedient means, sought to accommodate
the needs and abilities of every suffering being according
to his state of religious advancement. Such, at any rate,
was Buddhism as it developed in its Chinese versions under
the inspiration of Mahāyāna ideals.

We cannot, within the limits of our present assignment, deal
in any more detail with Chinese Buddhism as a system. In
any case, it is easy to realize that membership in a monastic community was always limited to a very small fraction
of the Chinese population, so that the religious vocation
would not be a mode of dealing with suffering applicable to
many people. This is not to say, however, that the highly
systematized Buddhist <u>Dharma</u> did not have profound influence
throughout Chinese society in general. One can easily see
that, in addition to impressing the universality of suffering upon the Chinese mind, Buddhism's basic teachings about
<u>karma</u> and impermanence have been part and parcel of the Chinese
worldview from literati elite to unlettered peasants.
Suffering could be accounted for, in this Buddhistic view,
by the deeds of a past existence that came to inevitable
fruition in this one. The sorts of suffering that came
from the relentless workings of time could be accepted with
resignation through the Buddhistic insight that all things

are transitory because they are the product of ceaselessly changing causes. This latter view was, indeed, a reinforcement of the pre-Buddhist idea of change as the essence of things, most fully explicated in the Yi Ching or Scripture of Change.

If Buddhism thus provided householders, who could not leave society to devote themselves to terminating rebirth, with what may be seen as essentially compensatory attitudes toward the problem of suffering, there were other, more positive religious responses. To accept suffering as an inescapable result of the karmic process is to become resigned to it; to emphasize the impermanence of all things is to take refuge in philosophy. These are so to speak last-ditch stands, consciously attempted psychological adjustments to what cannot be helped. But suffering was most generally perceived as affliction by agents who could be dealt with, agents from the invisible, but entirely real dimension of this world that we call the supernatural. Besides those afflictions which could not be understood in a pre-scientific culture as having "natural" causes, there were quite often supernatural agents at work even in cases where the natural causes could be identified.

Such a concept of inflictions by spiritual powers is an explanation that is common in cultures throughout the world, whether the powers are evil spirits, ancestors, minions of Satan, or even justly punishing agents of a god. The notions of supernatural powers are infinitely varied in details from one culture to another, but while they give much of the "local color," they are essentially the outcome of an identical kind of human reasoning. In the Chinese case it seems that the supernatural agents are reducible to malevolent spirits or displeased ancestors.[10]

One copes with supernatural afflictions by religious means.[11] The sufferer may divine to ascertain the precise nature of the offense for which he is being punished, or the evil spirit that is doing the attacking. Malevolent spirits which take up residence in a person's body may be exorcised. Otherwise the supernatural beings may be dealt with by the universally practiced means of supplication, sacrifice, or the making and carrying out of vows. Those who have not yet been attacked will take care to defend themselves by the use of talismans and charms.

Displeased ancestors are displeased because they have not been properly tended to by their surviving kinsfolk. They

have not received the sacrifices that are as necessary to
their existence as food is to the living. Or they have been
given as their spirit residence an uncomfortable grave.
They expect the same filial devotion in their post mortem
state as they would have received while alive. When it is
not manifested, they may bring afflictions upon their neg-
lectful descendants. If such a cause is suspected,
sufferers may divine to identify the problem, and rectify
their remissness by providing the proper sacrifices or
attending to the improvement of a burial site.[12]

While we need not detail the many forms which suffering
takes, it may be worthwhile to consider briefly the conspicuous case of disease, which was so devastating everywhere in the world until only yesterday. The recent
television series produced under auspices of Jonas Salk and
shown by public broadcasting stations, called "Microbes and
Men," reminded us that it was hardly a century ago that
doctors began to grasp the germ theory. More often than
not, people went to the hospital not to live but to die. In
the most extreme situations disease took unimaginable tolls
of lives, as in the great plagues of 14th century Europe.
As recently as the 1920's a massive study of rural areas in
central China indicated that "one-half of those born in
China die before they are twenty-eight years of age."[13]

Coping with disease has always been, and to a not inconsider-
able degree still remains, one of the most common functions
of religion; or, to put it in our terms, the universality
of disease has given rise to religious responses everywhere.
The ability of practical methods of healing is always
limited, and the benevolent powers of the supernatural
realm are often the only recourse, while on the other hand,
the cause of a disease may as likely be supernatural as
purely physical. The Chinese physician was supposed to be
versed in what we might call "natural philosophy," the
general theories concerning which applied to the human constitution as to the rest of nature. But, says Dr. Edward
Hume, "Of still greater importance to the Chinese doctor is
a full understanding of the spirits that form a part of the
vital essences whose balance results in health."[14] "Health
and disease are due to balance or imbalance of the living
forces which make up the universe. There are life-preserving
and life-destroying forces everywhere, acting alike on man
and on plants and animals. It is the concern of medicine to
neutralize the malevolent influences of the environment by
the help of friendly spirits, to bring to man's aid every
friendly force in nature, and to use for the patient's

restoration, medicaments that have not only what the West
calls pharmacological value, but that are also, in themselves,
akin to the forces of life and vigor."[15] In this passage is
clearly brought out the mingling of the natural and supernatural in Chinese medical theory and practice.

Healing in human cultures is never a monopoly of physicians;
in fact, the professionally trained physician is a relatively limited phenomenon. For many thousands of years all
healing was essentially faith healing. Its practitioners
were shamans or similar religious specialists who claimed
to transmit supernatural power to the benefit of the sick.
It is not surprising, then, that in traditional China religious responses to the physical suffering of disease took
the forms both of a pseudo- or proto-scientific praxis and
faith-healing. It is perhaps unnecessary to remind ourselves, at this point, that faith-healing is still, in the
modern scientific milieu of the West, a conspicuous religious phenomenon--whether practiced by religious specialists
or by psychiatrists.

The Quirks of Fate

It is above all when the particular worldview of any group
of people is suddenly faced with anomalies, when the expectations of regularity and dependability systematized in
that worldview are shaken, that the religious response is
evoked. One may not go so far as the coiner of a phrase,
famous during World War II, and accept that "there are no
atheists in foxholes," but certainly conditions of extreme
emergency call forth man's deep-seated hopes for supernatural succor. Crises such as earthquake or flood, drought
or famine, war or pestilence arouse people to their utmost
efforts to ward off disaster, but, as the saying goes, when
man has done all that is humanly possible, "the rest is in
the hands of the gods." One's final response may be hope-
less resignation, but before such a state, there will surely
be fervent prayer, beseeching the mercy of whatever gods
there be.

In all of this there is nothing unique about the Chinese
case. What is remarkable is the social results of such
situations. According to the Chinese worldview, the occur-
rence of these quirks of fate was to be accounted for by
the failure of Man, specifically as represented by the Son
of Heaven--the Emperor--to do his part in maintaining the
harmonious balance of natural operations. More than this,
the manifestations of maladjustments in such operations

were ominous of Heaven's displeasure with the rule of its
human representative, and thus of a possible "change of the
Mandate." In other words, it was a time of great danger
but also of great opportunity: the will of Heaven was un-
settled, and the legitimacy of the dynasty in question.
Such readings of crisis events must be counted among the
most common, basic causes for the many uprisings against
established authority that occurred throughout Chinese history, including the eruptions of rebellions by millenarian
sects.

Human Inadequacy

Human inadequacy is obviously such a broad category that it
might subsume almost all of the challenges and responses
that we have listed as religious. However, we use it here
to refer to those situations in which people undertake
activities whose outcome is of vital importance, and yet
which remain uncertain of success because of factors beyond
human control. An evident example of such an undertaking
is an activity whereby the group obtains its basic necessities. In a hunting culture life depends upon finding and
killing game; in an agrarian culture the crops must thrive
if subsistence is to be assured.

The Chinese peasant was among the world's most skilled,
knowledgeable, and diligent agriculturists, and whatever
human brains and hands could accomplish in the pre-scientific,
pre-modern technological age, he accomplished. But in the
last resort it is always nature that gives or withholds the
harvest, which was always apparent to the farmer. So, then,
to the powers that controlled nature's activities he must
address his supplications. Much of the peasant's religious
preoccupation is thus with the supernaturally caused blights
of weather and disease that could endanger his crops and
animals, and with the benevolent supernatural beings who
could protect them.

Similarly, the artisan, such as the caster of bronze or iron
or the firer of porcelain, was conscious of the limitation
of his own ability to guarantee success or failure.[16] His
undertakings must therefore be carried out under the auspices
of the deities concerned, who are invoked by elaborate
rituals. In China, not only such crafts, but ordinary mer-
cantile activities--in fact, the activities connected with
every occupation whatsoever--were likewise felt to be hazard-
ous without the protection of superhuman patrons. Man had
not yet attained the modern sense of self-confidence that

his own, unaided efforts are all-sufficient.

Meaninglessness of Life

Existence is inherently meaningless. Meaning is something
human beings, presumably alone among the creatures, somehow
create and project upon their environment. It is individually thought and felt, yet in many ways socially expressed
and nurtured. Even when it seems to be purely individual,
it has been, as we know, to a great extent "socialized" into
us. This is obvious, for example, in our ethical values,
which we absorb from our family and our community long before we give them any self-conscious consideration. It is
also true of the notions we hold about relationships between
man and the rest of the world, including the supernatural.
The creation, transmission, and reinforcement of certain
meanings that have been accepted within a culture as incon-
trovertible--"We hold these truths to be self-evident"--is
studied in anthropology and religion as myth and ritual.
Myth and ritual may in turn be subsumed under the comprehensive rubric of symbolism, which is a mode of expressing
meanings more concisely, immediately, and impressively than
verbal definition. Those kinds of meanings that are not
expressible in words may find expression in the arts, whose
products themselves never cease to evoke by their intriguing
ambiguity additional inexpressible meanings. In general,
one might say that profundity of meaning is in a spectrum
that goes inversely to verbal clarity: from words through
visual representation through kinetic and musical revelation.[17] From the point of view of religion, the extreme
end of this spectrum is just silence. In the highest truth
of Mahāyāna Buddhism this is enlightenment as to the essential "emptiness" (śūnyatā in the Sanscrit, or k'ung in
Chinese) of all things whatsoever. It is already expressed
in the words of the Lao Tzu text, several centuries before
the Common Era:

> "One who knows Tao does not talk about it; one who
> talks about it is one who knows it not. Block the
> road, shut your gate, subdue your ardor, do away
> with your inner divisions, dim your light, and be-
> come one with the dusty world. This is called
> realizing the original identity of all things..."
> (Chapter 56)

Meaning seems to involve two interrelated kinds of mental
constructs: the worldview, and the value system. By the

former we mean the work of the human mind that makes sense of, or confers order upon, a world of an infinite number and variety of phenomena. By the latter we mean the assigning of relative values to social relationships and all of the other products of human cultures. For life to have meaning in the religious sense of the word, the world must be recognized as a cosmos, a system in which the place of man is not only defined, but in some way important. We need not remark on the crisis which modernization has brought upon the West, and thence to the rest of the world, in regard to these matters. Our purpose here is to point out the ways in which the problem of meaninglessness was faced by the religious responses of the Chinese. It appears to me that these may be identified as the "gestalt" worldview, and the familistic society.

By the "gestalt" worldview I mean a conception of the universe as a great harmony (ta-t'ung in Chinese) in which all things have their place, and in which man is integrated. This view does not conceive a Creator apart from his creation; still less does it give man the position of "lord of creation." Of all creatures man is of course most intelligent and dominant, but he is still only one part of the great scheme of things, and unless he works in harmony with the great, overall powers of nature--that is, Heaven and Earth--he will suffer disaster. The cosmos in this Chinese view functions in a perceptibly orderly, dependable, and productive way, called, in fact, Tao (which means a way), and man's success and happiness was contingent upon his conforming with this Tao. Chinese philosophy is basically concerned with trying to figure out just what human Tao will best bring man into congruence with the natural Tao. It seems to me that the understanding of the world as a complex of vital relationships is satisfying to the human mind, particularly as man can realize that he is an essential element in the functioning of this system. Instead of being a stranger in a cold, indifferent, mechanical universe of unimaginably vast size, in the Chinese view man is related to the whole of the cosmos, which is more animate than inanimate. Nature--Heaven and Earth--is not just some sort of environment, which may be inimical to, or exploitable by man for his own selfish ends. It is a concord, even a moral concord, of living beings with whom man is in symbiotic relationships. This is a religious view that is largely successful in avoiding man's alienation in space.

Similarly, the famous familism of the Chinese was able to solve the problem of alienation in time. Ancestrism, the

carrying on of family relationships through time, provided
basic psychological security, just as the organization of
the family provided basic social security. Individualism
has some obvious advantages over familism; but the converse
is also true, and most obviously in the matter of religious
meaning. Where every question, including the meaning of
life, has to be solved by the individual, there will inevitably ensue a fragmentation and great uncertainty of
beliefs. Where people's feeling of accomplishment is based
upon the living of well defined roles within the small
society of the family, there is a greater degree of integration, and the matter of personal "beliefs" enters in hardly
at all. Ancestrism assured that the family system in which
the individual had been subordinated all of his or her life
was triumphant over death itself. It was a self-fulfilling
cycle of meanings from life to death and back to life. The
individual did not face the endless emptiness of time alone
and helpless; he was a link in a continuous chain of being
that was conceived as an organismic reality. This view
sanctioned and gave meaning to the elaborate codes of behavior (li) which worked to perpetuate the system, and thus
served the essential purpose of establishing social values.
When a person knew how to live, and that death did not cut
him off from life, existence was no longer meaningless.

Authority and Submission

The preceding words will already have indicated the extent
to which the religious view of the Chinese derived from
solutions to the problem of authority and submission within
the family. This is of course not to say that all Chinese
were always happy about their family system, in which from
our present-day point of view there was an intolerable repression of women and the young. Nevertheless, it seems to
have served human needs at least as well as any other family
system over a very long period of time. Insofar as psychological security is created by well-defined "rules of the
game," the Chinese system was admirably unambiguous, resting
upon the unquestionable authority of males and seniors, and
the generally accepted submission of females and juniors.
It was maintained not only by the binding custom of a traditional society, but additionally by extremely detailed
written codes whose custodians were the Confucian literati
elite. While modern scholars are much more interested in
Confucian teachings about ethics and statesmanship designed
for the small number of "superior men," I tend to see the
Confucian tradition as especially weighty for its inculcation

of the whole original Chinese view of authority and submission, within and without the family. In this respect it
is outstanding for the elaborateness with which it has ritu-
alized the myth. It is of course precisely because of this
identification of Confucianism and the traditional system
of authority and submission that Chinese in this century
have so often attacked Confucius as the great symbol of a
past whose traditionalism they wish to leave behind.

The relationship of authority and submission to religion is
found not only in the family system, but also in the political system. It is hardly necessary to labor the point
that all political and legal systems of pre-modern societies
have required ultimate religious sanctions. For one man to
maintain authority over all others he must be divine, as
against their humanness, or at least have divine commission.
For law to be authoritative it must refer beyond man to
divine--and hence unquestionable--authority. What will
happen in a modern world lacking such a superhuman source
to compel the submission of men, is still in considerable
doubt. In the case of traditional China, as is well known,
emperors derived their authority from Heaven, although not
themselves divine. The Mandate of Heaven remained with a
dynasty as long as members of its line ruled in accord
with Tao, and was transferred to another line when they
ceased to do so. Submission to this authority was an
acknowledgment of the ruler's supernatural election, but
rebellion against it was justified as the means whereby
Heaven was able to remove its Mandate from unworthy to
deserving representatives of man.

Omnipresence of Evil

Like all values, the moral law is a human construct and not
something given in nature. In fact, many would point to the
moral law as precisely that which raises man above the
animal level, where the governing law is simply big fish
eats small fish. A thorough consideration of the moral law
in the Chinese tradition is not possible here, but probably
everyone is at least aware of the great emphasis placed
upon it by the philosophers, especially K'ung (Confucius)
and his school. We raise the subject because it is the
existence of the moral law that produces the omnipresence
of evil. Whatever contravenes the accepted moral law is
evil,[18] and in the nature of things there will always be
plenty of contravention. Society takes punitive measures
against these evil actions, but often without conspicuous

success. The religious question arises as to why, in a cosmos that, particularly in China, is conceived as a moral order, evil should exist. Then there is the even more practical question as to why the moral law should be obeyed when evil men flout it with seeming impunity and benefit to themselves. This challenge to the conscience is what K'ung Tzu refers to when he says, "The victory (of right) in the (moral) struggle (within a man's heart) may be called virtue." (Lun Yü VI.20)

In many cultures the struggle between good and evil is projected onto the transcendental level and made into a struggle between the ultimate Powers of the universe, God and Devil, who use men as their pawns. The Chinese did not explain evil in such terms, despite their recognition of spiritual agencies in suffering.[19] They placed it squarely upon the shoulders of man himself, as a morally responsible agent.

The problem of evil did not receive satisfactory solution in China until the assimilation of Buddhism. It was Buddhism that offered a complete explanation for the existence of evil, and a complete rationalization for keeping the moral law whatever the temptations to flout it. Buddhism underlined the inevitability of suffering in all forms of existence, and equated evil with ignorance of the true nature of things. Men were evil because they did not realize that every evil thought and deed simply accumulated that karmic energy which would propel them into rebirth and even more suffering. To flout the moral law was to obtain only transsitory pleasure which led directly to greater pain. One could even rationalize one's own suffering at the hands of evildoers as a deserved retribution for one's own sins in a previous existence.

Death and Salvation

Nowadays, among students of religion in this country, death and dying are very popular. In the schema we are using here, the dying process may be subsumed under suffering. As for death itself, man has regarded it as the greatest suffering, as the end of suffering, or as the transition to a new condition--which in turn may be still more suffering, eternal bliss, or rebirth. In any case, death is indubitably sui generis, inevitable, and in our thoughts, particularly as we grow older. It is the one experience we know that all living beings share, but its mystery is not lessened thereby. The trouble is that no one has died and lived to tell about it.

The problem of death may be separated into two parts: the individual facing his own death in prospect; and the survivors facing the fact of another's death. The latter is of course from one point of view just another aspect of the former. In facing the prospect of death a broad range of defenses can readily be conceived, such as resolutely putting the subject out of mind; resigning oneself to accept it with the least resistance; embracing it eagerly in some great cause such as patriotism or religion; longing for it as the end of unbearable suffering; ordering one's life to be found worthy of translation to a better world; and so forth. Whatever of these attitudes eventuates in action, under the terms of our hypothesis we should have to denote as religious, and not merely psychological. Types of personal reactions will naturally vary from individual to individual, but are also considerably conditioned by the culture. Martyrdom, for instance, may be popular among certain groups but decidedly not among others. Suicide would be considered the appropriate response to dishonor among the Japanese samurai, but would be regarded as a sin by Christians. Furthermore, there are certainly great differences in the emotional feelings men have about their own death, depending upon individual psychological as well as cultural factors. Not least among the latter are the teachings about death and its aftermath in the formulated religion, and the extent to which the individual really believes in these teachings.

While we must remain ignorant of individual feelings, we are well informed about how the Chinese religion handled the problem of the survivors. Rituals of death, funerals, mourning, sacrifice, and assisting the soul in its post mortem circumstances are most prominent by far in this religion. It is no accident that in the most ambitious study ever to appear in a Western language, The Religious System of the Chinese, by J. J. M. de Groot,[20] three stout volumes are devoted entirely to the subject of "disposal of the dead," while the remaining three volumes deal with various topics that are inseparably involved with death, under the general heading of "the soul and ancestral worchip."

This elaborate cult of the dead served many important social functions,[21] but we shall here note only the religious aspects, as responses to the problem of death. The most fundamental fact, in this connection, is that it is

designed to affirm by every possible ritual the continuing
relationship of deceased and survivors. This is in striking
contrast to the purpose of death cults in many other cultures, where the dead are so feared that all emphasis is
placed upon assuring the total and irrevocable separation
of dead and living. Chinese religion comforts one facing
the prospect of death by the knowledge that he will, as it
were, remain a member of the family. The survivors, for
their part, are comforted by the belief that in performing
their many ritual tasks they are making this possible.

Buddhism introduced into this age-old native tradition some
complicating factors, as might be deduced from some of the
things we have already said. According to the native tradition the physical, or so-called yin, soul was placed with
the corpse in the grave, where it resided. The spiritual,
or so-called yang, soul was ensconced in its spirit tablet
upon the altar in the family home. After a few generations
this yang-soul would be removed in a new tablet to the company of the numerous spirits of the entire lineage, housed
in the lineage temple. But according to popular Buddhist
doctrine, the soul was forced, immediately upon death, to
undertake a difficult and dangerous journey in the under-
world, whose destination was the infernal courts of purga-
tory. There it would receive the most terrible punishments
for its many sins, and eventually it would be cast up by
the wheel to rebirth in some form commensurate with its
karma of the previous lifetime. Only the few who had led
morally upright lives could hope to escape this process
and be reborn directly upon death into the Western Paradise, as the Buddha-land of Amitābha was called.

The question naturally arises as to how these two theories
can be reconciled. I am not sure that they ever were, to a
degree that would satisfy a Western theologian, but the fact
remains that the Chinese cult of the dead did amalgamate
them. The fate of the ancestors was too vital to their
descendants for any possibility of salvation to be over-
looked. Sinful though he might have been, the deceased
could not be allowed to be subjected to the torments of
hell. Fortunately, through the power of the ordained religious, ritual and prayer could be brought to bear, and,
if properly performed and sincerely intended, the compassion
of the Buddha Amitābha would be moved to bring the subject
to the Western Paradise. Likewise, Taoist priests were
brought in to work for the salvation of the deceased, as
they had similar versions of the afterworld, and similar
powers of persuasion.

Salvation, the overcoming of Time, thus appears in two
guises in the Chinese religion. On the one hand it means
subsisting after death as an ancestor; on the other, it
means gaining the Buddha's Paradise or some form of bliss-
ful immortality according to Taoist notions. In either
case it depends ultimately upon the filiality of the survivors. This makes their responsibility for performing the
appropriate rituals very great. It also gives them the
satisfaction of feeling that they are able to cope with the
crisis of death by effective action.

iii

Let me now attempt to sum up the discussion. In the first
place, it was proposed that we look at "religion" as a
human way of coping with universal problems, or what is
often called the existential situation, and that we see if
there is not a "Chinese religion" identifiable in such
terms. We isolated seven human situations for our analysis, as follows: (1) Suffering. Special emphasis was laid
upon the insight brought to Chinese minds by Buddhism,
which equates existence with suffering and provides the
most thorough-going inquiry into the cause and cure of
suffering. We then described the suffering inflicted by
supernatural agents including resentful ghosts--the bereaved spirits of ancestors--and drew attention especially
to the role of the supernatural in disease and healing.
(2) Quirks of Fate. When overwhelmed by disasters that
upset the dependable regularity of nature, man's recourse
is supplication of superhuman help. In China, such irregu-
larities in nature were interpreted as signs of Heaven's
dissatisfaction with the ruling dynasty, and often inspired
rebellions and millenarian movements. (3) Human Inadequacy.
Man's limited ability to influence the outcome of vitally
important activities required him to seek the favorable
intervention of the superhuman powers concerned. (4)
Meaninglessness of Existence. We noted that "meanings" are
human invention, manifested religiously in myth and ritual,
and embodied finally in symbols. The two sorts of meanings
that we considered are the worldview and the value system.
We described the Chinese worldview as constituting a
"gestalt," in which man is well integrated. This integration overcame alienation in space. On the other hand,
alienation in time was countered by the sense of continuity
of living and dead in the family system. (5) Authority

and Submission. The familistic rather than individualistic
society gave the Chinese well-defined roles to play, which
largely prevented the crises of authority. In the State,
the concept of a Mandate of Heaven provided the ruling line
with the sacred legitimation essential in kingship; the
Mandate was revokable when the ruler failed to carry out his
responsibilities and was rejected by Heaven. (6) Omnipresence of Evil The existence of evil is created by the
creation of the moral law; both are human inventions. The
theoretical question is how evil can exist in a moral universe, but the practical question is the upholding of the
moral law in the face of the apparent success of evil. We
observed that good and evil are not given any transcendental
significance in China, and that moral responsibility is
placed directly upon man. The problem of evil was dealt
with most adequately by Buddhism, which equated it with
ignorance and explained it by the inescapable functioning
of karmic destiny. (7) Death and Salvation. While ack-
nowledging our inability to know the reaction of individual
Chinese to the prospect of death, we stressed the richness
of the rituals devised to comfort the survivors. We
pointed out that the basic purpose of these rituals is to
assure the continuing relationship of living and dead on
the one hand, and to assist the soul to a happy post mortem
state on the other. These two aims arose from the theoretically discrepant theories of the ancient native tradition and Buddhism, which were, however, successfully
blended in practice. Salvation, therefore, meant on the
one hand that one continues in the post mortem state to
receive the filial services of one's descendants, and on
the other that one would attain Buddhahood in the Western
Paradise or immortality in the Taoist realm.

This cannot, of course, be the whole of Chinese religion,
but it may suffice at least to convince us of that religion's essential reasonableness and similarity to the
religious responses of the rest of mankind. In this sense
it is eminently scrutable, arising from the same existential
situation men everywhere and always have faced.

NOTES

1. Apparently hard-core social scientists nowadays have left functionalism behind. James Dittes, himself a noted psychologist and former editor of the prestigious Journal for the Scientific Study of Religion, ironically observes that "social scientists . . . are suspicious of the functional and seem to assume that either religion serves discernible functions or it is true." James E. Dittes, "Beyond William James," in Charles Y. Glock and Phillip E. Hammond, editors, Beyond the Classics? Essays in the Scientific Study of Religion, New York (1973) p. 303.

2. Mircea Eliade, Patterns in Comparative Religion, English translation by Rosemary Sheed, Cleveland and New York (1963) p. xiii.

3. Claude Lévi-Strauss, The Savage Mind, English translation, University of Chicago (1966) p. 95.

4. This view of the raison d'etre of religion is hardly original. It was perhaps first enunciated most trenchantly by Malinowski. For a well-turned phrase, take this from his article on "Culture" in the Encyclopaedia of the Social Sciences (Vol. 4, 1931): "Religion is not born out of speculation or reflection, still less out of illusion or misapprehension (referring to an opinion of Sir James Frazer), but rather out of the real tragedies of human life, out of the conflict between human plans and realities." Quoted in William A. Lessa and Evon Z. Vogt, editors, Reader in Comparative Religion, Evanston, Ill., and White Plains, N. Y. (1958) p. 97. See also, in the same volume, an example of a similar view expressed more systematically by Talcott Parsons: "Religious Perspectives in Sociology and Social Psychology," pp. 118-124.

5. Max Weber calls such religious geniuses "prophets," and uses the term to denote both a "renewer of religion" and a "founder of religion" as, in his view, "the two types merge into one another." See Max Weber, The Sociology of Religion, English translation by Ephraim Fischoff, Boston (1963) p. 46. In the case of China, I have taken the position that K'ung Tzu (Confucius) may from the religious point of view be considered as The Prophet (sheng-jen), as one who proclaimed the Tao in its most authoritative form, and the Founder of the Ju School or the Great

Tradition. Thus he was a prophet in both of the senses in which the term is used by Weber. See my unpublished paper on "Imagining Confucius," in which I also note that H. H. Rowley already suggested the suitability of considering the ancient Chinese "sages" as prophets, in his Prophecy and Religion in Ancient China and Israel, University of London (1956).

6. See Lévi-Strauss again, for a good description of the latter phenomenon, in "The Sorcerer and His Magic," English version in his Structural Anthropology, Doubleday Anchor paperback (1967) p. 161. For a thorough psychological and physiological explanation, see Walter B. Cannon, "'Voodoo' Death," American Anthropologist 44 (1942) 169-181; reprinted in abridged form in Lessa & Vogt, Reader, op. cit., 270-276.

7. For the history of attempts along this line see Charles H. Long, "Primitive Religion," in Charles J. Adams, editor, A Reader's Guide to the Great Religions, 2nd edition, New York (1977) pp. 1-38; and E. E. Evans-Pritchard, Theories of Primitive Religion, Oxford University (1965).

8. Sir Edwin Arnold, "The Light of Asia," Book the Third. Reprinted in Lin Yutang, editor, The Wisdom of China and India, New York (1942) p. 421.

9. As a pampered young prince, kept from the harsh realities of the world in his palace, the future Buddha was brought to his destiny by seeing Four Signs during brief forays into the outside: an old man, a sick man, a corpse, and a holy man or "truth-seeker."

10. I am by now at least half-persuaded that these two categories are ultimately a single species: the "bereaved spirits," or the spirits of the deceased who have for one reason or another been deprived of the sacrifices that are due them. There seems not to be any principle in Chinese religion of evil operating for its own self-fulfillment. I have considered this question in more detail than is possible here in a paper entitled "Objectification of Divine Power: Some Chinese Modes," which will be published by Brigham Young University as part of a collection of papers given at a recent conference there.

11. We shall avoid fruitless arguments as to whether or not religion and magic are separate phenomena, and keep

to our criterion of coping by other than "practical"--i.e.
commonsense or technologically effective--means.

12. The siting of graves is the main business of feng-
shui, or "geomancy," a quite elaborately developed pseudo-
science. There is currently some difference of opinion as
to whether the deceased should be regarded as willing good
fortune or affliction upon the survivors, or as functioning
"mechanically" to focus these effects through the "scientifically" identifiable features of a good or bad site.
For a representative statement of the latter opinion see
Jack Potter, "Wind, Water, Bones and Stones: the Religious
World of the Cantonese Peasant," Journal of Oriental
Studies (University of Hong Kong) 8.1 (Jan. 1970) pp. 139-
153, reprinted in Laurence G. Thompson, editor, The Chinese
Way in Religion, Encino and Belmont, Calif. (1973). For
the former view, see Emily Ahern, The Cult of the Dead in
a Chinese Village, Stanford University (1973) especially
chapter 11.

13. John Lossing Buck, Land Utilization in China,
Shanghai (1937) p. 392.

14. Edward H. Hume, M.D., The Chinese Way in Medicine,
Johns Hopkins University (1940) p. 19.

15. Ibid., p. 5.

16. This universally encountered phenomenon has been
studied extensively in the case particularly of the metal-
smith. See, for instance, the illuminating work of Mircea
Eliade, The Forge and the Crucible, English translation by
Stephen Corrin, London (1962).

17. On this last point, compare Dan Sperber: "A representation is symbolic precisely to the extent that it is
not entirely explicable, that is to say, expressible by
semantic means. Semiological views are therefore not
merely inadequate (he is at this point expressly criticizing Levi-Strauss); they hide, from the outset, the
defining features of symbolism." Rethinking Symbolism,
English translation by Alice L. Morton, Cambridge University (1975) p. 113. This is perhaps an even keener perception than that of Coomaraswamy, who has accurately
pointed out that "Art is concerned with the nature of
things, and only incidentally, if at all, with their
appearance. . . ," Ananda Coomaraswamy, Christian and
Oriental Philosophy of Art, New York (1956) p. 93.

18. Eberhard has reminded us that the Chinese language does not distinguish between sin and crime. "The same words that are used in social contexts are used in religious contexts. . . All crimes (<u>tsui</u> and <u>kuo</u>) are sins, but not all violations of the moral code set up by the deities are crimes and punished by the laws of the realm." Wolfram Eberhard, <u>Guilt and Sin in Traditional China</u>, University of California (1967) p. 13.

19. On the foregoing, see my paper cited above, "Objectification of Divine Power. . ."

20. Leiden (1892-1910); reprinted in Taipei (1964).

21. These functions have been a major subject of research by anthropologists working in Taiwan and Hong Kong's New Territories during the past fifteen years or so. The literature is too large to cite here.

III – A RELIGIOUS DIMENSION IN CHINESE COMMUNIST THOUGHT

Richard C. Bush

Much has been said recently about the ways in which communism in China appears to be a religion, has religious aspects or dimensions, is analogous to or functions as a religion. Regardless of how the question is put, both scholars and those with general interest in China tend to find the questions intriguing.

The Great Cultural Revolution which began in 1966 seems to have intensified discussion of what is now called Maoism and religion. When thousands of enthusiastic young people waved their little red books of Mao's sayings, sang songs about Chairman Mao as the red sun shining in their hearts, and proclaimed to their elders the right word for every problem, the liturgical note was unmistakable. Professor Paul Rule has seen in the descent of these Red Guards on the capitol city of Peking a pilgrimage motif,[1] which may also be seen as people visit Mao's boyhood home in Hunan and his home for his middle years in Yenan. The great emphasis on confession of bourgeois sins of the past, as well as those which surface again in the present, along with the sense of great release and joy that accompanies the acceptance of the confessor after he has confessed to his peers in a study group, parallels similar patterns in several religious contexts.

Moral as well as ritual practices have also evoked comparisons with religious movements. Especially the stress on self-sacrifice for the good of the people, the dedication to a simple life of service in memory of those who gave so much, is reminiscent of countless religio-ethical codes. Moral rules and codes can be found in non-religious contexts as well, but rarely is the moral life followed so continuously and so passionately apart from religious motivation.

The result of all of this is the "new Socialist man," a model of virtue and dedication who in every crisis reacts with the wisdom born of reading and studying the teachings of Chairman Mao, who chooses to be Red rather than expert if the choice is demanded, whose only thought is to serve the people in the name of Chairman Mao. He parallels the new convert in just about every way, including evangelistic fervor to convince and win those who have not yet seen the light. Tempered in the fires of class struggle, he knows who he is and thus continues in the vanguard of revolution.

All this is well and good. Few will argue with the proposition that the singing and quoting of sayings from and about Chairman Mao sounds liturgical, that there is a religious intensity about the way people follow the moral codes of the new China, and that the "new creature in Mao" who emerges from this process looks and acts like one in any religion who, being born again or emancipated, is a model of piety and virtue. Our impressions of religiousness, however, are based on data from the area of practice, both ritual activity and moral life, without any parallel impressions based on belief or doctrine. Most people, however, expect belief in a god or in some being or power to be present in a movement if it is to be classified as a religion. Both the classical Marxists and Chinese Communist thinkers past and present stoutly maintain that they are atheists, that belief in gods or spirits, along with other religious trappings, is an opiate used by rulers and upper classes to keep the masses in submission. Any idea of ultimate mind or spirit, however impersonal, is impossible because idealist metaphysics is excluded as illusory, and materialist metaphysics, which is almost a contradiction in terms, automatically excludes any spiritual reality. If there is no theological foundation, no recognition of and thinking about god, and if there is no ultimate reality, no philosophical absolute such as mind or spirit, then where is the basis for thinking of communism as a religion? If there is no ultimate reality, no god or philosophical absolute, can one even speak of a religious analogy or of communion functioning as a religion?

The study of the history of religions reveals several examples of distinctly religious movements whose followers neither believe in nor worship a deity, and which do not speak of any ultimate being in a metaphysical sense. Buddhism, of course, is the example which immediately comes to mind: the Buddha is not a god and calls neither for devotion to any god nor any thought about a transcendent Being. In one of his dialogues the Buddha tells Malunkyaputta that the question of the existence or non-existence of an absolute reality is not a good question, that the existence or non-existence of suffering and what we may do about it is a question very much worth discussing. Gautama neither says that an ultimate reality such as god exists, nor does he say god does not exist. The fact that Buddhas and Bodhisattvas function as gods in China and Japan, at least in popular piety, does not alter the basic Buddhist theoretical stance: no affirmation or denial of ultimate reality such as god. What is real is <u>karma</u>, actions producing rebirth, which means no first cause or prime mover or prime originator, only the process, the continuum. Thus the real for Buddhism is not being but becoming; the Void of Madhyamika philosophy is not emptiness in a negative sense but alive with meaning and purpose and value. And yet few would question that Buddhism is a religion.

Although belief in a god or some ultimate Being is not in the last analysis a <u>sine qua non</u> of a religion, there must be some "idea of the holy," a sense of something sacred or transcendent. In my own working definition of religion I have suggested that religion is a way of thought, practice, and grouping by which people approach and/or respond to that powerful reality (or realities) which they experience as having a profound effect on their existence. In the Judeo-Christian-Islamic tradition that reality is one almighty god, but in this discussion we are talking about another religious and philosophical context, however much Marxism may betray its Judeo-Christian ancestry. Although there need be no reality in the Western, Judeo-Christian sense, if we are to talk about communism in China as a religion, somewhere in that system of thought there should be a real power or powerful reality which is making things happen and to which people attempt to relate their lives.

I recall a course in graduate school in which Wilhelm Pauck, practically limiting the Reformation to Luther, quoted that

Reformer as saying (or meaning): "The world is a hullabaloo
and God is making the hubbub." I know that for Communists,
as for Buddhists, there is no god who is making a hubbub,
but the world is a hullabaloo everywhere you look. Something is happening and there has to be an explanation or
interpretation or theory of just what is going on and maybe
why.

Two further comments of an introductory nature are necessary. First, the fact that Communists disavow being
followers of a religion does not necessarily mean that that
communism is not to be considered a religion. Christians,
Buddhists, Chinese people generally, and a host of others
who are devoted to some movement classified as a religion,
refuse to consider that movement as a religion or themselves
as religious. It is always other people, especially "those
peasants," who are religious; we follow a philosophy of life
or the gospel or whatever the in-word happens to be.

In the second place, it is difficult to regard whatever
Marxist theoreticians say about religion (including what
they say about their own religiousness or lack of it) as
being entirely conclusive until we have more convincing
evidence of their having read beyond Feuerbach and his
circle. Feuerbach's radical criticism of religion can open
the student to new insights; it can also provide blinders
which prevent the student from seeing anything else. Even
when writers in Red Flag and Historical Research and other
more thoughtful or scholarly journals in the People's Republic of China were writing about religion in the fifties
and early sixties, they gave little evidence of having read
or considered any of the significant Western or Japanese
works on religion of this century. Some serious consideration of the work of Otto, Van Der Leeuw, Heiler, Wach,
Eliade, et al., by Chinese philosophers might open up some
interesting avenues of thought and discussion which they
have regarded as useless or unrewarding.

My purpose in this paper, therefore, is to examine the
thought of Mao Tse-tung and several others with respect to
the question of ultimate reality. There is no concern on
my part to find any hidden or implicit doctrine of god or
a theology. I am trying to see if there is any awareness
of something real, ultimate, and other in the writings of
Mao and his associates. I have long suspected that there
is a greater sense of an ongoing, ultimate reality in Mao's
thought than has been recognized in the literature, and
this study has confirmed such hunches.

Most interpreters of Mao's thought concentrate on his so-called philosophical essays, "On Practice" and "On Contradiction." In the first of these essays Mao is working at a theory of knowledge, which he says begins as man, by participation in production, class struggle, political life, scientific and artistic pursuits, takes the first step in gaining knowledge about the world. This social practice alone is the criterion of truth, not subjective feelings, for theory is based on practice. Theory or concepts or logical knowledge arise from the data perceived in practice in a most interesting way:

> As social practice continues, things that give rise to man's sense perceptions and impressions in the course of his practice are repeated many times; then a sudden change (leap) takes place in the brain in the process of cognition, and concepts are formed. Concepts are no longer the phenomena, the separate aspects and the external relations of things; they grasp the essence, the totality and the internal relations of things. Between concepts and sense perceptions there is not only a quantitative but also a qualitative difference.[2]

The possibility, even the necessity of conceptual knowledge, making it possible for one to know "the totality, the essence and the internal relations of things and . . . the inner contradictions in the surrounding world," is most significant.

A few pages further in the essay Mao uses the term rational knowledge to describe the second stage. From "superficial perceptual knowledge, as shown in the indiscriminate anti-foreign struggles" of nineteenth century movements, the Chinese people moved to a second stage of rational knowledge. The first stage is not thereby denigrated, for personal participation in the struggle to change reality, direct contact with the phenomena of the world, is necessary if one is to get at the "essence" which is basic to rational knowledge.[3] The data of perception must correspond to reality if they are to be adequate for correct concepts.

There was the leap from perception (derived from practice) to concepts, which is followed by a leap back to practice.

> Marxist philosophy holds that the most important problem does not lie in understanding the laws of the objective world and thus being able to explain

it, but in applying the knowledge of these laws actively to change the world. . . . Marxism emphasizes the importance of theory precisely and only because it can guide action. . . . Knowledge begins with practice, and theoretical knowledge is acquired through practice and must then return to practice.[4]

The truth of Marxism-Leninism is due to the fact that "it has been verified in the subsequent practice of revolutionary national struggle."[5] It is clear that the struggle goes on, from which perceptual knowledge arises and is transformed into conceptual knowledge, and then is put to the test in struggle again. Thus there is continual movement, dialectic to the core, rather than any fixed body of knowledge or truth. Lenin's statement that "truth is a process" immediately comes to mind.[6]

The change that takes place in the process is even more important:

. . . Generally speaking, whether in the practice of changing nature or of changing society, men's original ideas, theories, plans or programmes are seldom realized without any alteration.[7]

Not only do we effect changes; we ourselves are changed in the process. Man concludes the essay with a sense of destiny as he refers to the responsibility which rests on the shoulders of the proletariat. The task is bipolar:

The struggle of the proletariat and the revolutionary people to change the world comprises the fulfillment of the following tasks: to change the objective world and, at the same time, their own subjective world--to change their cognitive ability and change the relations between the subjective and the objective world.[8]

Theoretical knowledge allows us to see among other things the inherent contradiction in a thing, and thus we are led to the second essay, "On Contradiction." External causes do not cause anything to develop. Development takes place because of the internal contradict within, or what Lenin called "the contradictory, mutually exclusive, opposite tendencies in all phenomena and processes of nature (including mind and society)."[9] Contradiction is actually a process in which a new unity of opposites continually emerge.

The old unity with its constituent opposites yields
to a new unity with its constituent opposites, where-
upon a new process emerges to replace the old. The
old process ends and the new one begins. The new
process contains new contradictions and begins its
own history of the development of contradictions.[10]

One sees contradiction in nature and in society, in class
struggle and in military struggle, between idealism and
materialism in philosophy. The need to stress individual,
concrete contradictions is balanced with the need to see
the whole. Certain dogmatists

> do not understand that we have to study the par-
> ticularity of contradiction and know the particular
> essence of individual things before we can ade-
> quately know the universality of contradiction and
> the common essence of things, and . . . they do not
> understand that after knowing the common essence of
> things, we must go further and study the concrete
> things that have not yet been thoroughly studied or
> have only just emerged.[11]

Then one may move on to the universality of contradiction:

> To deny contradiction is to deny everything. This
> is a universal truth for all times and all coun-
> tries, which admits of no exception. Hence the
> general character, the absoluteness of contradic-
> tion. But this general character is contained in
> every individual character; without individual
> character there can be no general character. . . .
> It is because each contradiction is particular that
> individual character arises. All individual char-
> acter exists conditionally and temporarily, and
> hence is relative.[12]

Some contradictions are antagonistic ones, some are not.
Those which are non-antagonistic at one time may become
antagonistic, and vice versa. Antagonism will disappear
under socialism; contradiction goes on. The ongoing dialectic process is probably more antagonistic than the
traditional yin-yang dialectic, but not unlike it in the
movement of opposites within a particular sphere. Many of
us have jumped immediately to a connection between Maoist
contradiction and the yin-yang polarity, and James C.
Hsiung has noted a minimal influence on the early Mao of
the ancient idea.

In his Marxist stage, Mao's theory of "contradictions" reflects this heritage. His theory that
contradictions manifest not only "mutual contention" but also "mutual complementarity" (hsiang-
ch'eng) and that contradictions may be nonanti-
thetical as well as antithetical recalls the
"mutual pervasion" (complementarity) of yin and
yang.[13]

Certainly the yin-yang concept allows for contention and conflict and Mao's theory of contradiction allows for complementarity and pervasion, but the emphasis in each case
clearly is not the same. The living quality of the process
is set forth most clearly in the following passage:

> Why is it that "the human mind should take these
> opposites not as dead, rigid, but as living, con-
> ditional, mobile, transforming themselves into
> one another?" Because that is just how things
> are in objective reality. The fact is that the
> unity or identity of opposites in objective things
> is not dead or rigid, but is living, conditional,
> mobile, temporary and relative; in given condi-
> tions, every contradictory aspect transforms itself
> into its opposite.[14]

The reactionary classes and metaphysicians see opposites as
dead, etc.

> The task of Communists is to expose the fallacies
> of the reactionaries and metaphysicians to propagate
> the dialectics inherent in things, and to accelerate
> the transformation of things and achieve the goal
> of revolution.[15]

This movement of contradictions, the old giving way to the
new in an endless process of change, yet with the focus ever
on the particular contradiction at hand is best illustrated
by class struggle throughout history. Mao cites examples
of the struggle "The class struggles of the peasants, the
peasant uprisings and peasant wars constituted the real
motive force of historical development in Chinese feudal
society" because these uprisings and wars "dealt a blow to
the feudal regime of the time, and hence more or less
furthered the growth of the social productive forces."[16]
Mao cites examples of struggle with the Kuomintang and with
the Japanese to explain the way in which opposites are
transformed into each other and how "the contradiction of

a thing (itself a unity of opposites) could become intensified or stimulated (<u>chi-hua</u>) to the point of changing the unity."[17] A great deal of flexibility is allowed, even demanded, in order to deal with this constantly changing situation. And in the process men attain that knowledge which comes from practice as described earlier. Wakeman summarizes:

> As the proletariat came to understand the essence of capitalism by fighting it, or as the May Fourth generation (in contrast to the indiscriminately xenophobic Taiping Rebels or Boxers) arrived at a rational knowledge of imperialism by opposing it, men grew through practice to know their own historical task and thereby changed from members of a "class in itself" (<u>tzü-tsai chieh-chi</u>) to being part of a "class for itself" (<u>tzü-wei chieh-chi</u>).[18]

In his discussion of "On Practice," Wakeman points up the difference precisely at this point between Marx and Mao, stating that Marx generalized laws from history, which laws Mao believed in, but he saw his major purpose not as deriving laws but that of "guiding human society through revolutionary change by showing men how to make and remake themselves and their environment by dialectical 'unity of knowing and doing' (<u>chih hsing t'ung-i</u>)."[19] The fact that Wang Yang-ming spoke of the unity of knowledge and action as <u>chih hsing ho-i</u>, involving only a different term for unity, is not the only reason for noting a possible influence of Wang upon Mao's thinking, as we shall see later. As Mao saw it, very similar to Wang Yang-ming, knowledge had to be more than cognition. It had to involve continuity, "the entire realization of a process that began in cognition and was wholly completed in action."[20]

A remark by Mao in his essay "On the Correct Handling of Contradictions among the People" summarizes the drift of what has been said above concerning history as a movement of contradictions. In response to criticisms of the government and the Party which had been voiced from many quarters during the Hundred Flowers Period, Mao distinguished between two continuing contradictions--that between the people and the enemy and that among the people themselves. Mao reaffirmed that "the ceaseless emergence and ceaseless resolution of contradictions is the dialectical law of the development of things."[21] To emphasize the "ceaseless" aspect of the operation of this dialectical law he went on to say:

What is correct invariably develops in the course
of struggle with what is wrong. The true, the good
and the beautiful always exist by contrast with the
false, the evil and the ugly, and grow in struggle
with the latter. As soon as a wrong thing is rejected and a particular truth accepted by mankind,
new truths begin their struggle with new errors.
Such struggles will never end. This is the law of
development of truth and, naturally, of Marxism as
well.[22]

All of the themes in Mao's writings are echoed again and
again by his disciples who reiterate in various ways the
idea of the continuing dialectic process. Only three months
after Mao's speech on handling contradictions, China Youth
carried an article by Meng Wen affirming the universality
of contradictions which, as settled, are followed by new
ones. "Contradictions are the motive force of progress in
all matters and a phenomenon found in Nature as well as in
our social life."[23]

In the same 1957 article on contradictions Mao had spoken
of the "unity of opposites," relating it to a dialectic of
unity-criticism-unity. In a 1960 article in Red Flag Wang
Jo-shui proceeded to discuss the identity of thinking and
being, rejecting both the idealist metaphysics of Hegel and
what he called the materialist metaphysics of Feuerbach.
"Being" in this discussion is not the absolute being of
metaphysics but "material being" which is the primary nature
of the world and unites the world. Thinking "belongs to
the secondary nature" and is subjective in character. For
our purposes Wang's statement of the way practice bridges
the gap between the subjective and the objective will
suffice.

It is only in the process of practice that an
objective thing will be reflected in the human
consciousness, while man can realize his purpose
through practice, thereby converting subjective
things into objective things, and proving whether
his subjective view is in keeping with the objective view. On the basis of practice, subjectivity
and objectivity continue incessantly to transmute,
to generate contradictions, and to solve contradictions, which is the historical and concrete
unification of subjectivity and objectivity.[24]

An Chi-wen followed much the same line in talking about the

"constant interaction between thought and existence, that changes of existence give rise to changes of thought," that changes of man's thought have effects on changes of existence."[25] An Chi-wen, however, seems to stress a more significant role for thought affecting existence than is customary in a Marxist thinker and makes the following rather startling statement:

Life in human society has two aspects: material and spiritual. Material life is the base, while spiritual life is the expression of material life and has effects on material life. Material and spiritual lives are the two interdependent aspects of life in human society.[26]

Reference to "spirit" may be startling, and refers of course to the human spirit and not to any ultimate spirit, but the same terminology was used by a shipyard Party Committee in 1976 who quote from Mao's "Where Do Correct Ideas Come From" the dictum that in the hands of the masses "ideas turn into a material force which changes society and changes the world." The shipyard workers say that Mao's teaching

profoundly reveals the dialectics of matter turning into spirit and spirit turning into matter and illustrates the importance of spirit to matter and revolutionary theory to revolutionary practice. . . . Marxism-Leninism-Mao Tse-tung Thought provides us with a powerful, ideological weapon for knowing and transforming the world (and for fighting counter-revolutionaries like Liu Shao-ch'i, Lin Piao and Teng Hsiao-p'ing) . . . and shattering the spiritual fetters imposed by the bourgeoisie. This will inevitably generate tremendous socialist enthusiasm and promote the development of production at a pace that was unattainable in the past. Spirit can turn into matter and this is the basic reason why our shipyard has continuously won fresh victories in both revolution and production.[27]

Lest anyone be tempted to draw the conclusion that Chinese Communist thought is tending in the direction of a prior role for thinking or spirit, one should be reminded that Yao Wen-yuan, aesthetic arbiter during the Cultural Revolution and member of the "gang of four," was scathingly rebuked for maintaining that the view that "social being comes before thinking and objectivity before subjectivity," classical Marxist doctrine, "distorts dialectical materialism." Whether he said such or not is immaterial. Such a statement is attributed to him and he is therefore accused of advocating subjective idealist metaphysics.[28]

The ongoing dialectic process which centers in contradiction may be most frequently discerned in references to the class struggle and to history, which are combined of course since history is the history of class struggle. Lenin is quoted: "History has confirmed long ago that great revolutionary struggles will produce great people." Chairman Mao is quoted: "Class struggle is the key link and everything else hinges upon it." And those who quote him go on to say: "All strivings in history, whether political ideological or religious, were manifestations of class struggle in greater or lesser degrees."[29] A writer named Chin Nan calls attention to the Marxist theory "that class struggle is the motive force for the development of class society . . ." with the result that work "will have a correct orientation and be done well" if class struggle is the key link which "starts the locomotive of revolution."[30] When the earthquake hit an area of Hopei Province on July 28, 1976, a comment in Red Flag maintained that "Man Will Triumph over Nature" because of his revolutionary spirit developed in class struggle, which is "the great motive force propelling history forward," and the way to handle right deviationists like Teng Hsiao-p'ing and other problems.

Although these writers we have considered, from philosopher types to laborers in a shipyard, may sound the same note as Chairman Mao because it is the thing to do, one must acknowledge that the tenor of thought we have been describing has become dominant in the People's Republic of China. Chinese Communist thought, whether that of Mao or of others who deal with ideas, contains the rudiments of a metaphysic in which the truly real, that which ultimately keeps the hullabaloo going, is neither the divine mind or spirit of the classic Western idealist, nor the reality of the means of production of Marxist materialists. It is the process whereby a unity of opposites occurs, thus involving an internal contradiction which is the occasion of yet another unity of opposites. The process never ends. It certainly involves material things like the earth and instruments of production and workers and guns and human beings, but the process is more than these elements. The classical Marxist phrase is "the dialectic of history," which does indeed have a "transcendent" character, although that word seems no more appropriate in this context than does the word "immanent."[31] It does have the character of the "other" which is not quite comprehended in or by the hullabaloo.

As Goldman put it, "the transcendental element present in this faith (Marxism) is not supernatural and does not take us outside or beyond history; it merely takes us beyond the individual."[32]

There is an aura to the dialectic process which is inescapable and infectious. There is a compulsion to relate to that which is happening and to be swept up by it, to struggle with class enemies and with one's closest associates and family members, to carry the revolution through to the end. To be continuously and endlessly involved in making revolution is not to engage in wild forays but is to act in accordance with one's fundamental concept of reality, seen not as being that is spiritual or material, but seen as process, movement, dialectic, and revolution.

That Mao has this understanding of reality seems relatively clear. That he conceived of the dialectic process, contradiction, and the movement of history as ultimate reality and that it therefore functioned as a metaphysic in his thought, represents, of course, my own reading of what he has said. This understanding of reality, as I have described it, is not strange for a person like Mao whose thought was taking shape in the early years of this century in China. Various influences on Mao's early thought have been analyzed in a most penetrating way by Frederic Wakeman in History and Will, to which reference already has been made in this paper. The likely influence of Wang Yang-ming's "unity of knowledge and action," as well as certain similarities between Mao's theory of contradiction and the ancient yin-yang idea, have been discussed above.

Wakeman goes on to add a possible stimulus on the young Mao of the seventeenth century philosopher Wang Fu-chih's theory of change, mediated through a Wang Fu-chih Study Society in Changsha which Mao attended. In his attempt to overcome Sung Neo-Confucian dualism of principle and material force, Wang emphasized the latter power or force called ch'i.

It fills the universe. And as it completely provides for the flourish and transformation of all things, it is all the more spatially unrestricted. As it is not spatially restricted, it operates in time and proceeds with time. From morning to evening, from spring to summer, and from the present tracing back to the past, there is no time at

which it does not operate, and there is no time
at which it does not produce.[33]

Although Mao was later to regard K'ang Yu-wei as a utopian
visionary, he was greatly impressed by K'ang's ideas and
activities in pragmatic reform. Wakeman has detailed how
Mao, through his Changsha First Normal School teacher,
Yang Ch'ang-chi, came to know the thought of K'ang Yu-wei
and his disciple Liang Ch'i-ch'ao, as well as Wang Fu-chih.
K'ang also placed much stress on the notion of a vital
force or primal force working through all of life and history, which he associated with the Confucian idea of jen,
so that his notion of a primal ether becomes a kind of
spiritual electricity. For his disciple T'an Ssu-t'ung
this became a transcendent ethical force. Another disciple, Liang Ch'i-ch'ao, did not hold back from the prospect of revolutionary killing and bloodshed as did K'ang,
holding that destruction was necessary if constructive
achievement was to follow, and if men were to move toward
the utopian goal K'ang had envisioned. From this milieu
of ideas which Mao encountered in Changsha, whether from
teachers like Yang or from reading in the periodicals of
the time, Mao received much that was to shape his later
thought. Wakeman finds that Mao gained there his idea of
the importance of the will, but is not prepared to say
without qualification that the ideas of a force working
in history or of contradiction were formed in Mao's mind
during this period. There is, however, the distinct possibility that the basic directions of Mao's thought were
being shaped during this period. He clearly shifted from
reformism to revolution, from utopian views to involvement
in class struggle. The basic theoretical stance in which
he saw that the world and society are in constant change
and that human beings must be involved in the ups and downs
of this change, was adopted by Mao during his early years
and then absorbed into his mature Marxist stance.[34]

Wakeman also traces influences from various Western thinkers
such as Hegel, Kant, Paulsen and Green, but these influences
are only tangential at best to the present discussion.
There are, of course, the obvious or direct lines from Marx
and Lenin, but it is the overall influence from his Chinese
heritage, which we have sampled in a most incomplete way,
and the ways in which certain modern thinkers in particular
may have shaped or stimulated his thought, that I have
found most impressive.

If the type of metaphysical thought we have found in Mao

should seem strange to us, it might be interesting to think
for just a moment of Alfred North Whitehead, perhaps the
greatest philosopher of the English speaking world in the
first half of the twentieth century. It is not that White-
headian and Marxist philosophies have anything particularly
in common. There is a profound strain of Platonic idealism
in Whitehead, and he does arrive at an idea of God, which
is enough on either count to make him anathema to Marxists.

A glance at some of the beginning statements on creativity
in Process and Reality is rather productive. Creativity

> is that ultimate principle by which the many, which
> are the universe disjunctively, become the one
> actual occasion, which is the universe conjunctive-
> ly. It lies in the nature of things that the many
> enter into complex unity.
>
> . . . .
>
> The ultimate metaphysical principle is the advance
> from disjunction to conjunction, creating a novel
> entity other than the entities given in disjunction.[35]

There seems to be no move back to the many, as in Mao's
thought, but there is the idea of an occasion within which
there are separate parts as a creative event. God is
spoken of as a principle of concretion, and that concept
is lacking in what the Judeo-Christian tradition has
called transcendence.

There is a reality for Whitehead, but it is not the substance reality of the great chain of being; it is rather
a process and this process equals reality. It is, in John
Cobb's language, "not a static entity undergoing change.
It is, rather, itself the active ongoingness of things."[36]

Whitehead is a thinker. Mao is a revolutionary. The
thought of the two men is worlds apart, but each from a
very different perspective conceives of the true reality
of the world as active, not static, and as an ongoing
process. My point in comparing them is to assert that the
theological and philosophical concept of being which has
seemed so necessary to a religious orientation in the West
is not necessary, and that there is at least this one metaphysical option which is viable. In the introduction to
Process and Reality, Whitehead pointed out that his philosophy of organism, as he termed it, seemed closer to

"some strains of Indian or Chinese thought" than to European
thought or the religions which arose in the Middle East.[37]
Whitehead's philosophy at least provides a vehicle for a
greater lai-wang or "coming toward" for contemporary
thought in China and the West. A most stimulating dialogue could well take place (someday!) between Mao's
intellectual heirs and process theologians such as John
Cobb, to whom reference has been made, and Schubert Ogden
in Protestant circles, as well as David Griffin within the
Catholic theological community, all of whom have found the
thought of Whitehead a viable alternative to substance or
being metaphysics in constructing Christian theology.

As Mao Tse-tung is the revolutionary man of action, so any
aspect of his thought can never be seen as theory alone.
What I regard as a process metaphysic in his thought is
central to any discussion of a religious dimension in
Chinese Communist thought because it does demand commitment and action. You cannot sit and contemplate the
reality. You must approach it or respond to it with those
words and actions, moral life and rituals, which are appropriate to that reality. If the reality is an ongoing
process, then you must move with it. And, as we saw in
the discussion of epistemology, one cannot perceive and
then conceptualize and then put the concepts to work without being changed in the process. You must be changed.
That clearly is the message of Chinese Communist thought.
The change, which we are told leads to a new Socialist
man, is rooted in a recognizable ongoing reality.

Because the people emerge from this struggle with a new
importance, their role as the makers of history realized
and acclaimed, one might readily argue that the reality in
Chinese Communist thought lies in another but related
direction, namely, the people. It is the men and women
who engage in revolution and carry it through to the end,
who exemplify in their daily lives the virtues and values
of the new morality, who are the reality. This would tend
to be the humanism which my colleagues see in the current
scene. I have no objection to this, in fact it would be
vain to deny that there is a profound humanism here, particularly in the sense of a concern and feeling for human
beings. My question, however, is whether we have anything
more than humanism in the strictest sense of that term,
the philosophy or "religion" which says there is nothing
but man.

Benjamin I. Schwartz points out in this regard that non-

Chinese admirers of the People's Republic of China have
drawn:

> the conclusion that the peasantry and the poor have
> now inherited the messianic task which Marx assigned
> to the industrial proletariat, and see in this the
> new gospel of the Chinese revolution, (but) Mao
> himself has never drawn this conclusion. In spite
> of the role of the peasantry in the Chinese revolu-
> tion, in spite of the strain in Maoism toward a
> populist-nationalist formula, Mao has never attrib-
> uted to the peasantry or the poor as such the
> transcendent virtues and capacities suggested by
> the word "proletariat."[38]

In spite of the fact that Mao does not attribute transcendent qualities to the peasants, it is quite possible
that the people as a whole, led by the peasants and the
workers, implicitly are invested with such qualities and
function as an ultimate reality.

If the basic point of this paper is true--that there is a
powerful reality in Chinese Communist thought, conceived
not as being but as process--then two consequences follow.
The first is that there is a much sounder ground for
speaking in genuinely religious terms of a doctrine of
salvation, of the redeemed individual and society, of the
significance of the moral life and cultic acts, and of the
communal bonds experienced in various groupings. Secondly,
one is more inclined to take with a grain of salt such a
statement as "We Communists are atheists." Technically
the statement is true, but it is hardly operative for
people who talk and act in terms of a reality which is
basic to the world, to human life, and to history.
Denials of the existence of such a reality, like the refusal of the Buddha to discuss the existence of the atman,
should not blind one to the presence of reality as process,
and therefore to a more likely basis for thoughtful relationships than we might have realized.

NOTES

1. Paul Rule, "Is Maoism Open to the Transcendent?," in The New China: A Catholic Response, Michael Chu, S. J., ed. (New York: Paulist Press, 1977), p. 29.

2. Selected Works of Mao Tse-tung, Volume I (Peking: Foreign Languages Press, 1965), p. 298.

3. Ibid., p. 301.

4. Ibid., p. 304.

5. Ibid., p. 305.

6. Philosophical Notebooks, p. 156; quoted in Arthur A. Cohen, The Communism of Mao Tse-tung (Chicago: University of Chicago Press, 1964), p. 10.

7. Selected Works, I, p. 305.

8. Ibid., p. 308.

9. Quoted in Selected Works, I, p. 316.

10. Ibid., p. 318.

11. Ibid., p. 321.

12. Ibid., p. 330.

13. James Chieh Hsiung, Ideology and Practice (New York: Praeger, 1970), p. 140.

14. Selected Works, I, p. 340.

15. Ibid.

16. "The Chinese Revolution and the Chinese Communist Party," in Selected Works of Mao Tse-tung, Volume II (Peking: Foreign Languages Press, 1965), p. 308.

17. Frederic Wakeman, Jr., History and Will (Berkeley: University of California Press, 1973), pp. 298-299.

18. Ibid., p. 232.

19. Ibid., pp. 234-235.

20. Ibid., p. 233.

21. K. Fan, ed., Mao Tse-tung and Lin Piao: Post-Revolutionary Writings (Garden City, N. Y.: Doubleday and Company, 1972), p. 165.

22. Ibid., p. 183.

23. Chung Kuo Ch'ing N'ien, 206, May 1, 1957; Excerpts from China Mainland Magazines, 95 (August 10, 1957), p. 4.

24. "On the Problem of the Identity of Thinking and Being," Hung Ch'i, 11, 1960; Chinese Studies in Philosophy, III, 2 (Winter 1971-72), p. 161.

25. Chinese Studies in Philosophy, III, 2 (Winter, 1971-72), p. 111.

26. Ibid., p. 113.

27. "Spirit Can Be Turned into Matter," Hung Ch'i, 8 (August 1, 1976); Selections from People's Republic of China Magazines, 886-887 (August 30-September 7, 1976), pp. 51-52.

28. Jen-min Jih-pao, March 29, 1977; Selections from People's Republic of China Press, 6335-6339 (May 9-13, 1977), pp. 11-14.

29. "Reverse the Reversal of History," Li-shih Yen-chiu, 1 (February 20, 1976); SPRCM, 874 (June 7, 1976), p. 32.

30. "Class Struggle is the Key Link, Everything Else Hinges on It," Li-shih Yen-chiu, 2 (April 20, 1976); SPRCM, 878 (July 6, 1976), pp. 8, 13.

31. Ninian Smart, Mao (London: Fontana/Collins, 1974), p. 84, appears to be hung up on the lack of the transcendent, though he acknowledges "a certain transcendence of the empirical."

32. From Lucien Goldman, The Hidden God, as quoted in George Lichtheim, The Concept of Ideology and Other Essays (New York: Random House, 1967), p. 278.

33. Ch'an Wing-tsit, A Source Book in Chinese Philosophy (Princeton, N. J.: Princeton University Press, 1963), p. 698.

34. For all of this discussion of early influences on Mao Tse-tung I am indebted to Wakeman's History and Will, already cited several times.

35. A. N. Whitehead, Process and Reality (New York: Macmillan, 1929), pp. 31-32.

36. John B. Cobb, Jr., A Christian Natural Theology (Philadelphia: Westminster Press, 1965), p. 139.

37. Process and Reality, p. 11.

38. Communism and China: Ideology in Flux (Cambridge: Harvard University Press, 1968), p. 41.

IV – CHINESE RELIGION AND WESTERN SCHOLARSHIP

N. J. Girardot

Throughout the historical development of the Western study of China, Chinese culture has generally remained an anomaly, a "special case." This is the almost paradigmatic attitude in the history of Western scholarship that tended to see China as unique in the history of world civilizations-- especially in the sense that what seemed to make China special, or even a welcome anomaly, was its seemingly non-religious and non-mythological nature. At the very least, this view tended to assert that religion and myth did not significantly impinge on the essence of the purely philosophical "great tradition":

> Above all else, China must be seen as a special case in the history of world religions since there was never any "deification of sensuality". . . . How comes it to pass that China has escaped this pitfall of the nations? It is certainly not from an individual love of virtue on their part, for they are an extremely licentious people in word and deed-- yet their literature, their religious worship, and their public life are singularly pure when contrasted with all other heathen nations.[1]

Aside from the overblown rhetoric, and gratuitous tone, of

this quotation from a Victorian scholar writing in the pages of the China Review, the myth of a "Confucian China" which was "singularly pure" with respect to religion is still found embodied in Western scholarship. It is, therefore, generally accurate to say that in comparison to Indian religious tradition, the history of Chinese religions has been particularly distorted and neglected.[2]

There has always been an ambivalence with regard to the Western vision of China, an ambivalence that is present even today--that is, a recognition of China's "otherness" yet a conviction that hidden within that darkness were lessons of extreme significance for Western man. It could very well be said that the history of the West's attempt to fathom the obscurity, difference, or special nature of China with regard to religion is a revealing case study not only in the history of scholarship, but also as a reflection on the West's own understanding of itself--especially those rationalistic and romantic "imaginary visions" of the exotic East that were always more important than any objective understanding. We are thus involved in an appraisal of a history that was, from the earliest period, seeing a reality darkly through a prismatic glass largely of its own making. Shadow as much as substance has shaped the West's perception of China.

Dream and Reality: The Early Period
of the Western Encounter with China

The first contacts of the Western world with China are but vague traces lost in the mists of history and we can do little more than pick out threads of hazy conjecture and legend. Although at one time it was the scholarly fashion to trace the origin of Chinese civilization back to the Ancient Near East, to some ancient Indo-European culture, or to one of the lost tribes of Israel, all that can really be said about the earliest records of East and West relations is that there was a dim awareness in pre-Christian Roman sources of a land of silk-producing people called the "Seres." A little later there are additional references to a "Sinae" (or "Thinai") in Greek and Roman works on geography of the first and second centuries A.D. This name of "Sinae" was not directly linked with the earlier "Seres," but seemed to refer similarly to a legendary land of savage, silk manufacturing peoples living at the end of the world.[3] This attitude is indicative of the fact that, like China's own view of itself as the "central kingdom," it was

impossible to conceive of any other civilized culture existing beyond the center of the world in the West, the Roman
Empire.

A few centuries later than these earliest Western accounts
of what was probably China, a Byzantine historian known as
Theophylactos of Simocatta briefly wrote of a strange country called "Taugast" which can only have been a description
of China based on information received from the Central
Asiatic Turkish tribes.[4] This is the most accurate early
account of China in the West, but it is still only slightly
advanced over the strictly legendary notions of previous
eras.

There was considerable economic and cultural contact, if
not intellectual interchange, through such routes as the
Silk Road in Central Asia even during the earliest periods
of Chinese and Western history; but the obscurity of this
period prevents us from knowing anything more than the
meager information conveyed by the various legendary and
semihistorical accounts found in both Western and Chinese
sources. Nevertheless, the legendary aspect is not without significance. It is precisely a historically embel-
lished fabulation of Chinese civilization that will be
seized upon by Europe after receiving the accounts of
Marco Polo and the later, Jesuit writers. It is this that
initiates the process of making China into something of a
"special case" among other non-Western cultures. Indeed,
a case could be made to support the contention that our
view of China, both popular and scholarly, has remained in
the realm of legend and myth.[5] Of course, this is also
the case for China's own view of the West. Most important,
however, is that the "legendary" self-image of the Confucian tradition proved especially seductive for the Western
scholarly view of China, providing a medium of debilitating
synthesis with the mythical preconceptions of China already
established in the Western mind.[6]

The first real knowledge of China did not come until the
thirteenth century with the travels of the Franciscan
missionaries, Giovanni de Piano Carpini and William of
Rubruk, to the Mongolian empire of Ghengiz Khan. Neither
of these two men actually reached China proper, but they
did mention China incidentally, now called "Kitai" or
"Cathay," in their accounts of the Mongol empire. What is
noteworthy is that the intrusion of the missionary attitude
is already becoming significant for the shaping of the
Western understanding of China, particularly Chinese

religion. There is an obvious need on the part of the early
Catholic missionaries to pay particular attention to the
religious status of the people encountered on their jour-
neys. Thus, Carpini's short description of Kitai is given
over primarily to a consideration of the religious situation. It is also obvious that to describe what could be
considered really religious it was necessary to find some
connection, however strained, with Christianity. In a
pattern that repeats itself throughout this history, non-
Western religious or intellectual phenomena were simply
forced to fit with some Christian doctrine; if anything
else was left over it was either ignored or relegated to
the level of blind superstition and paganism. Therefore,
at this early date, such things as Confucianism, Taoism,
and Buddhism were not seen as separate entities. From a
perspective that is clearly colored by the Nestorian Christian congregations that existed in the Mongol empire at the
time, Carpini optimistically states that while the people
of Kitai are "heathens" it is also said that:

> They possess the Old and the New Testaments, and
> accounts of the lives of the Fathers, and have
> hermits and buildings which are similar to our
> churches, and in which they pray at fixed times.
> They say that they also have a number of saints
> like ours. They pray only to one God, and honour
> our Lord Jesus Christ and believe in an eternal
> life. On the other hand baptism is completely
> unknown amongst them. They honour and esteem our
> Holy Scriptures, regard Christians favourably, and
> carry out very many works of mercy; in short, they
> seem to be very kind and benevolent people. . . .
> They speak a remarkable language of their own, and
> are the cleverest experts in the world on all the
> inventions of human ingenuity. Their country is
> very rich in cereals, wine, gold, silver, silk and
> everything that human nature needs for its suste-
> nance.[7]

Two aspects in Carpini's account are significant. First,
the feeling that somehow there must already be a foreknowl-
edge of Christian revelation in China and, second, the
exalted vision of the wealth, cleverness, and grandeur of
the Chinese kingdom. Both of these views, particularly the
second factor as emphasized by Marco Polo, became constant
factors in the West's conviction in the legendary uniqueness
of China--a basically optimistic view not radically altered
till the nineteenth-century invasion of the Protestant

missionaries.

More important for the thirteenth century than either of
the accounts of the two Franciscans were the sensational
writings of Marco Polo (1254-1324) who gave Europe the first
detailed direct descriptions of China proper. On the basis
of these very vivid travel reports concerning the magnifi-
cent material splendor of the Mongolian empire and Chinese
civilization, the West began to think seriously, or at least
with amazed interest, about China. In fact, the accuracy
of these accounts is outstanding for the period and they
are still an important historical source for the description of the Chinese civilization of the Sung dynasty.[8]

The impact of Polo's journals was important because
of its laudatory descriptions of the "fabulous" nature of
Chinese civilization which became a factor in the setting
of China apart in a special category among other non-
Western nations. China had now definitely started to become something of a Hyperborean vision for the West. As
Henri Baudet has observed, this "fantastic" view of China,
and later the vision of the "Mysterious East" as a collective reference for what was other than Western culture,
can be seen to have been a surprisingly formative factor
in the development of the Western historiographical consciousness.[9] China as the first exemplar of "The East"
was already beginning to take on the raiments of the West's
own mythical nostalgia for paradise. Thus, in many ways
the reaction to Polo's descriptions of China was a reflection on the West's own longing for perfection, a quest for
a paradise removed from the realm of eternity and that
could be located geographically and historically. Even
in Polo's cryptic references to what was probably Chinese
Buddhism, as R. Welbon remarks, there is a foretaste of
the longing for the "Noble Savage" that was to become so
popular in the later European mind.[10] That the discovery
of China was a fillip to the Western desire for a "paradise
on earth" is, as Baudet and Welbon have suggested, an instance in the emergent historical consciousness of the West
and was a crucial element in the resulting development of
the scholarly study of non-Western cultures and religions.

1) The Jesuit Mission: Christianization of Confucianism

The next really significant, even definitive moment, in the
shaping of the basic attitudes later adopted by sinology is
the period of the great Jesuit missions to China during the

sixteenth and seventeenth centuries. The earlier missionary views of China's "mightie kingdome" and "politike
governement,"[11] and the Christian imprint on its religious
beliefs, are only a glimmer of what is to be greatly magni-
fied by the Jesuits. It is with the more acute and intimate
observations of the Jesuits concerning the intellectual
life of China that for the first time a real distinction
is drawn between the three principal religious traditions.
But the Jesuits also discover that one is "'more famous
than the rest'" and "is derived from 'the doctrine of one
Confucius a notable philosopher.'"[12]

The fact that the West should at this point discover that
Confucianism, as a superior form of philosophical and social
wisdom, was also a superior form of religion or the only
real religion in China at all--"No other Chinese doctrine
'approacheth so neere unto the trueth as this doeth'"[13]--
is the natural result of the Jesuits' efforts to establish
an intellectual rapport with the ruling elite of Chinese
society, the Confucian literati. Where all forms of Chinese
belief were previously seen as a confused whole and shared
in the general respect paid to the greatness of Chinese
civilization, this discovery of Confucianism on the part
of the Jesuits marks a decisive shift in the fortunes of
the other Chinese religions. If the noble philosophical,
ethical, and ritual principles of Confucianism were solely
responsible for the mighty civilization, government, and
perfect society of China, as the Confucian elite claimed
them to be, then the imprint of the true Christian religion
must be discernible in it and not in the other religions.
Consequently, Confucianism as the essence of the "Great
Tradition" of Chinese culture became the single focus of
attention, a situation that to some extent is still dominant in sinological studies.

There is no question of the genius of such outstanding
figures as Matteo Ricci and other Jesuit missionaries; but
it may also have been an unfortunate accident of history
that the West is so heavily indebted in its intellectual
understanding of China to this most "mandarin" group of
Western observers. There seems to have been almost a
natural affinity between the Jesuits and the Confucians--
that is, a wary intercourse between two classes of literati
both harboring their own cherished preconceptions and self-
images but finding agreement in a particular rationalistic
and dogmatic view of Chinese civilization. This was a view
that left little room for what was seen by Confucian and
Jesuit alike as the degenerate heretical cults of Buddhism

and Taoism, those elements that contributed nothing to the
humanistic superiority of Chinese culture and society.
Thus, Matteo Ricci in his book Storia dell' Introduzione
del Christianesimo in China valued Confucianism highly but
"condemns Taoism as well as folk religion for their paganism and detestable idolatry."[14] Hans Steininger notes
that Kircher was of the same opinion and "he makes the
derogatory remark that Taoism only appealed to the common
people ('. . . respondet plebeis'), and this opinion is
shared by all early Jesuit missionaries."[15] For these
reasons, Dawson has rightly said that "the Chinese view of
a Confucian dominated homogeneous culture corresponded so
closely with what the Jesuits needed to believe that the
'false sects' of Taoism and Buddhism were left out of
account and a very distorted view of Chinese thought was
transmitted to Europe."[16]

In many respects the Jesuits were willing converts to the
Chinese literati's official self-image. But, of course,
given their role as Christian missionaries, the Jesuits
strove to make the Confucian image of Chinese civilization
fit more readily with Christian doctrines. The precedent
for this kind of tinkering with history had already been
established, so it is not surprising to find that the
Jesuits studied the ancient Chinese classics with the
basic intention of seeing whether the Chinese had at some
time believed in a personal creator God. The results of
these studies, which were extensive and can be considered
as significant scholarly contributions since they were the
first substantial translations of Chinese works into
Western languages, produced two ostensibly conflicting
opinions reflecting the polarities of the earlier missionary attitude. The first was the more optimistic and self-
consciously convincing opinion that found that there was a
sort of incipient primitive awareness of God represented
by the ancient figures of Shang Ti and T'ien (T'ien-chu).
The second view was more pessimistic, not so important for
the Jesuits but to become relatively more persuasive for
the Protestant missionaries of the nineteenth century,
finding that there was only materialism and pagan fetish-
ism. While there was some disagreement, the Jesuits in
the main opted for a rather optimistic combination of the
two extremes so that the original dim awareness of a Supreme
deity was preserved only by Confucianism and was, they
judged, "derivative of the teachings of ancient Judaism
carried to China after the Noachide dispersion."[17] But
the false sects of Taoism and Buddhism "opposed and partially corrupted this ancient teaching," reveled in their

pagan idolatry and prevented the full flowering of a belief in the true God in Confucianism.[18] It is at this point that the real aversion to a proper and complete history of Chinese religions becomes manifest and represents an attitude that, while not so theologically grounded, is still a factor in the reluctance to deal with Taoism and Chinese Buddhism.

Despite the Jesuits' efforts to reinterpret the Confucian understanding of Chinese tradition in a Christian context, there was always an evident artificial cast to their efforts. Consequently, their Christian apologetics were not really so important for the later development of scholarship. As a matter of fact, the forced Christianizing of Chinese history and the attempt to justify and rationalize Chinese ancestor worship so that it could exist alongside Catholic beliefs proved ultimately unacceptable for both the Confucian elite and the Jesuits' own authorities in Rome. Indeed, it was a factor in the eventual decline of the Jesuit mission in China and one of the problems leading to the censorship of the Jesuits in Europe in 1715. On the one hand, the Jesuits were too religious for the Confucians and, on the other hand, too irreligious, rationalizing, and Confucian for the Catholic authorities in Rome. Wolfgang Franke mentions that the makeshift attempt to find Christianity in Confucianism eventually proved to be an affront to the very Confucian elite the Jesuits were trying to please. As Franke says:

> In particular, the thinking of the educated class, formed by Confucianism, was agnostic and unfavorable to all metaphysics, and concentrated on this world and its problems, and consequently made difficult the spread of a religious doctrine largely oriented towards the next world. As a result of its metaphysical element, therefore, Christianity was frequently regarded by members of the educated class as being on the same level as the highly superstitious Buddhist and Taoist popular religion.[19]

In an ironic reversal, the Jesuits themselves were found to be but propagators of a "false sect." The need to avoid a "Christian," or any kind of "religious" interpretation of Chinese civilization, began to assert itself as the most significant factor in the later development of secularized European thought.

2) The "Natural Religion" of the Enlightenment:
   "Sancte Confucius, Ora Pro Nobis"

The theological effort of the Jesuits lost much of its
validity in the age of the Enlightenment during the eighteenth century, a period that was to absorb even more completely the view of China as a pre-eminently rational and
philosophical civilization. It was an easy step for
eighteenth century Europe to agree wholeheartedly with the
Confucian disapproval of the necessity to find Christian
elements in the Chinese tradition. Institutionalized
religion, whether Christian or pagan, was no longer important for the Western intelligentsia. Only the humanistic philosophy of pure Reason had the mark of true wisdom
and enlightenment, and was seen as a kind of "natural" religion superior even to Christianity which was now seen as
only another form of superstition.[20] And the great para-
gon of pure philosophical wisdom was seen to be Confucianism since it manifested its fruits both in terms of its
own rational, agnostic self-image and the perfect utilitarian social order it produced.

While the Jesuits' vision of China's social and political
perfection was held to be "an example and model even for
Christians," the eighteenth century had no need to be so
smugly Christian in its assessment of the lessons China
could teach Europe.[21] In fact, the eighteenth century
Enlightenment only knew of China through the glowing
accounts of the Jesuits and their early translations of
the Confucian classics, but the interpretation of these
documents was put into a newly dechristianized context of
rationalism and pure philosophy cut away from the spiritual
and intellectual authority of the Church.

China, therefore, influenced the dechristianization of
European thought and, at times, became the most important
example of the great goal of pure reason the Enlightenment
was striving for. As Baudet has so insightfully seen, this
trend was already anticipated by the Jesuits of the previous century who were "in danger of losing sight of their
missionary purpose" in their delight over finding such a
perfect and rationally ordered society.[22] For the eighteenth century this vision of perfection transmitted by the
Jesuits led to a sinophilia of remarkable proportions.
The China seen, however, was not so much the real China
but rather the culmination of the synthetic Confucian and
European visions of rational perfection:

China was seen through the eyes of the Jesuits as
an immense, remarkable land of perfect peace. Before long their irreligiousness was to rank in
Europe as the Chinese virtue par excellence. Consciously and positively atheist, the only nobility
they acknowledged are their men of letters, and it
was on this account that Voltaire paid tribute to
them as intellectuals in every sense of the word.
The Far East became the source of inspiration for
an almost purely "foreignist" sentiment /sweeping
Europe/ . . . . This sentiment found its fullest
expression at the aesthetic level--in interior
decorating and gardening, in fashion, decoration
and other elements of style. For after all, the
Chinese style was by definition synonymous with
perfect beauty.[23]

In an age that sought to overthrow God and the saints of
the Catholic Church, Confucius became the new patron saint
of the "natural" faiths of deism, atheism, and agnosticism.
Leibnitz and Wolff thus saw the great value Confucian
philosophy would have for a "natural theology" and the
achievement of a "great harmony" in the social order; and
in the overtly atheistic period of French encyclopaedism,
Voltaire admired China because "he found with Confucianism
what he missed in the Christian Church, i.e. religion and
ethics based on reason, without revelation, mystery and
miracle."[24]

Another factor that favorably impressed and attracted the
European intellectuals was that China was seen to be
governed by a philosophical elite. The Enlightenment
thinkers tended to feel that the religious and political
control of the Catholic Church had proven its bankruptcy
for European society and that it was time for the light of
pure reason cultivated by a group of secular intellectuals
to be given the chance to guide the socio-political fortunes of Europe. Needless to say, China became the great
model of a society not dominated by priests but successfully guided by a special class of pure philosophers.

Furthermore, the role that China has had to play in the
overall "discovery of History" and the resultant rise of
the historiographical and scientific study of human culture
is especially significant in seeing how deeply the myth of
the philosophical purity of Chinese civilization became
rooted in Western consciousness. As China apparently had
no need for a religious cosmogony involving an otherworldly
Creator God, so did the West tend to see this as

verification of the necessity to replace the old superstitious cosmogonies of Christianity with an ideology of
the rational perfectability of man through human history.
For the philosophes of the eighteenth century, human
reason alone was held to be the basis for "creation," now
seen historically rather than metaphysically, and the only
tool necessary for social and moral perfection.[25] In many
respects, the impressive "perfection" of Chinese society
had already vindicated the rightness of these feelings
since Confucianism did not claim to ground its ideology on
any religious principles or a mythical Creator God. It
seemed that China had discovered the "truth" of human history and reason even before the West. This was the basis
for China's special perfection and superiority among
nations.

China is still held to be a little more "perfect" or
"philosophical" than other non-Western cultures because of
its pragmatism and unique "historical-mindedness"--espe-
cially in relation to other Asian cultures like India
which were seen to be always wallowing in crude varieties
of myth and religion.[26] The eighteenth century, then,
initiates a deceptive coalescence between the Confucian
self-image of Chinese culture and the developing historiographical and positivistic zeitgeist of Europe. This
deception tended to prevent the possibility of a proper
history of Chinese religions and the full assessment of
those "little traditions" running alongside and inter-
penetrating the Confucian "great tradition."

The Seventeenth and Eighteenth Century Legacy:
The Philosophical Purity of Chinese Civilization

Because of its importance for the nineteenth century development of the discipline of sinology, I want here to
examine some of the more salient features of the Confucian
self-image as it presented itself to the West during the
seventeenth, eighteenth, and nineteenth centuries. It
must be kept in mind that this period generally represents
the height of Neo-Confucian orthodoxy and dogmatism; and
that, for example, if Europe had made intellectual contact
with China during some other less monolithically doctri-
naire period of Chinese history this image might have been
significantly different. To summarize some of the dominant
features of the Confucian vision of Chinese culture that
bear on the later attitudes accepted by sinology, the
following points can be enumerated:[27]

(1) The basic self-supporting Confucian image of
Chinese culture was that its greatness rested on a sym-
metrical socio-political, intellectual, and moral order
continuous with the civilization established by the great
model emperors of antiquity. A. Wright has noted that
the Chinese notion of "civilization" contains none of the
European implication of civitas or the idea of the progressive elaboration of civilization as an outgrowth of
the development of the city-state. The term wen for
"civilization" was initially only used to translate the
Western concept. The word that China traditionally used
to refer to its own civilization and culture was t'ien
hsia, a concept implying that the whole order of Chinese
culture and society was "under Heaven"--that is, a pre-
existent, self-contained, coherent, and static entity
passed down from ancient times.[28] Anything that was not
Chinese--or to a certain extent not Confucian--was not
"under Heaven" and, therefore, barbarian and vulgar (su).
This is the "central kingdom" mentality that held China
to be the cultural, political, and even geographical
center of the world, completely self-sufficient and
superior to other nations.

(2) The Confucian classics, as the storehouse of the
ancient wisdom of the legendary sage kings, were taken as
the only proper objects of concern for a learned gentleman. As the great model gentleman, Confucius, said that
he only transmitted the wisdom of the past so did the
literati who assumed his mantle take it as their moral
and intellectual imperative to pass on the precepts
gleaned from the Classical texts. Thus, the Chinese classical tradition was founded primarily on a Confucian
scholarship of philological exegesis and commentary on a
corpus of works declared to be "The Books."

Starting with the Jesuits, the classical tradition was the
exclusive object of concern for Western scholars, and the
same attitudes and biases of the literati were generally
adopted by the developing discipline of sinology. Emulating the Confucian school, Western scholarship has on
the whole remained a philologically oriented exegetical
tradition based on the classical texts. The mesmerizing
quality of this is shown by the fact that even after Western scholarship had recognized the less than objective and
historical basis for this approach, the "great tradition"
of Confucianism continued to consume most of the efforts
of the Chinese specialists. The "little traditions" of
Taoism and Buddhism were simply ignored or, as an after-

thought, fitted into the pre-existing scheme established as the "great tradition."[29]

(3) One aspect of the Confucian self-image that has been particularly damaging for scholarship was the pseudo-historical and rationalized schema that has tended to make the Chinese appear so historically and philosophically minded that there was no need to consider the role of mythology. As Maspero has pointed out in his discussion of the Shu Ching (the classic most fully containing the lore of the sage kings), the Confucian "historical" system is actually founded on ancient mythic themes concerning the civilizing labors of various local culture hero deities.[30] During the Han dynasty, however, these mythic themes were rationalized, systematized, and transposed into human terms, thus giving rise to a single, official history of Chinese culture.[31]

(4) Another persuasive aspect of the Confucian self-image was its humanistic emphasis on man and society and, consequently, its apparent exclusion of myth and religion in favor of a utilitarian philosophy without any super-natural foundations. This is to a large extent the basis for the Confucian "agnosticism" or "atheism" that so impressed the Europe of the eighteenth century. Huston Smith has correctly noted that the "utilitarian interpretation of Chinese thought" fits well with the prejudices of modern academia which is inclined toward rational humanism and is pleased, as were Voltaire and the Enlightenment sinophiles, to find it anticipated by the sophist self-image of the Chinese.[32] Because the Confucians had at a very early time lowered their mythic vision to the level of man, society, and history (Granet's "preoccupations politiques"),[33] it can be said that the Chinese self-image was utilitarian and anti-metaphysical in comparison with the traditional Western transcendental view of a personal Creator God (only overthrown in the eighteenth century). But while not metaphysical in the Western sense, there is still a kind of hidden cosmogonic, mythic, or religious transcendence implied.[34]

(5) The last point I want to make about the Confucian self-image and its influence on sinological attitudes concerns the exaggerated aesthetic preoccupations of the Ming and Ch'ing periods. Artistic appreciation and interpretation was but part of the general principle that all cultural manifestations were to be judged in terms of the laws of aesthetic elegance (ya) established by the classical models

of art and literature in the past.[35] This can be seen as
a reflection of the self-image of the Confucian elite con-
trasting itself with the mass level of the peasants and
their "vulgar" (su) forms of popular literature, art, and
religion--all of which were more blatantly concerned with
mythological, legendary, and folkloric themes. By the
Ming dynasty the aesthetic principles of the elite tradition were so rationally abstract and artificially constructed from what were deemed to be the proper Confucian
canons of interpretation that almost all evaluation of
artistic and literary symbolism was cut away from the more
concrete and primitive sources of myth, religion, and
folklore. Despite criticism coming especially from the
French school of sinology, the aesthetic mode in Chinese
studies has continued to prevail, and this has usually
meant that the interpretation of the meaning of Chinese
artistic and religious expression has never gotten much
beyond the cliché that somehow Chinese culture had a very
refined and aesthetic "feeling for nature."[36]

The purely philosophical, humanistic, historical, utilitarian, rational and aesthetic homogeneity of Chinese
culture--these are still pretty much the dominant ideas
in the Western mind concerning traditional China. But,
there is a modicum of truth behind these impressions which
makes it very difficult to break out of their narrowing
horizons. What is disturbing is that these truisms were
frequently used as blanket assumptions about the overall
nature of China. There was never very much effort to
determine exactly where their truth or falsity was for
specific elements of Chinese culture and, at the same time,
where other factors such as religion and myth might be introduced in order to perceive a less channelized and pre-
digested version of the truth.

China and the History of Religions

Ironically, if the influence of China during the eighteenth
and early nineteenth centuries was primarily supportive of
Europe's growing irreligiousness, it was also true that
the study of the classical Confucian works "gave a decisive
impulsion to the development of the history of religions."[37]
This was the age that was dethroning the Christian God but
also, for the first time, seriously confronting the gods
of non-European man.[38] Reichwein notes that it is "remarkable to observe how, in the course of the eighteenth century, three names unite to form a triple constellation--

Mohammed, Confucius, Zoroaster."[39]

But this was only a brief interlude for Confucius and China. More important was the fact that since China was conveniently found to be so much less tainted with the usual Western norms of "religion," it became relatively easy to regard Confucius as basically only a moral teacher or philosopher rather than a founder of a religion. Thus, the strongest stimulus to the early development of the comparative history of religions eventually came from Islam which was much more obviously "religious" with its monotheistic beliefs.

It is also during this age that the groundwork was being laid for the development of Western historiographical science, with sinology as a natural outgrowth, once it was possible to move beyond the simplistic vogues of sinophilism and chinoiserie. In many respects, the basic attitudes concerning the nature of Chinese civilization discussed in the previous section were already being inculcated in the incipient tradition of sinology. The history of sinology really begins in the lingering sinophilia of the Jesuits and enlightenment.[40]

There is an additional dimension that is of importance here both in relation to the development of sinology and the history of religions as Western historiographical disciplines. This is the trend of "Orientalism" that became a part of the West's effort to believe itself possessing the only true "historical" tradition.[41] It, therefore, became necessary to see what was non-European as something totally "other" than Western culture; and this, in turn, gave rise to the theories of cultural polarity between two great imaginary cultural entities--the "East" and the "West."[42]

In terms of the changing Western vision of China, the perspective of Orientalism sought to establish a categorical distinction between the European and Chinese sense of "history." Thus, while Chinese civilization had achieved a remarkably stable social order it suffered from the fact that it was not subject to the dynamic historical process that Europe saw itself to be undergoing in the form of scientific and technological progress. China was historically minded, especially in comparison with other "Eastern" cultures, but its idea of history was seen to have remained retarded, static, conservative, cyclic--in sum, qualitatively different from, and inferior to the

"history" of Western culture.[43] It is on this basis that
a growing pessimism about China and all other "oriental"
cultures becomes evident, a feeling that reaches its apo-
gee in the mid and late nineteenth century.

From a previous status of admired perfection, China was
now seen as too perfect, a civilization immune to progressive change and dynamic development. For the growing
tradition of European history seeking to define a "universal history" in order to understand Western technological, economic, and colonial expansion, the Chinese
became the "people of the eternal standstill" and, as a
corollary, the "East" became a category that was defined
in contrast to the "West." This has a direct bearing on
the history of the history of religions in that this kind
of orientalism implied that, since there was no real progressive change or development in the East, it was only
necessary to study the ancient texts of the cultures in
order to uncover the basic key ideas that were preserved
as static eternal values. This was felt to be the crucial
method of interpretation for all of the non-historical
cultures of the East, and resulted in the goal to unveil
an "altorientalische Weltanschauung."[44] This also implied
that whatever was discovered about one culture applied
collectively to all of the other Eastern cultures. In
John Steadman's terminology, this is one aspect of the
"myth of Asia" that is still a part of our consciousness
about non-European cultures.[45]

In the case of sinology, this approach was strengthened
by the authority of native Chinese scholarship which saw
all of Chinese culture as only an efflorescence of the
original principles of Confucian philosophy found in the
ancient Classics. For sinology, being not only a product
of the Western historiographic consciousness but also sub-
servient to the values of the Confucian literati, it
became established that the study of Chinese thought meant
primarily the study of the Confucian classical tradition
which, by definition, was purely philosophical. There
was a single original "Weltanschauung" or "great tradition" (which has been variously labeled as "Universismus,"
"Sinism," or "Siniticism")[46] that was basically philosophical in nature and was the fountainhead for all of the
different currents of Chinese thought. In this sense,
other cultural forms like the early Taoism of Lao Tzu and
Chuang Tzu were also purely philosophical in nature. Taoism in its original state was like Confucianism said itself to be--philosophical, non-mythological, non-religious,
and had no real connection with later corruptions and

false religious sects. Early Taoism, being closer to the
original source of all Chinese wisdom, could partake of
the classical purity most fully manifested by the Confucian
tradition.

This has affected the history of religions in that, even
though the concern for the "ancient wisdom" of the East
was a primary motivation for the rise of "comparative
religions," it seemed necessary in the case of Chinese
thought, more than any other Asian tradition, to divorce
the aspect of religion entirely from the study of the
weltanschauung found in the ancient classics. Another
factor affecting the history of religions' distorted
evaluation of China was the resurgent intrusion of Indian
culture into the field of European taste at the end of
the eighteenth century and the beginning of the nineteenth,
and the resulting concern with the Indo-European hypothesis which so dramatically and "scientifically" (i.e.
comparatively) seemed to link India and Europe.[47]

India's effect on the West was largely the reverse of
China. Since India appeared to be so blatantly caught up
in the throes of religion, myth, and mysticism, it became
the focus of the newly intense European vogue for "comparative religions." This was given definitive form somewhat later through the translations of the "Sacred Books
of the East" under the direction of Frederick Max Müller,
the great preponderance of which were devoted to Indian
materials. In general, "Indian mysticism ousted Chinese
illumination, and played in the nineteenth century a part
similar to, if less noticeable than, that which the latter
had played a century before"[48]--a fact which reflects a
movement of European spiritual attitudes towards romanticism after the great upsurge of the Enlightenment had
burned itself out.

India became the model for what was assumed to be an integral Oriental mysticism. Such individual cases as
Chinese, Japanese, and other Asian religions were but
facets of a unified religious vision or archetypal "per-
ennial philosophy" that could be more directly and aptly
investigated in Indian culture. The great bulk of scholarship in the formative period of Religionswissenschaft
was consequently devoted to studies of Indian phenomena.
Being seen as something of the great mother culture for
Eastern religion and having an additional Indo-European
relation with the West, the study of India in the history
of religions has almost entirely eclipsed the occasional

half-hearted investigations of Taoism, Chinese Buddhism, Chinese folk religion, and Japanese religions. It is certainly true, as B. Earhart has noted, that:

> It is difficult to overestimate the influence of Western research in Indian philology, mythology, and religion on the founding of the History of Religions   Indian studies began early, and, more important, there was the very natural connection between matters "Indian" and "European." The familiar adjective "Indo-European" has been applied to philology, mythology, and even religion. Thus, the various disciplines dealing with India, such as Indology, philology, and Buddhology, came to be grafted onto the earlier European studies of languages, classics, and religion. Because of this long-standing interest and because of the voluminous scholarly research available, the study of the History of Religions in the West--even to this day--has been associated first and foremost with the religions of India.[49]

In the final analysis, the study of Chinese culture was left to the growing body of "Chinese specialists" molded in the spirit of the enlightenment. China, therefore, tended to remain a special case with regard to its seemingly unique non-religious nature. Here, perhaps, is the point of bifurcation for sinology and the history of religions--sinology has generally adhered to the strongly positivistic vision of China while the early study of "comparative religions" got excessively mired in the more romantic, and just as distorting, vision of "The Mystic East." Even when China was considered as a part of the study of world religions, the interpretation has frequently been modeled on Indian patterns of religious thought and practice--the belief that India was the key for all forms of Eastern "mysticism." This has given rise to a plague of dilettantish efforts to discover the occult secrets of the mysterious East to which, unfortunately, the history of religions has been sometimes both a conscious and unconscious handmaiden.[50] Understandably, this has made the Chinese specialists react all the more strongly against these tendencies by re-asserting their own treasured cliches concerning the purely philosophical nature of Chinese tradition.

Sinology, as the more respectable offspring of the Western

scholarly tradition with its rationalistic inclinations,
has tended to entrench itself in a position which generally denigrates the value of religion and mythology for
Chinese thought. There is still a lingering and somewhat
anachronistic disdain for "comparative religions" among
sinologists that unfortunately fails to recognize that the
history of religions is just as open to a critical examination of its own historical and methodological shortcomings
as sinology is and has, in fact, progressed beyond the
distorted excesses of the old romanticized stereotypes of
"comparative religions."[51] In sum, and for reasons built
respectively on paradigmatic models of China or India,
both sinology and the history of religions (né "comparative religions") are two of the most deformed step-
children of the Western historiographical legacy.

The Nineteenth Century and After

In the China of the nineteenth century with its protracted
and accelerated contact with Western science, technology
and imperialism, the self-image of the Confucial literati
was buffeted and suffering disintegration; and this is
reflected in a rather decisive shift in European attitudes
toward China. Europocentrism was the byword in historical
studies and the tradition of Orientalism became even more
confident in its pessimistic evaluation of Eastern culture.

The previous feelings of optimism displayed by the enthusiastic sinophilism of the seventeenth and eighteenth
centuries finally gave way to the newly aggressive political and religious doctrine of the dynamic progressivism
of the West--its technological and capitalistic expansion
directed toward the acquisition of colonies and spheres of
influence all baptised by a similarly aggressive imperialistic missionary policy. The new Protestant mission to
China, in distinction to the earlier Jesuit mission, saw
itself fulfilling a divine mandate to convert the poor
unfortunate masses of the non-Christian world to the
blessings of Western civilization and Christianity which,
by this time, were seen to be one and the same thing.
This supremely self-confident and righteous attitude,
which now included definite racial connotations (the
"yellow peril"), could not help but see China more pessi-
mistically.[52]

In place of sympathy, respect, and understanding there was
substituted, in many cases, contempt; whatever was "other"

than Western civilization or Christianity was seen to be
necessarily evil, the ravings of heathen minds. For
Protestant and Catholic missionaries of this period the
"heathen Chinese" were no longer perfect in any way, but
simply "peculiar" and in need of the saving word of the
Christian God. Even Confucianism became as much a "false
sect" as the previously condemned Taoism and Buddhism
Dawson has pointed out that this new attitude was possibly
the most damaging factor for the history of Chinese religions, since the overall bias against the "heathen Chinese" seriously "retarded the proper study of Chinese
religion."[52] Dawson continues:

> Most of the writing on this subject used to be
> done by missionaries whose main purpose was to
> describe obstacles to the progress of Christian-
> ity for the benefit of prospective missionaries.
> They tended to assume that religious experience
> has much less variety than is, in fact, the case;
> and this made them ask the wrong questions about
> the nature of Confucianism, Taoism and Buddhism,
> treating them as if they were of the same general
> nature as Christianity, though markedly inferior.[54]

While this affirmation of the inferiority of non-Western
cultures was becoming so psychologically important for the
West, there was still a lingering residue of the previous
feeling that somehow China was different from the other
more overtly heathen civilizations. The Chinese were indeed inferior, but possibly not so inferior or pagan as
other nations. Thus, we can see two emergent positions.
One of these was the more secular scholarly tradition of
agnostic positivism and rationalism (dominating the later
development of sinology) which found that it was exactly
the fact that the Chinese had no real religion, Christian
in nature or otherwise, that made them a special culture
less inferior than other Eastern countries.[55] The other
position was that of the nineteenth century Protestant and
Catholic missionary scholars who, in resurrecting the old
Jesuit apologetics, envisioned an original pure monotheism
reflected in the earliest forms of Confucianism and Taoism
which had only suffered a fall into paganism with the introduction of the blatantly heathen Buddhism from India--the
real origin of paganism and pantheism in the East. The
investigation of the hypothetical original Chinese monotheism was in terms of the precedents set in the seventeenth and eighteenth centuries--that is, an exclusive
concern with the ancient literary classics of the Confucian

school.[56]

This, of course, is not to say that there have not been any
lasting contributions made during this period to the history of Chinese religions. In fact, despite the distortion
and neglect, the missionary scholars of the nineteenth
century did lay a substantial foundation of translation
and ethnographic documentation in the area of Chinese
religion. Among other works one need only think of Legge's
careful and still valuable translations of The Chinese
Classics and The Texts of Taoism (1891); Leon Weiger's
Bibliographie, Le Canon, Les Index (1911) and his Les
pères du systeme taoïste (1913); the massive compilations
of popular religious practice in Doré's Recherches sur
les superstitions en Chine (15 vols., 1914-29) and
J. J. M. de Groot's The Religious System of China (6
vols., 1892).[57]

Conclusion

It will be increasingly necessary for sinology to criti-
cally examine its own historical and methodological legacy
if progress is to be made toward an interpretive understanding of the history of Chinese religions. Arthur
Wright has observed that because of the past, "Chinese
studies remain a retarded and underdeveloped field of
Western scholarship";[58] and, consequently, there is a
need for the specialized areas of philological and historical research to be coupled with more expansive interdisciplinary perspectives--synthetic and theoretical
perspectives that must take into special consideration
the long neglected problems of religion and myth.

The relevance of this task is especially clear today since
there are signs of an important interdisciplinary revival
in the study of Chinese religions--a convergence of disciplines embracing both the humanistic disciplines and
theology.[59] It should be clear that only a serious
assessment of the past missionary attempt to fathom an
"other" religious tradition like China's can lead to the
kind of theology of missions relevant to the contemporary
pluralistic situation. Theology can no longer afford to
insulate itself from the humanistic disciplines. It must,
rather, begin to form a working partnership with such
disciplines and with the history of religions most particularly. In this way the past can inform the future
with respect to the meaning and nature of intercultural

missionary activities.

As a final comment let me simply say that such reconsiderations of China as a theater for the shifting shadow-play of the Western imagination have as much of a critical bearing on our evaluation of contemporary China--Marxist and ostensibly "non-religious" in nature--as it does on the past. Viewed historically, the self-proclaimed non-religious, or even anti-religious, nature of Maoism is in some ways ironically similar to the self-image of medieval Confucianism. Whatever the specific instance of China as a "special case" for either missionary or secular scholarship, we will only approach an understanding of China, past and present, in relation to a more critical evaluation of the genius of China's religious and cultural heritage and the history of the changing Western visions of that heritage.

It is above all necessary that sinology, the history of religions, and theology together exorcise some of their respective chimeras concerning China. This is not to say that we will ever overcome our need for "Chinese shadows," but it does suggest that any meaningful historical and interpretive enterprise must be continually, and purgatively, made aware of the projective nature of those shifting shadows. To paraphrase the great Chinese mystic, Chuang Tzu: "between shadow and substance, dream and reality, butterfly and man, there must be some distinction! This is called the Transformation of Things."[60]

NOTES

1. Anonymous ("S"), "Cosmogony and Religion," China Review 4 (1875): 12.

2. See C. K. Yang, Religion in Chinese Society (Berkeley: University of California Press, 1967); H. Smith, "Transcendence in Traditional China," Religious Studies 2 (1969): 185-96; A. Wright, "The Study of Chinese Civilization," Journal of The History of Ideas 21 (1960): 232-55; L. Thompson, "The Myth of Confucian China," unpublished ms; and with respect to the neglect of the "little traditions," N. J. Girardot, "Part of the Way," History of Religions 11 (1972): 319-337.

3. See W. Franke, China and the West (Columbia, S. C.: University of South Carolina Press, 1967): 1-?.

4. Ibid., p. 3.

5. See, for example, J. Steadman, The Myth of Asia (New York: Simon and Shuster, 1969); and Henri Baudet, Paradise on Earth, Some Thoughts on European Images of Non-European Man (New Haven: Yale University Press, 1965).

6. See below and Wright, "Chinese Civilization," pp. 235ff.

7. Quoted by Franke, China and West, p. 8.

8. Ibid., p. 11ff; and especially L. Olschki, Marco Polo's Asia (Berkeley: University of California Press, 1960).

9. See Baudet, Paradise on Earth, pp. 74ff.

10. R. Welbon, The Buddhist Nirvana and Its Western Interpreters (Chicago: University of Chicago Press, 1968), pp. 15ff. See also M. Eliade, "The Quest for the 'Origins' of Religion," in The Quest (Chicago: University of Chicago Press, 1969), pp. 37-53.

11. See D. F. Lach, Asia in the Making of Europe (Chicago: University of Chicago Press, 1965), concerning the work of the Spanish monk, Gonzales de Mendoza, pp. 744-786.

12. _Ibid._, p. 815, quoting R. Hakluyt's _The Principal Navigations, Voyages, Traffiques, and Discoveries of the English Nation_ (Glasgow, 1904) which gave extracts from the reports of Ricci and the other Jesuits. More generally on the Jesuits in China see George H. Dunne, _Generation of Giants_ (Notre Dame: University of Notre Dame Press, 1962).

13. Quoted in Lach, _Asia in the Making of Europe_, p. 815.

14. Hans Steininger, "The Religions of China," in _Historia Religionum_ (Leiden: Brill, 1968) Vol. 1, p. 512.

15. _Ibid._, p. 512.

16. Raymond Dawson, _The Chinese Chameleon, An Analysis of European Conceptions of Chinese Civilization_ (London: Oxford University Press, 1967), p. 47.

17. _Ibid._, p. 46.

18. _Ibid._, p. 45f.

19. Franke, _China and The West_, p. 53.

20. See Frank E. Manuel, _The Eighteenth Century Confronts the Gods_ (New York: Atheneum, 1967); A. Reichwein, _China and Europe_ (New York: Alfred A. Knopf, 1925); Basil Guy, _The French Image of China Before and After Voltaire_ (Geneva: n.p., 1963); and V. Pinot's _La Chine et la formation de l'esprit philosophique en France_ (Paris: n.p., 1932).

21. Dawson, _Chinese Chameleon_, pp. 33ff.

22. Baudet, _Paradise on Earth_, p. 44.

23. _Ibid._, p. 44.

24. Friedrich Heiler, "The Influence of the Eastern Religions on the European Intellectual and Spiritual Life," _Proceedings of the lXth International Congress for the History of Religions, Tokyo and Kyoto_ 1958 (Tokyo: Maruzen, 1960), p. 710. See also A. Owen Aldridge's "Voltaire and the Cult of China," Taipei, 1970 (mimeographed).

25. See Baudet, _Paradise on Earth_, pp. 74ff; and, more

generally, A. O. Lovejoy, Essays in the History of Ideas (Baltimore: Johns Hopkins University Press, 1948), pp. 80ff.

26. See D. Bodde, "Myths of Ancient China," in S. N. Kramer, ed. Mythologies of the Ancient World (Garden City: Anchor Books, 1961), p. 403. On the persistence of the Western vision of India see Stephen Miller, "Passages to India: Hindu Culture and Western Minds," The American Spectator 11 (August-September 1978): 5-10.

27. Concerning most of these points see Wright, "Chinese Civilization," pp. 235ff.

28. Ibid., p. 236.

29. See A. Wright's discussion, "A Historian's Reflections on the Taoist Tradition," History of Religions 9 (1969-70), pp. 248-55. For an early example of this tendency see M. Abel Rémusat, Mélanges posthumes d'histoire et de litterature Orientales (Paris: n.p., 1843), p. 164.

30. H. Maspero, "Légendes mythologiques dans le Chou King /Shu Ching/," Journal Asiatique 205 (1924): pp. 1-2.

31. On the overall problem of Chinese myth see N. J. Girardot, "The Problems of Creation Mythology in the Study of Chinese Religion," History of Religions 15 (1976): 289-318.

32. Smith, "Transcendence," pp. 185-87.

33. See M. Granet, La pensée Chinois (Paris: Albin Michel, 1968), p. 283.

34. See Girardot, "Creation Mythology," pp. 289ff; and Smith, "Transcendence," pp. 188ff.

35. See R. Stein's discussion of this in "Jardins en miniature d'extreme-orient," Bulletin de l'école francaise de l'extreme-orient 42 (1942): pp. 22ff. See, for example, the explanations offered for Chinese symbolism in such works as Doré's Recherches sur les superstitions en Chine which is based on the interpretations offered by traditional Chinese scholarship. It can also be said that this reliance on the Chinese classical tradition has rendered most of the Western works on Chinese symbolism and myth useless for a proper hermeneutics of the history of Chinese religions--

such works as William Mayers' The Chinese Reader's Manual
(London: Trubner, 1874), V. R. Burkhardt's Chinese Creeds
and Customs, C. A. S. William's Outlines of Chinese Symbol-
ism (Shanghai: n.p., 1931), and E. T. C. Werner's A
Dictionary of Chinese Mythology (Shanghai: Kelly and
Walsh, 1932) and his Myths and Legends of China (New York:
Farrar and Rinehart, 1922).

36. See especially the remarks by Herman Köster,
Symbolik des chinesischen Universismus (Stuttgart: Hierse-
mann, 1958), pp. 9-13.

37. Reichwein, China and Europe, pp. 77-78.

38. See Manuel, Eighteenth Century.

39. Reichwein, China and Europe, p. 78.

40. Wright, "Chinese Civilization," p. 240.

41. Ibid., pp. 241f. For a fascinating discussion of
"Orientalism" and the study of Islam see Edward Said,
Orientalism (New York: Pantheon Books, 1978).

42. See R. Dawson, "Western Conceptions of Chinese
Civilization," in The Legacy of China, ed. R. Dawson
(Oxford: Clarendon Press, 1964), p. 18ff.

43. Dawson, "Western Conceptions," pp. 14ff.

44. See Wright, "Chinese Civilization," pp. 241f.

45. See Steadman, Myth of Asia, pp. 23-45.

46. The notion of "universismus" originates with
J. J. M. de Groot's Universismus (Berlin: n.p., 1918).
H. G. Creel in an early, and since repudiated work, coined
the term "Sinism." See his Sinism, A Study of the Evolution of the Chinese Worldview (Chicago: Open Court, 1929).
Wright, in "The Study of Chinese Civilization," p. 254,
also mentions other such theories of the altorientalische
Weltanschauung variety: F. C. F. Northrop's "undifferentiated aesthetic continuum" and Lily Abegg's "envelopmental
logic." For criticism of Creel's contribution to this type
of theorizing, see M. T. Price's "Sinism--A Historical
Critique of H. G. Creel's Case for Its Pre-Confucian In-
digeneity," Journal of the History of Ideas 48 (1948):
214-236.

47. See Reichwein, China and Europe, p. 153; and especially B. Feldman and R. D. Richardson, The Rise of Modern Mythology 1680-1860 (Bloomington: Indiana University Press, 1972); pp. 349-64; R. Schwab, La renaissance orientale (Paris: Payot, 1950); and A. Leslie Willson, A Mythical Image: The Ideal of India in German Romanticism (Durham: Duke University Press, 1964).

48. Reichwein, China and Europe, p. 153. See also Eric J. Sharpe, Comparative Religion, A History (New York: Charles Scribner's Sons, 1975), pp. 27-46, 144-171.

49. B. Earhart, "Toward a Unified Interpretation of Japanese Religion," in The History of Religions, ed. by J. Kitagawa (Chicago: University of Chicago Press, 1967), p. 198. In a survey of American popular opinion concerning Eastern cultures Harold R. Isaacs (Images of Asia /New York: Capricorn Books, 1962/, p. 249) notes that: "Images of India as a land of religion, of Indians as a people deeply and peculiarly concerned with the religious life, are among the most commanding of all that appear in the course of this exploration. Indeed, the whole notion of the 'mysticism of the East,' if it is located anywhere at all, is more generally attached to India than it is, certainly, to China, Japan, or any of the Moslem parts of Asia. The subject of religion came up seldom or not at all in connection with China. In relation to India, it came up soon and often and for many was uppermost and controlling."

50. While not dilettantish, the works of the influential scholars, Mircea Eliade and Ananda Coomeraswamy, reveal a similar rooting in a kind of archetypal vision of Indian religion--see Guilford Dudley III, Religion on Trial, Mircea Eliade and His Critics (Philadelphia: Temple University Press, 1977), pp. 105-118; and Philip Rawson's review essay on Roger Lipsey's Coomaraswamy (/Princeton: Princeton University Press, 1978/, 3 vols.) in New York Review of Books 26 (February 22, 1979): 15-17.

51. See, for example, the rather unsatisfactory discussion of these problems among Chinese specialists in H. G. Creel, ed., Conference on Chinese Civilization in Liberal Education (Chicago: University of Chicago Press, 1959). Starting on p. 141 there is a debate over the use and meaning of the term "philosophy" in Chinese studies with Creel admitting that there is a significant difference between the Western and Chinese understanding of the term.

For want of a resolution, it was finally suggested by G. L. Anderson that it might be necessary to see Chinese "philosophy" in a cultural "jacket" or context that includes religion. As Anderson said: "If there is no Chinese jacket (and it does not seem to be emerging from the discussion here), perhaps the reason for this is that the dividing line between Chinese religion and philosophy is not as clear (at least to us) as it is in the West conveniently between departments of religion and departments of philosophy" (p. 159). The conference then went on to reject the possibility that the history of religions, or as they put it, "comparative religions," might have something to contribute. They stated rather narrowly that "there is the superficial business, of course, of not being really able to offer much in the way of comparative religion. It is not a fashionable subject. It seems to have gone out about 1935 and has not been revived. As Mr. Chan /Wing-tsit/ pointed out, it is a subject which people who don't know very much regard as controversial. If you are teaching Buddhism you should do it under a philosophy rubric. Even so, I /G. L. Anderson/ wonder if the Chinese jacket is not really a mixture of Chinese religion and philosophy, and if Chinese philosophy should be treated in this fashion" (p. 159).

52. On the Western mythos of the "yellow peril," see the interesting study by Richard Austin Thompson, The Yellow Peril, 1890-1924 (New York: Arno Press, 1979).

53. Dawson, Chinese Chameleon, p. 146.

54. Ibid., p. 146.

55. See above, note 1, concerning the China Review.

56. See, for example, C. B. Day, Chinese Peasant Cults (Teipei: Ch'eng Wen Reprint ed., 1969), p. 176. Much of this debate pertains to the so-called "term controversy" concerning the proper Chinese translation for "God"; see Donald Treadgold, The West in Russia and China. Volume 2: China 1582-1949 (Cambridge: Cambridge University Press, 1973), pp. 20-26.

57. It should be noted that most of these works are concerned with documentation rather than interpretation. As Wright notes, it has always been the French school of sinology that has been "the center of methodological innovation" and that Chavannes' work constitutes a major break

with the past leading "the way towards a new critical method in dealing with the Chinese past" ("Chinese Civilization," pp. 241, 246). (See also P. Demiéville, "Aperçu historique des études sinologiques en France," Acta Asiatica 11 (1966), 56-110). This legacy was continued by Maspero who "used and developed the methods of Chavannes" and "also pioneered in other fields of research outside the orthodox limits of earlier Chinese scholarship. His were the first systematic studies in economic history and in the history of Taoism, the dissident tradition so long disdained by the Chinese Literati" (Wright, p. 247). On Doré and de Groot see D. C. Yu, "Chinese Folk Religion," History of Religions 12 (1973), 378-87.

58. Wright, "Chinese Civilization," p. 253. See also his remarks in Studies in Chinese Thought, pp. 1-18.

59. See, for example, the Bulletins of the newly founded Society for the Study of Chinese Religions, and the special symposium on "Current Perspectives in the Study of Chinese Religions," History of Religions 17 (1978), 209-432.

60. Chuang Tzu, chapter two; see Burton Watson, The Complete Works of Chuang Tzu (New York: Columbia University Press, 1968), p. 49.

PART TWO

THE CHRISTIAN ENCOUNTER
WITH CHINA

INTRODUCTION

Yu-ming Shaw

Part two of this volume addresses historical and theological aspects of the encounter between China and Christianity. Three historical analyses follow a theological and missiological reflection on this intriguing relationship.

Langdon Gilkey's paper, the keynote speech that began the Notre Dame conference, sets the tone for a theological analysis of the meaning and future course of the Christian encounter with China. Rejecting the old term of "mission," which he finds to be "historically and theologically misleading," he suggests the substitution of "covenant"--a covenant to be established with the Chinese similar to that made with the Greek tradition by the early Christians. The hope implied by this new concept of covenant is that just as the great synthesis had developed between the gospel and the Hellenistic culture, a new synthesis between modern Christianity and the new China can also be brought about. From this synthetic perspective, Gilkey moves to a discussion of the two levels of this covenant: cultural and religious. On the cultural level, he feels that Confucian and Maoist China have much to offer to the Christian West: the communal emphasis of Chinese life, the social concerns of Chinese state policies, and the harmony between man and nature. On the religious level, the West has much to contribute to China: the Christian concepts of transcendence, sin, and grace. He believes that these Christian religious concepts can complement and enrich the religious dimension of Maoist culture.

In covering the ground for a proper encounter between Christianity and China, Gilkey maintains a delicate balance between accepting the positive aspects of Confucian and Maoist China on the one hand and affirming the universal relevance of the Christian faith on the other. The succeeding three papers examine the historical record of this encounter with China.

Eric Hanson's paper examines the response of the Chinese State, whether Confucian or Communist, toward the importation of Catholicism into China during the last several centuries. His conclusion is that the Chinese official response has constantly been unwelcoming, with periodic tolerance when domestic or international considerations demanded it.

Yu-ming Shaw's paper focuses on the response of the Chinese intellectuals toward religion, especially Christianity, in the early part of the twentieth century. His conclusion is simple: "Religion was a dead issue in the minds of most of the Chinese intellectuals in the early decades of this century, and perhaps even until the present. Religion, especially Christianity, suffered that inevitable fate both because of the effective work of its detractors and because of the larger historical forces that were at work at the time."

While Hanson's and Shaw's papers have documented the negative aspects of the Chinese response to Christianity, Donald Treadgold's paper, a keynote speech on the second day of the conference, "The Problem of Christianity in Non-Western Cultures: The Case of China," provides us with some comforting thoughts. He praises the Jesuit-Cathay synthesis; the religious tenacity, if not loyalty, of the Chinese T'ai-p'ings; the beneficial and significant influences of Christianity in Chinese culture or politics; and the permanence of the Chinese humanistic or Confucian tradition which has and will endure the threat from whatever external or internal spiritual or mundane forces. But the main burden of his speech is to offer some criticism, based on an extensive comparative historical perspective, of what he terms the "mistaken" views of the encounter between Christianity and China. He criticizes the narrow reading of Western

imperialism as having been exclusively harmful; the inaccurate notion that the Maoist revolution was entirely of
indigenous origin; the defeatist conviction that the
Christian Church has to come to terms with Maoist atheism;
the naive expectation of a peaceful co-existence between
Christianity and Marxism; and, lastly, the erroneous perception of the PRC (People's Republic of China) as representing "something like the march of God on earth."
Treadgold is not reserved in comparing the PRC with Stalin-
ist Russia and believes that the former has not exempted
itself from all the attendant evils of a totalitarian rule.
He therefore urges caution in converting "the /Chinese/
story of human suffering into Heilsgeschichte."

I – THE COVENANT WITH THE CHINESE

Langdon Gilkey

The Model of Covenant

I have lived relatively long as a young ignoramus in China,
and been twice to Japan as a visitor. Thus I can smell
oriental smells, whiff oriental meanings, and feel oriental
shapes and forms almost as well as anyone. I am a relative
"know-nothing" about Chinese religions, cultural and political history, and about present day Maoism. I know too
little about the Chinese present, therefore, to try to
suggest concrete ways in which Western Christians may relate their faith to this new reality. What I may be able
to do is to discuss theological principles according to
which such an interrelationship may be assayed.

Our question concerns the relation of Christianity or of
Christian faith to the new, powerful, promising, and
attractive reality of China. This question is usually
posed as the question of "mission," of bringing or of not
bringing our gospel, our religion, our church to the
Chinese. Such a posing of the question--with, let me
admit, immense backing from both Bible and tradition--is,
I shall suggest, historically and theologically misleading,
or better, almost fatally tempting. Its implications are
that our religion, in its present forms is transcultural.

As a result the question that is then put is: in what ways
do their culture and their religious life need our religion
and so our church? Already latent here, I suggest, are the
seeds of the imperialism, and the ultimate ineffectiveness--
for in spiritual matters the two are opposite sides of the
same coin--of recent Christian invasions of China.

In the place of this model of "mission" I would like to
propose the model of "covenant." By covenant in this context I mean the patristic concept of the "covenant with
the Greeks" through which the Fathers--or some of the more
liberal of them--legitimated the synthesis of Hellenistic
culture and the gospel, out of which synthesis what we now
call Christianity arose. Here, therefore, we are speaking
of our history and of the formation of our religion--so
immediately everything is less, much less imperialistic and
utterly different! This is, I say, a more helpful and
accurate model with which to ponder the subject of our
conference, the relation of Christianity to the old and
to the new China.

The Catholic religion, and so of course ultimately Protestantism too, resulted from the movement of an apocalyptic
branch of Hebraic religion into the new and alien world of
late Hellenism. This was a world replete with social,
political, and ethical norms and goals strange to those of
the earliest Christian communities, and a world reflective-
ly structured by alien philosophical categories and permeated with a religious orientation utterly different from
their own. Out of a slow, deep and essential interpenetration of these two realities arose our Christian religion:
an interpenetration in the areas of rite, of symbol, of
ethical obligation, of forms of church organization, and
finally, of categories and concepts of reflective thought.
Hellenistic culture was transformed in part--unfortunately
only in part!--by the Christian leaven. In turn Christianity was expressed and made real within forms and categories of the Hellenistic world.

Heresy appeared when the religious dimensions of Hellenistic
life quite overcame the affirmations of the gospel. No
historian, however, can deny that both the orthodoxy that
combatted and conquered heresy, and the creeds that sealed
the victory, were themselves saturated with the categories
of Hellenistic culture and permeated with the characteristics and aims of Hellenistic religion. This synthesis,
pace Harnack, was immensely creative and anyway inevitable.
It expressed and uncovered elements in the gospel essential

to its full witness; and it was surely in part this Hellenistic component that made it possible for the gospel to be
a basic formative factor of medieval culture and so of
subsequent Western civilization.

One other "covenant" may be mentioned; the covenant with
the modern West. Modernity's science, its history, its
psychology, its political, economic and social norms and
goals, its moral and human self-understanding, its sense of
time, history and human destiny, have impinged, as both a
lure and a threat, on the older synthesis with Hellenism.
Liberal and post-liberal Protestantism sought for two
hundred years to establish a creative covenant with the
modern Renaissance and Enlightenment; Catholicism is
finally seeking to do so as well.

Think what the implications of this covenant are for
"missions"! Much of what we most treasure and defend in
modern Christianity has arisen from this synthesis: its
acceptance of pluralism, its tolerance, its emphasis on
autonomy, its awareness that all dogmas and forms of religion are historically relative, its drive to transform
the world in the name of justice and of love. As Hellenism
once did, modern life, in its synthesis with Christianity,
has uncovered and emphasized invaluable elements of the
gospel latent and even denied before.

We cannot repudiate this paradigm of the covenant and be
ourselves as contemporary Christians. We know in ourselves
and in those we respect that a living Christianity always
appears in the form of a "covenant" with the cultural life
in which it seeks to live. The absence of such a covenant
or synthesis heralds either imperialism, the heteronomous
imposition of an alien synthesis on the life of a new
culture, or--and this is always the final result--ineffec-
tiveness, emptiness and disappearance.

The church has consistently refused to apply the model of
covenant in relation to other cultures. Forgetting how its
own synthesis arose, the church has sought to send other
cultures this synthesis. Or, put another way, it has sought
to send itself: its traditional language and concepts, its
dogmas, doctrines and theologies, its institutional structures and forms, its rites and liturgies, its rules and
norms. One cannot, as a modern Western Christian, look at
any of these traditional forms of dogma, law or polity and
not feel their Hellenic origin and so what is to us their
anachronistic character. We are all dedicated to bringing

this whole religious corpus "up to date": in theology, liturgy, canon law, moral philosophy, church structure. And yet we, who can hardly wait to bring this inherited corpus into the deepest union with the forms of the modern culture we share, are apt to feel an infinite risk when we contemplate, if we do, a synthesis with another cultural substance entirely.

I need not press the irony in all this. Do we think these forms save us, or that God cannot use the forms of others as he has used ours? Can he not establish a covenant with the Chinese as well as with pagan Hellenism and pagan modernity? Would not a Chinese Christian feel the same need of "aggiornamento" in terms of his culture as we feel in terms of ours--and one that goes not only into the peripheral realms of social polity but one that penetrates-- as does ours--to the very heart to rites, liturgy, theology and moral understanding?

Preliminary Cautions

Three comments should be made before we turn directly to the issue before us. The first is that at least at the present there is hardly any prospect of the sort of synthesis that historically the covenant principle has represented, namely, a deep interpenetration of Christianity and Chinese culture. Christianity has little present prospect of entering massively the Chinese scene. Only Hellenistic Christians could create the synthesis that became orthodoxy; only moderns can write contemporary Catholic theology. Interested Westerners are probably like early Bedouin converts trying to foresee the forms of the 4th and 5th century creeds!

We, to be sure, are deeply influenced by the present Chinese civilization; correspondingly we are asking the question about our relation, as Western Christians, to that culture. They are scarcely asking that question! At present it is their theoria and faith, their patterns of being human, that are impinging with power on us. Our questions, let us be clear, may (like theirs) be really more about the shape of future Western culture and of our Christianity than about theirs!

Secondly, a further word should be said about imperialism. A religion can be imperialistic on two scores, interrelated but separable. 1) Religion is imperial when it accompanies,

appeals to and profits from the military, economic and
political power of its culture. This we have done enthu-
siastically: first with Constantine, and then across the
globe, the Church accepted security, wealth, prestige,
honor and glory from Caesar--and has in our day paid for
it both in Caesar's coin and in the honor of our Lord's
name. 2) A religion is imperialistic when the cultural
forms which it inevitably bears--for no religion but has
a cultural expression--are made absolute and so are forced
upon that new cultural situation. In the case of Christian mission the Western cultural forms and institutions
of Christianity were regarded as identical with the gospel
and the grace being mediated, by both Catholics and Protestants. Thus instead of pointing beyond itself to its
non-Western Lord and its transcendent God, Christianity
pointed to itself as a Western religion--and sealed its
own doom.

These two forms of imperialism are avoidable if one is
aware of them--and if we understand that God's covenants
are wider than we think, as his rain falls on all. The
greatest present danger is that we may, in consciously
rejecting both military and economic power and Western
social, economic and political culture, fail to see how
Western our religion and our Church are, and so seek again
to move our religion and our church into union with the
new China.

As is evident, the question of imperialism is not directly
related to the question of the universality of a religious
reality. In order to avoid imperialism one does not need
to repudiate the claim of a religion to universal relevance. Universal religions--Buddhism, Christianity,
liberal democracy and Marxism--can proceed into new cultural situations without imperialism, solely by means of the
persuasive power and relevance of their message, and have
sometimes done so. On the other hand, each has proceeded
into new situations imperialistically. Let us also note
that anyone who demotes Christianity from the status of a
universal faith to a "culture religion," relevant only in
its own cultural and historical situation, has already
relinquished Christianity and adopted in its place some
other universalist faith, possibly liberal democracy or
Marxism.

Each universal faith tends quite naturally to reduce the
status and pretensions of its victims and its rivals. For
each realizes, and rightly, that the essential structure

of its own belief is radically compromised if its claims to universal relevance are rejected. The theological trick in all these matters--for cultural systems such as liberalism and Marxism quite as well as for explicit religions such as Buddhism and Christianity--is to preserve the sense of universal relevance, and so of truth, along with that clear sense of our own relativity which alone can dissolve imperialism and generate charity.

Thirdly, we should note that there are two different levels of any cultural whole with which a religion is to make synthesis, and correspondingly two different levels of religion. This was true of Hellenism and of the modern West, and it is surely also true of present China. There is first of all the level of cultural life as such: science of forms of inquiry and of truth; social and political thought; forms of art; social and personal norms, mores and goals; and so on. Second there is the religious dimension, a dimension that appears in each cultural whole however "secular" it may regard itself to be, a dimension that is explicitly expressed in organized religion. In an avowedly secular culture such as the modern West or Maoism, the cultural life as such is all that is recognized. Most discussions of a synthesis of Maoism with Christianity that I have seen, have only this secular level of Chinese reality in mind.

The Cultural Covenant

We shall, then, first seek to deal with the cultural level. How might Christian faith relate to the social, political, economic and moral reality of present China? It is on this level that to me the clearest gains for Christianity and for our common future appear. The synthesis of Christianity with the modern West has had many creative results. But undoubtedly this covenant has brought with it an emphasis on the individual: his or her salvation in heaven; his or her conscience, autonomy and freedom of spirit; his or her property and its rights--all of which, for better or for worse, have reconstructed Christianity from the medieval and feudal phenomenon it was into a democratic and bourgeois one. I do not wish by any means to repudiate this inheritance in its entirety. But it is, especially in its American variants, desperately weak on the communal side.

The embeddedness of the individual in responsibility to the community, the ineradicability and value of relationships

and their obligations, the priority, therefore, of community
obligations over obligations to the self, the absolute importance of the category of the "common good"--all of these
emphases are peculiarly oriental, as the Confucian tradition
in both China and Japan witnesses. They reappear in modern,
progressive and so creative form in Maoist thought and in
the reality of the new life in China: in the principles of
the Mass Line, in the polarity of elite and peasant, in the
emphasis on the social origin and character of knowing and
of theory, and in the identity of the substance of China
with the whole People of China. The same creative rebal-
ancing of forces appears in the subordination of technology
to the people's needs, of the authority of the expert and
the power of the pragmatic technician to the political and
moral goals of society, and in the insistence that all
theory be reinterpreted through praxis.

These phenomena are not just the politicization of life, the
absolutization of an ideology, as many American observers
maintain. They represent in principle the reintegration of
elements of culture sundered in our own cultural experience
and so in destructive conflict and dissolution. In the West
there is a continuing struggle between the individual and
the community, between rational organization and moral purpose, between technology and human need. We perceive our
sundered and self-destructive reality, but our theories
remain only theories, separated as protests from the sundered reality. In China the beginning of a reunion of these
separated polarities appears as an actual and a powerful
social reality (compound of Confucianism and Socialism)
that seems to have effected not only a redirecting of public
policy but even more of individual motivation and of obligation. As Western life created a new pluralistic society and
a new individual autonomy--as well as new theories about
each--so Chinese life seems to be creating a new society and
a new individual oriented towards the common good, using
Marxist theory and Western technology and rationalization
for human purposes. If, as I believe, the central social
and political crisis facing us at present requires a new
synthesis of the tradition of individual freedom with the
communal character of human existence, then it is surely
modern China that will provide the inspiration and the guidance for the creation of that synthesis.

The Religious Covenant

Every cultural whole, however, has a religious as well as a

cultural dimension, a religious substance which maintains cultural life's unity, power and meaning. Each culture expresses in all its cultural forms a particular vision of what is ultimately real, true and valuable, and lives out in all aspects of its life that stance towards being and meaning. Such a view of culture as having a religious substance has been expressed in varying ways in 19th and 20th century theoretical sociology and anthropology; it has been set in theological form by Tillich, and in a poorman's version by myself. Let us note that it represents an antagonistic position both to the exhaustively secular interpretation of culture of the Enlightenment and of Marxism, and to the natural-supernatural interpretation of culture of traditional theology. For here the natural is permeated with the supernatural, while, as we have argued, the church is also expressive in all its religious forms of its cultural locus.

Needless to say, this religious dimension of culture's life complicates the relation of a religion such as Christianity to any given culture. For therewith the problem arises not only of the relation of Christian faith to the culture as such, but also its relation to the _religious_ elements of that culture. It has historically been here especially that the real issues of a covenant of a synthesis have appeared.

Concerning this problem the Church has been clear in theory and ambivalent in practice. Heresy is constituted by a capitulation to the _religious_ idolatries of a culture, not by a use of its cultural forms. The gnostic, Arian and Manicheean heresies sought to set into Christian symbolic forms the religious visions of the Hellenistic world. They were countered by peculiarly Christian symbols expressing a non-Hellenistic religious orientation: _ex nihilo_, Trinity, Incarnation, resurrection of the body, etc. We should note, however, that none of the orthodox fathers eschewed Hellenistic cultural categories in expressing what became orthodoxy. In order to effect their Christian opposition to Hellenistic religion they used the categories of Hellenistic culture.

The same point could be made about the so-called "neo-orthodox" in the modern synthesis. In order to express their "orthodox" theology meaningfully, they used modern categories of interpretation, and they deliberately sought _not_ to combat the secular science, history, psychology and so on of their time. In order to express a _traditional_

theological position, they counter what they regard as the
false religious dimensions of modern culture: its rampant
individualism, its scientism, its principle of autonomous
self-sufficiency, its belief in progress and so on.

The problem of the relation of Christian faith to the religious dimension of culture--when the liberal consciously
accepts culture and even the orthodox must use cultural
concepts--dominates the theological controversies of both
the ancient and the modern church. It can hardly fail to
be the most important issue in our problem: the relation
of Christianity to either the old or the new China.

A synthesis is possible and necessary only when each side
has something to offer. I have indicated at length what
ancient and present Chinese cultural reality may offer to
the West and to Christianity: the strong moral and communal emphasis of Confucianism, now refashioned in an egalitarian rather than a hierarchical manner and oriented
forward to new possibilities in history rather than back-
ward to a sacred past. Here both the Confucian tradition
and the Marxist tradition have been transformed in relation
to one another, a genuine covenant, a monument to Mao's
genius. That the very different Western cultural emphasis
on criticism, individual autonomy and the value of the
person has in the past and even in the present something
to offer China, I do not doubt. But what does Christianity
have to contribute?

I shall try to suggest an answer in three points. All involve transcendence and our relation to it. Since Christianity is a religion, and thus a mode of being in relation
to the divine, what it has to offer is primarily a new form
of that relation, a form which transforms but does not replace the various aspects of cultural life in the world.
Correspondingly, what the faith offers to Maoism is essentially a new shape to the religious dimension of Maoism--
as Christianity sought to do with Hellenism and with Western
modernity. Christianity does not replace the cultural life
with which it is in covenant; it has no science, politics,
sociology or economics to offer of its own. Hopefully by
transforming the religious substance of the culture into
one of its own shape, (here is the relevance of the symbol
of the Kingdom) it will transform and deepen all of these
common aspects of culture into a more perfect realization
of what they themselves intend. Our three points, then,
seek to clarify how the Christian tradition might reshape
the religious dimension of Maoism into a truer and more

creative form. Clearly my argument is circular: Maoism is incomplete on these three issues only when viewed from a Christian (or some other) perspective. From its own perspective it naturally needs no complementary principles, no grace beyond what it may itself provide. But this circularity is characteristic of all intercultural and interreligious discourse, and so, while it is well to recognize it, it should not deter us.

Point One. That there is a religious dimension to Maoism is undoubted. Like its sister, Western Marxism and its distant cousin, the liberal view of Evolutionary Progress, Maoism presents a global viewpoint encompassing a view of reality as a whole and of its meaning, as a whole. This viewpoint is set in a symbolic structure of remarkable depth and consistency, that calls for participatory faith, commitment and obedience. The symbolic structure stabilizes and shapes institutions and the forms and the values of communal existence; it grounds the meanings of daily life; it structures the patterns of education; and it guides political action. Above all, in answering the deepest questions of the meaning of life, it relates human beings to the categories of the absolute and the sacred, and thus provides their fundamental principles of judgment and renewal, the grounds of confidence and hope, and so the possibility of their creative existence. This is not to say the Maoism is a "religion"; it is only to say that like any fundamental cultural reality, it contains and lives from a religious substance and religious dimension.

Now my first question is: what happens when this religious dimension is latent or in fact denied, as is the case in China? The denial does not remove the religious elements: the sense of the relation to the ultimate reality of process, to the meaning of history, to the promise of future fulfillment. Mao's genius is clearly evident in the way he prevented that claim to absoluteness from settling onto and rendering ultimate any particular plan or theory: the elite vanguard, the proletariat or peasants, the party, the nation. There is here a sense of transcendence that is able, to a remarkable degree, to be permanently critical of each of the polarities of socialism in process.

The preservation of transcendence is crucial lest absoluteness settle again (as it did in Russia) on theory and on the party elite, or lest the religious dimension itself be entirely lost in a pragmatic expertise ultimately indistinguishable from Western counterparts. Modern history is replete with creative cultural experiments whose religious dimensions were unheeded and suppressed. The meanings of such a culture can then disintegrate into superficial triviality. Its norms and its call to justice can dissolve--and finally, in reaction, the absolute can return in primitive, parochial, and demonic form. A cultural whole--and the more redemptive it is the more the risk-- that understands itself to be "religionless" is continually in danger of a profanization that loses its essential religious substance, or of a self-absolutization that leads to the demonic. Both have occurred, often in quick succession, in the West, and both still threaten us. China is by no means invulnerable to this possibility. Where the transcendent is not known and acknowledged, the creativity of a cultural substance is always in danger.

Point Two. The necessity of the transformation of social institutions--of the structures of government, of property, of the relations of production, of the interrelations of social groups and classes--has been one of the major creative themes of modern world culture. It is the central theme of the forces of liberation everywhere. This theme has historically been a creative result of the covenant of Christianity with secular modernity. Its roots are, to be sure, in important part Biblical. But it has been only in modern history that it has, for various reasons, become part of the self-interpretation of the Church and so of her understanding of her obligations. What does Christian faith, if it recognizes this "demand" for the transforming of the institutions of society as its own obligation have to say to a movement and a society centrally devoted to that transformation?

The answer, obviously itself dependent on a Christian view of our historic existence, is grounded in a distinction between our estrangement on the one hand and its consequences in cultural life on the other, between what has traditionally been called "sin" and what we might term "fate." The warped and unjust institutions of our common life of government, property, race, group, family, sexuality--can and do become a "fate" for those who live under their domination. Such institutions, incarnating injustice, can be inescapable for those born into them; they prevent and constrict our freedom to constitute ourselves and to share in the determination of our own destiny; they separate us from one another and from all meaning and worth. The suffering that arises from unjust social institutions is the clearest sign of the fallen character of history, and, as modern theology has pointed out, of the ravages of sin in history.

Since such institutional structures are the result of sin, and since they create suffering and encourage further sin, they defy the will of God for human community and are an offence to the Kingdom. On the basis of scripture and of the implications of every basic Christian symbol, therefore, the eradication, in so far as it is possible, of "fate" in this sense is an ultimate obligation of the gospel. Liberation theology, and the thrust of Maoism--as of the humanitarian movements of the 18th and 19th centuries--are essential aspects of theology. Correspondingly, both faith and theology are required to unite themselves with authentic political, economic and social movements of liberation whenever the latter appear. True theology is inescapably political theology dedicated to social liberation.

On the other hand, warped institutions are not the cause but the effects of history's most fundamental problem. Consequently, political and economic liberation, however crucial, is not the sum total of the gospel. For these institutions in this distorted form do not appear from nowhere; their warped character is not itself uncaused, a simple "given" necessarily if inexplicably present in historical life. On the contrary, this warped character--as liberal democracy and Marxism knew well--is a removable, alterable aspect of historical life, or there is no point at all in the effort to ameliorate it. Human creativity has helped to create and fashion these institutions; the estrangement of our creativity accounts, therefore, for the element of distortion and injustice present in all of them.

Thus even the very creativity of each cultural whole is involved in the end in the ultimately oppressive character of its institutions--as the bourgeois democratic culture of the West and its most creative gift to the world, technology, clearly illustrate. How hopefully that culture once viewed the "innocent," "just" and unambiguous future that it dreamed it would create! How evident it is now that the very principles that formed that dream constitute the anatomy of our present problems, dilemmas, and suffering! Each creative moment of history's life rightly rejects and transforms the warped social destiny that it inherits; each believes that thereby it has rid history of its most fundamental problem, the root source of its evil--as liberal democracy and its protestant equivalent viewed feudal aristocracy and authoritarianism and their Catholic justification. However creative, each in turn reenacts in its own forms our common

human estrangement, and produces for its children and for
others its own fated destiny: warped institutions which call
for transformation.

A deep spiritual estrangement runs through history and itself needs healing. As freedom falls into sin in history,
so the creative destiny we seek to bequeath to our children
itself falls into fate. The transformation of that social
"fate" is a necessary task, but the redemption of the freedom that continually falls, and in falling recreates historical fate, calls for what our creative and even
revolutionary action in the world cannot provide.

This truth is seen implicitly by Mao when he speaks of the
need for the transformation of the inner person as well as
for the transformation of institutions, and when he recognizes the permanence of the contradictions of historical
life and the continual reappearance of both "proleteriat"
and "bourgeois" even in socialism. Social transformation
deals with the consequences of estrangement and alienation,
not with its deeper causes. Thus estrangement and its consequences will reappear even when the given forms of fate
in our time have been radically reduced. An explicit
dealing with the problem of sin, as well as with fate, is
essential--and this a social philosophy can never finally
either promise or achieve. Our commitment in Christianity,
as Augustine argued, is in the end based on the self-
understanding that discovers our problem, and so the human
problem, to be one of estrangement or sin, and that calls
therefore for the answer of a grace beyond cultural possibilities and the possibilities of our own intelligence and
will. On this self-understanding the relevance of Christian faith to every cultural situation is based.

Point Three. There is a remarkable sense in Maoism of both
the mystery and the meaning of historical process, and the
dialectical interrelation of mystery and meaning. For historical process is here viewed as a process of struggle
between opposing but interdependent polarities, each dependent on the other but each critical of the other and bal-
ancing it. This struggle is seen as necessary in order to
preserve justice and harmony; yet risk is also necessary in
order to prevent their separation and destruction. Out of
the relativity of the parts and the chaos of surface events
arises, therefore, a deeper meaning. Here is a picture of
a creative process with religious depth, with an intrinsic
principle of self-criticism and with hidden but profound
telos and meaning latent within it.

From the Christian perspective, this view presents a profound interpretation of the providence of God as it works
in history, a hidden purpose working through judgment and
new possibilities to create deeper meaning. It is however
intrinsic to the Christian perspective that an even deeper
dialectic appears in the course of history, a dialectic
symbolized not by providence but by the Cross and the
Resurrection. For us, as we have seen, the dialectical
process of creation, opposition and struggle is at once a
process of a human creativity enmeshed in sin, and a process qualified by judgment and grace. The transcendent is
present in the process as the ground of creativity and of
new possibility, of a dynamic surge through struggle into
the new--as Mao recognizes. But the transcendent is also
over against the process as the principle of judgment, of
prophetic criticism of those who rule and even of those who
revolt, a principle of judgment of all in order that all
may be rescued. This dialectic, which is the heart of
Christianity, can never be present unless the transcendent
is recognized as transcendent, unless judgment on even the
creative, the wise and the good is made explicit, unless
grace appears as powerlessness and suffering as well as
victory, and life appears after and through death. The
Cross and the Resurrection hover over the creative process
as the sole principles of its continuing creativity.

Unless even what is most creative knows its mortality and
is willing to die, it can hardly live without destruction.
Unless life arises in history continually out of the possibility and reality of death, it can hardly live. This
Christian principle is dimly foreshadowed in the principle
of dialectical opposition, and more clearly seen in the
principles of continual revolution and the Mass Line. However, only as explicit, only as internalized, only as
appropriated in and through the presence of repentance and
of grace can it be real and permanent. Only if the life
of the human spirit dwells explicitly in humility, repentance, trust and hope in the presence of the eternal can
that life enact this final dialectic and be creative. The
Christian symbols centered on the Cross and Resurrection,
do not "save us"; grace does. But they can create for us
a self-understanding and an ultimate horizon within which
we find ourselves coram deo, in the presence of God, reconciled, reoriented and reborn in an inward stance where
presence and grace may be received. This gospel must be
heard anew, both here and there.

The supreme irony of history--and the supreme illustration

of history's <u>need</u> for this message! -- was that this gospel
of judgment on all (even on us ourselves) that grace may
be present in all, was proclaimed via gunboats, commercial
goods, technology and the self-affirming ego of the West,
not to mention the power and authority of the triumphant
Church! It would be equally ironical if it were to appear
once again, in a land now deeply devoted to the masses, in
the guise of a new ecclesiastical invasion of the mainland,
planned and enacted with all the devotion, resources and
ingenuity of the vast <u>ecclesia</u>.

Only a community <u>itself</u> under judgment that grace may come
to <u>it</u>, can give <u>this</u> message to a China newly reborn in
history out of near death. Only a mission that eschews
its own power and glory can communicate this message of
judgment on and grace to the culture and religion of the
new China. The Church had too long proclaimed justice,
reconciliation, repentance, love and unity to the world,
and quite forgotten to apply these stern requirements to
its own life and even to its own mission. The word of
God's judgment and grace must first be heard within,
acknowledged and appropriated by ourselves, if we are to
speak that word in the Spirit to others. If the church
merely brings its own culture and its own religion, its
Western forms and rites and its ecclesiastical might and
power--even if these proclaim the Cross in <u>our</u> eyes--it
will rightly be rejected again. A mission that dies itself, that sacrifices what it is in the world--in culture,
in religion, in theological formulations and in ecclesiastical might--in favor of the transcendent to which it seeks
to witness, can be heard--both in China and here. For
that alone is the voice, and the commission, that comes
to us from the Cross and from beyond the tomb.

II – POLITICAL ASPECTS OF CHINESE CATHOLICISM

Eric O. Hanson

On March 17, 1960 the Shanghai Intermediate People's Court condemned Shanghai Catholic Bishop Ignatius Kung to life imprisonment. The same trial sentenced fourteen other Chinese priests and four missionaries. Of the foreigners, only the American Maryknoll Bishop James E. Walsh remained in China. The PRC finally expelled him in 1970. The Court charged all those indicted with espionage and counter-revolutionary activity.[1]

Two hundred and thirteen years earlier during the great Christian persecution of 1746-48, a local mandarin in the same area of Kiangnan (Kiangsu and Anhui Provinces) captured two European missionaries and a Chinese priest. One of the missionaries carried a list of Chinese Christians. The government used this list to round up the Christians and force them to apostacize. Some, like Joseph T'ang Te-kuang, refused and died in prison after torture. The Ch'ing Magistrate sentenced the two missionaries to be strangled. They died in their cells on the night of August 13, 1748.[2]

One hundred and thirty-one years before this strangulation, the Ming persecution initiated by Shen Chueh forced most of the Jesuits of the Empire who escaped deportation to

hide at the home of the famous Catholic scholar Yang T'ing-
yun in neighboring Hangchow. Shen, the vice-president of
the Nanking Board of Rites, distinguished himself as one
of history's most implacable enemies of Catholicism. In
May 1616 Shen presented a memorial to the throne which
called for the death of all the missionaries and their converts. Finally, after further memorials and counter-
memorials, an imperial edict of February 14, 1617 ordered
the expulsion of the Jesuits from China. Shen's contemporary, the Jesuit Camillo di Costanzo, tries to account for
Shen's hatred of Catholics by citing examples in which
Shen or friends publicly lost face in debates with Hsu
Kuang-ch'i or other Chinese Christians or by saying that
Shen wished to use anti-foreignism to gain the post of
Grand Secretary. The historian Dunne, however, emphasizes
the horror that Sung-orthodoxy bureaucrats felt for the
new religious heresy. In their minds Catholicism threat-
ened to subvert the State.[3]

The central thesis of this article is that during the last
four hundred years Chinese State policy toward religion
has remained constant. The political-religious categories
of the Ming continue to guide government religious policy
in the People's Republic. State Catholic policy derives
from State policy toward religion in general. As a foreign
institutional[4] religion, the Catholic Church has always
been unwelcome, but at times it has been tolerated because
of its domestic and international uses. When the State
perceived the Church as a heterodox sect, however, it
sought to obliterate it. In response to this constant
State policy, the Catholic Church has adopted various
political strategies in its quest for organizational survival and expansion.

The basic choice facing the Church has been whether to
support the State ideology or to challenge it. When Catholics have supported the Confucian[5] or Nationalist regimes,
they have stressed the complementarity of Church and State
ideologies. The sixteenth century Jesuit Matteo Ricci
donned the mandarin gown and sought to harmonize Confucian
thought and Christian doctrine. The twentieth century
Archbishop of Nanking, Paul Yu Pin, not only composed a
Catholic rite to honor the ancestors,[6] but also assured the
Nationalist government that Catholics make superb anti-
Communists.

During these times when the Church supported the State, it
also stressed the political, cultural, and scientific advantages that Catholicism offered the Chinese government. The

seventeenth and eighteenth century Jesuits made themselves
welcome by serving Ming and Ch'ing Emperors at Peking.
Ricci first approached the court in 1601 as a mathematician
and astronomer. He constructed Western clocks, spheres,
globes, quadrants, and sextants. Ricci's successor Adam
Schall not only reformed the Chinese calendar, but in 1642
cast twenty cannons for the Ming defense of Peking against
the Manchus. Schall's successor Verbiest superintended
the casting of three hundred cannons for the Manchu K'ang-
hsi Emperor. The Jesuits also assisted the Chinese in
negotiating the treaty of Nerchinsk with Russia in 1689.
The K'ang-hsi Emperor finally rewarded his missionary
courtiers with an act of Christian toleration three years
later. Even during the Christian persecution which
followed the Rites Decision, the Jesuits continued to act
as astronomers, interpreters, cartographers, painters,
engravers, architects, and engineers at the court of
Ch'ien-lung (1736-1795).

When the Vatican supported Kuomintang nationalism in the
early twentieth century, it called for an early restitution
of China's full international rights. During the 1950s
American prelates like New York's Cardinal Spellman lobbied
to gain United States political and financial support for
Chiang Kai-shek against the People's Republic.[7]

Such ideological complementarity and foreign and domestic
service encouraged the Confucian and National Chinese
States to tolerate Catholicism. Weighed against such
positive elements, however, were the negative factors of
the degree of political threat posed by Catholics and the
political cost of their repression. Did the Church possess
such strong horizontal and vertical linkages to other dis-
affected groups that it constituted an immediate revolutionary danger to the State? Did Catholics have such
cohesive internal ideological and structural unity that
suppression would entail a long and bloody struggle?

The ability of the Chinese State to carry out its policy
toward the Catholic Church at any particular time depended
on three factors. First, it depended on the international
balance of power between the Chinese State and the Western
government sponsoring Catholicism. The stronger the political power of Portugal, France, or the United States
vis-a-vis the Chinese State, the less freedom of action
the Chinese government had with regard to the Church.
During the last half of the nineteenth century Peking
acquiesced to the revolutionary spread of missionaries

into the interior under the threat of foreign gunboats.
Prince Kung, however, made clear that he did this only to
gain time. He declared that as soon as the balance of
power shifted, he would expel the missionaries.[8] Basic
Chinese policy had not changed. The Chinese had to wait
ninety years, however, for this shift of power.

The second factor regarding implementation of Chinese State
religious policy concerns the domestic strength and political technology of a particular Chinese government. The
Ch'ing under K'ang-hsi could execute its policies much more
effectively than the eunuch-ridden governments of the late
Ming. Mao Tse-tung had a control of Mainland China that
Chiang Kai-shek never attained. The Communist revolution
in political participation is also relevant. Townsend has
documented the CCP's accomplishments in mass mobilization.[9]
This advancement in "political technology" meant changes
in both government and Church strategy.

The third factor concerns the indigenization of the Catholic Church. At its most basic level, the problematic of
Chinese State-Catholic Church relations concerns East-West
cultural interaction. Both the Chinese State and the
Catholic Church are historical institutions formed in a
particular political-religious culture. The dissimilar
traditional cultures of Medieval Europe and classical
China gave the two institutions different expectations
concerning the relationship between politics and religion.
The Catholic Church left its European political-religious
culture and came to China. Catholic missionary expansion
presents a specific case of a religious institution formed
in one political-religious culture interacting with a
government and society based on different ideological and
organizational principles.

Battle for Ecclesiastical Control of Kiangnan

This Catholic missionary expansion into China produced two
patterns. In the first pattern the Church projected a Chinese political-religious form in an attempt to win the
national elite. Ricci joined the intelligentsia and sought
to harmonize Catholicism with Confucian values. The early
Jesuits served the Ming and Ch'ing States in Peking. Rome's
Rites Decision of 1715, however, condemned ancestor ritual
and resulted in the proscription of Catholicism. Peking
classified the Church as a popular heretical sect.[10] In
their effort to survive, local Catholic congregations

adopted peasant organizational forms. Lay leaders directed
the local congregations and the phenomenon of virgins
emerged.

China in the late nineteenth century represents the second
pattern. French power enabled the Church to regain its
Western political-religious form, but at the cost of sepa-
rating itself from the mainstream of Chinese society. The
crucial battle for control of the Chinese Church was fought
in Kiangnan. The extension of French military power into
the Shanghai area facilitated the large scale return of the
French Jesuits to this area. The Jesuits returned in 1842
at the request of the Vicar Apostolic[11] de Besi. The European ecclesiastics immediately clashed with Chinese elements of local Church autonomy developed during Ch'ing
proscription. The French Jesuit Hermand describes the
situation from a Western point of view when he remarks
that during proscription Kiangnan Catholics had introduced
many abuses and blames these abuses on the infrequency of
clerical visits.[12] Other European clerics criticized the
Kiangnan Catholics for cowardice. The Vincentian priest
Baldus wrote, "The Christians in the Shanghai area enjoy
a well-merited reputation for timidity. . . . There were
only a few persecutions in Kiangnan, and, as everything in
China revolves around money, they bought the peace of the
Mandarins."[13] Such gratuitous remarks hardly endeared the
missionaries to the Chinese Christian families, many of
whom had sacrificed their entire fortunes to remain Catholic.

The missionaries clashed with the hui chang (lay leaders
of local congregations) over the question of local financial control. The laymen, having become accustomed to
complete financial autonomy, refused to yield it to the
Europeans. La Serviere says that although the influential
families showed great respect for the priest, if he broached
the subject of Church finances, he risked revolt.[14]

French diplomatic maneuvers strengthened the missionary
position. Paris dispatched the special envoy Lagrene to
secure French interests in China. Lagrene obtained an
imperial rescript of March 18, 1846 which restored to the
Church certain of its former properties. The following
August Bishop de Besi and the Jesuit Superior Father Gotte-
land employed the services of the French and English consuls
to begin negotiations on this issue with the Shanghai
authorities. As French political power expanded in the
next decade, the Jesuits moved further and further into the
interior while laying claim to Church property.

The priests' second problem, the ecclesiastical power of women (especially the "virgins"), proved insoluble by foreign authoritarian imposition at the national level. The virgins' liturgical and religious role depended on their place in the local community. While the missionaries appreciated the dedication of these single women, they also considered them a source of scandal. In 1840 Lavaissiere wrote that his great task was to eliminate night visits by the virgins and to compel them to show less familiarity with their relatives and neighbors.[15] Bishop de Besi, on the other hand, worried about their power vis-a-vis the priest. The Jesuits determined to solve these problems by "regularizing" the virgins' life in imitation of Western nuns. In 1869 a group of French nuns founded a native Chinese congregation, the Association of the Presentation of the Blessed Virgin (Presentadines). The new congregation would "replace the virgins."[16] The French Helpers of the Holy Souls gave the aspirants two years of spiritual formation at Zicawei, and supervised them in the apostolate for one year. They were then sent into the countryside in groups of two or three. By 1922 there were 217 Presentadines. However, the ancient institution of the virgin remained. The Jesuits asserted that the Presentadines had "a better formation and a more abundant spiritual life, and that they were more directly under the authority of the Mission Superior."[17] (Italics mine.) While the virgins strengthened local autonomy, the Presentadines extended French ecclesiastical control.

Virgin participation in the liturgy sparked the main missionary-Chinese confrontation of this period. The virgins in the prefectural city of Sungkiang were accustomed to chanting prayers in Chinese during Mass. In 1845 de Besi ordered the prayers recited by the entire congregation, men and women alternately. Since Chinese custom restrained public conversation between men and women, a storm of protest broke out. Finally, an ex-catechist issued a pamphlet attacking the Bishop and his Jesuit supporters as unworthy of Ricci and the early missionaries.[18] The Bishop replied by censoring the protestors and requiring public penances before they could return to the sacraments.

This local battle soon became an international issue. During this same period Rome and Lisbon were feuding over the Portuguese king's right to appoint bishops to Chinese dioceses according to the ancient padroado.[19] The king named a Vincentian seminary professor in Macao, Miranda, as Bishop of Nanking. Miranda would replace de Besi who had been

appointed by Rome without Portuguese consent. The Sungkiang Christians saw their chance to get rid of de Besi and
wrote to the king of Portugal. They listed their griev-
ances and offered an episcopal residence for Miranda. The
Chinese priests showed more discretion. They met at Suchow
and decided to send gifts to Miranda along with a joint
letter that promised an enthusiastic reception if he
arrived with Roman approbation. Miranda foresaw an ecclesiastical battle and never left Macao. De Besi then transferred the pastor of Sungkiang, Matthew Sen, to another
parish. Sen refused to submit to the order and de Besi
suspended him. The next vicar apostolic Maresca finally
settled the Sungkiang controversy. He lessened the ecclesiastical penalties and offered a liturgical compromise.[20]
The Sungkiang confrontation demonstrates the depth of Chinese popular and clerical resistance to the new missionary
ecclesiastical domination.

The Jesuits also feuded with de Besi over the control of
money given by European Catholics for the use of the
Jesuits in China. Rome separated the antagonists by
dividing de Besi's jurisdiction and appointing the more
acceptable Maresca as Vicar Apostolic of Kiangnan in 1848.
Rome appointed the first Jesuit Vicar Borgniet in 1856.
The Jesuits then ordered the Chinese secular priests to
live in Jesuit houses as subjects of Jesuit discipline.[21]

The Taiping rebellion (1850-1864) solidified Jesuit ecclesiastical control. The Taiping destroyed Catholic villages
and forced the Christians to flee to Shanghai and Jesuit
protection. After the Ch'ing armies restored order the
Jesuits rebuilt rural churches with European money. More
and more Jesuits arrived from France. The Jesuit historian
Colombel summarizes the result:

> From that time even in the temporal order the
> priest was under no obligation to the Christians,
> but on the contrary the Christians received
> almost everything from the priest. The rela-
> tions of the priest to his Christians were no
> longer what they had been before the rebellion.
> The priest was really master of his chretiente
> (community of Christians)."[22]

Before the coming of the foreigners Sungkiang, not Shanghai,
had the most important Christian community in the area.
But as Shanghai expanded into a large commercial city, more
and more people left their rice paddies and went to Shanghai

to seek their fortune. Many Catholics joined this migra-
tion. Shanghai's satellite village of Zicawei became a
great Catholic center. Next to the tomb of Hsu Kuang-ch'i
the Jesuits built a giant complex that consisted of the
bishop's residence, major and minor seminaries for diocesan clergy, a Jesuit scholasticate, observatory, two
orphanages, three high schools, and a teacher's college.[24]
Shanghai Catholicism had deep roots in its rural past.

The Chinese-Vatican Alliance Against
French Ecclesiastical Imperialism

The Treaties of Tientsin (1858-1860) permitted European
powers to send missionaries to live and work in the interior. This set off a scramble among the European religious orders for mission "spheres of influence." The competing groups showed little or no cooperation. Jesuits
and Vincentians nourished their historic mutual enmity.
Germans looked down on Latins. The French made no attempt
to hide their disdain for non-Frenchmen, occidental or
oriental. When Vincent Lebbe reached the Peking Seminary
in 1901, for example, he found that European priests and
Chinese priests ate at different tables, with only whites
occupying the head table. Chinese seminarians pursued a
far less advanced course of study than European ones:

> The missionaries were haunted by the fear that
> pride would drive the Chinese to revolt, and so
> the great thing was to keep them in a state of
> humility. . . . And of course they were expected
> to fill only subordinate positions in any case.[25]

France assumed the role of protector of the Chinese Catholic
Church during the nineteenth century.[26] She maintained her
role despite later protests from the Vatican itself. Finally, during the 1920s the Chinese Church and Rome established
direct relations. The legal basis of the French protector-
ate derived from the treaties following the English and
French victory in the Arrow War of 1848. The four treaties
(English, French, American and Russian) all contained a
toleration clause that stipulated

> persons teaching it (Christianity) or professing it,
> therefore, shall alike be entitled to the protection
> of the Chinese authorities; nor shall any such,
> peaceably pursuing their calling, and not offending
> against the laws, be persecuted or interfered with.[27]

This clause, which caused much dispute in later years, in its broadest interpretation placed every Christian under the protection of foreign consuls. The French and Russian treaties also provided that missionaries who carried their passports were free to travel throughout all of China. The French went one step further in the Peking Convention of 1860 when the French interpreter, Father Delamarre, inserted an additional sentence in the Chinese version. It read: "It is in addition permitted to French Missionaries to rent and purchase land in all the provinces, and to erect buildings thereon at pleasure."28

The French missionaries themselves welcomed special government protection. In 1901 Bishop Reynaud of Ningpo put forth an extreme statement of this nationalist position in an anonymous pamphlet entitled, "France in Chekiang." He defended French claims in the area on the basis of French military intervention:

> If ever any other country were to make claims as regards the Chekiang district, France would have the right to stop her and say, "Do not come here to disturb the rest of all my dead. Look at all these tombs bearing my name. . . . Here also under the flagstones lie big-hearted soldiers, my sons. . ." One has only to reverse a couple of words for "France in Chekiang" to become quite naturally "Chekiang in France."29

The French Bishop of Ningpo never considered that Chekiang might belong to China.

As the Catholic missionary effort in China grew, the Vatican attempted to bypass French government control. In 1886 the Holy See initiated negotiations to establish direct contact with the Chinese government, but France put up such threatening opposition that Rome dropped the idea.30

The Chinese government initiated the second attempt at establishing direct relations. In July 1918 it issued a presidential mandate appointing a Chinese minister to the Vatican. Rome responded by appointing a nuncio to Peking. France and Italy protested vigorously. Late in August the Chinese government announced that due to certain inconveniences, negotiations with the Vatican would not be resumed until after the War. The following day the Vatican announced that the Pope hoped to send a religious delegation to China soon, but for the moment rescinded the political initiative.[31]

On November 30, 1919 the Vatican took the offensive in the question of missionary-Chinese relations. The Pope issued the encyclical **Maximum Illud** which deplored the effects of European nationalism on the Catholic Church in China, and called for eventual Church administration by the Chinese clergy. The missionary clergy in China gave the letter a lukewarm response.[32]

In late 1922 Pope Pius XI sent a delegation headed by the very able Archbishop Celso Costantini to China. Rome pointed out that his mission was exclusively religious and educational.[33] However, the Chinese President received him immediately and the Apostolic Delegate often represented the Church at political events. Costantini became the architect of the new Vatican policy toward China. In 1923 the Pope appointed two native priests to head their respective missions. On October 28, 1926 Pius consecrated six Chinese bishops.[34] This policy, which seems obvious today, caused great controversy during that time of the Unequal Treaties.

These Vatican initiatives marked a notable change in the public stance of Chinese Catholics. Since the Boxer Rebellion, Protestants had assumed a certain prominence in public affairs, but the less well-educated Catholic community with its conservative missionary leadership had basically ignored national and international affairs to concentrate on building local Catholic communities. In August 1928, the Pope addressed a pastoral letter to the Church and the people of China. He expressed his joy at the termination of the Chinese civil war and stated that Catholics would be exemplary citizens of the new China. The Church, he said, "professes, teaches and preaches respect and obedience to legitimately constituted authority." He hoped that Chinese national rights would soon gain international recognition, and asked only "the liberty and security of common law" for the Catholic missionaries and laity.[35]

A few months later Archbishop Costantini attended the State funeral of Sun Yat-sen. The Chinese government received him with all the honors accorded representatives of other powers. At the grave he made the three ceremonial bows, presented his wreath and repeated the bows.[36] The occasion signaled that from then on the Holy See and China would deal directly with each other. It also indicated that the Church was taking a new look at the old Rites problem.

On December 8, 1939 Rome issued revised instructions on the
question of Catholic participation in Confucian ceremonies.
The instructions reversed the ruling of 1715 and permitted
Catholics to participate in services before a likeness or
tablet of Confucius. Yu Pin hailed this decree as the beginning of a new era of Vatican respect for China's cultural traditions. The bishop felt that the Church must
return "to the traditional method of approach exemplified
by Father Ricci." The literati must be reached. "Once
they are converted to Catholicism, the conversion of the
rest of the nation will follow as a matter of course."[37]

Post-1949 and the Future

The preceding discussion offers three continuities for
understanding the post-1949 PRC-Catholic Church struggle
and for predicting future political possibilities for the
Catholic Church.

(1) The establishment of the People's Republic in 1949
meant that the balance of political power had shifted
again. Once more the Catholic Church had to find its
place in a political-religious tradition that emphasized
penetration, regulation, and control of institutional religion and obliteration of heterodox sects. Just as both
Peking's favor and State persecution proved unsatisfactory
during the Ming and the Ch'ing, so neither alternative
appeared particularly promising in 1949. This dilemma
underlay the Vatican Internuncio Riberi's attempt to go
to Peking and the government's refusal to receive him.[38]
The 1955 Shanghai arrests crushed Bishop Kung's separation
of religious independence from patriotic duty.[39] The Chinese elite have not tolerated strong institutional religions except in periods of social, political and economic
crisis. They are not likely to do so in the future. The
major difficulty is not the philosophical tension between
Marxism and Christianity, but the political-religious conflict between a strong Asian State and a strong institutional religion formed by the Western political-religious
tradition. Vietnam, therefore, not Russia, is the best
comparative case.[40]

(2) Catholicism and Protestantism played very different
political and cultural roles in China. Chinese Protestantism never developed a strong presence at the local level,[41]
but during the late nineteenth and early twentieth centuries
it enjoyed considerable influence among the national elite.

The leading Protestant missionary nations to China, Great Britain and the United States, represented the new liberal capitalism that might save China. Just as Catholicism was rooted in the small peasant churches scattered over the countryside,[42] Protestantism built many of China's famous colleges and universities.

After 1949, however, the Protestant churches found themselves in a bad political position. Compared with Catholicism they lacked both Western hierarchical unity at the national level and strong traditional roots at the local level. After the PRC confiscated their educational and social institutions, Protestant churches offered no substantial service to the State. The Protestant liberal wing tried to elaborate an ideology of State support, but fundamentalists like Wang Ming-tao rejected such "idolatry." Protestantism appeared most dangerous during the Korean War because of its links to American Mission Boards. Denominationalism and the liberal-fundamentalist split weakened its institutional unity.

This split between fundamentalist and "social gospel"[43] Christians still influences the stance of Western Protestants toward China. Liberals tend to praise the "social gospel" of Mao and warn against precipitous direct evangelism. Fundamentalists stress the "godless" nature of the PRC and become enthusiastic about such projects as radio and Bible evangelism. Vatican II, however, lessened the distance between Protestantism and Catholicism. Pope John XXIII sought to make peace with the modern world. Aggiornamento thus expedited ecumenism, but also produced internal Catholic liberal-conservative tensions analogous to centuries-old Protestant problems.

For Chinese whose families have been Catholic for many generations, Vatican II requires some difficult adjustments. This difficulty is compounded by four factors: (a) Vatican II was a response to a liberal democratic modernization that China has not experienced; (b) Chinese Catholic strength centered in traditionally-oriented rural peasants, not urbanized intellectuals; (c) the Chinese Catholic Church has been traditionally anti-Communist; and (d) the Sino-Vatican alliance against French imperialism strengthened Chinese Catholic devotion to the Pope and appreciation of his ecclesiastical prerogatives.

(3) Catholic missionary expansion produced three political paradoxes in China. First, the strong foreign political

power that protected the Church from State interference also
reinforced foreign ecclesiastical forms that endangered
local Catholicism during persecution. Just as a missionary's big nose ruined any disguise, so foreign organizations
dominated by missionary clergy made an easy State target.
Second, precisely because a foreign organization was a
ready target, the more Catholicism assimilated itself to
the local community, the more it became a political threat.
The Shanghai Church put up such a fierce struggle against
the Communist government because it had a Chinese bishop,
an educated Chinese clergy, and could draw on the indigenous political strengths of family loyalties, amorphous
Chinese organization, and traditional rituals. PRC propaganda promoted the Three-Self Movement as a means to
sinicize the Church, but it soon became clear that there
was a "right" and a "wrong" way to be "Chinese."

The third paradox concerns the Catholic feeling of sepa-
rateness from Chinese society. This made the Church both
less and more of a political threat at the same time.
Since both Catholic and popular sectarians like the I Kuan
Tao had been persecuted simultaneously by both Confucian
and Communist governments, one might guess they had formed
alliances for mutual defense, but Communist[44] and Catholic[45]
evidence is unanimous in rejecting this hypothesis. On
the contrary, the heretical Taiping drove Kiangnan local
Catholicism into Shanghai and ecclesiastical dependency on
the French Jesuits. The Chinese Catholics of Taiwan still
consider themselves "a people apart" from their "superstitious" neighbors.[46] This attitude results naturally from
the social fact that conversion means withdrawing from the
religious ceremonies that constitute the local political
community.[47] The popular mind still identifies Catholicism
with foreigners. This Chinese Catholic feeling of separate-
ness translates into a failure to form wider external
political alliances and thus limits the Church as a political threat. However, it also produced a "bastion mentality" of organizational cohesiveness among old Mainland
Catholics that proved very resistant to State penetration.

NOTES

1. New China News Agency from Shanghai, March 19, and from Peking and Tientsin, March 20, 1960, collected in Survey of China Mainland Press, March 25, 1960, pp. 1-5.

2. Joseph Krahl, S.J., China Missions in Crisis: Bishop Laimbeckhoven and His Times, 1738-1787 (Rome: Gregorian University, 1964), pp. 52-54.

3. George H. Dunne, S.J., Generation of Giants (Notre Dame: University of Notre Dame Press, 1962), pp. 128-51. Dunne's book is an excellent description of the work of Ricci and the early Jesuits. This article emphasizes less well known aspects of Chinese Catholic Church history that are necessary for a political-religious explanation of both earlier and later periods.

4. See C. K. Yang, "Institutional Religion and Its Weak Position in Modern Chinese Society," in Religion in Chinese Society (Berkeley: University of California Press, 1961), pp. 301-9.

5. Beginning with the Sung, Confucianism regained its position after many centuries of Buddhist eclipse. Sung Neo-Confucianism "sought to show that it could offer every-thing desirable that Buddhism could, and more." H. G. Creel, Chinese Thought: From Confucius to Mao Tse-tung (Chicago: University of Chicago Press, 1953), p. 204. Creel later says that during the last four centuries two new forces have arisen to play major roles in the development of Chinese thought. The first was the Han Learning which called for a return to the earlier simpler teachings of Confucius and Mencius. The second force was the coming of the West. State Confucianism, of course, contains elements from both legalism and Taoism. The primary referent in this article, however, is the State itself, not Confucianism as a philosophical current.

6. A Chinese Bishops' Conference press release (Taipei: News Secretariat, n.d.) describes a ceremony for the veneration of Heaven and the ancestors which took place in Tainan on New Year's Day, February 11, 1975. Cardinal Yu Pin and Tainan Mayor Chang Li-tang presided. The press release ends by saying that the participants came to a "deeper understanding of this Chinese tradition with regard to the Catholic teaching."

7. See Robert I. Gannon, The Cardinal Spellman Story (Garden City, N. Y.: Doubleday and Company, Inc., 1962), especially pp. 308-9; Ross Y. Koen, The China Lobby in American Politics (New York: Macmillan, 1960). For a PRC attack on Cardinal Spellman, see Jen min jih pao /People's Daily/, April 16, 1951.

8. Paul A. Cohen, China and Christianity: the Missionary Movement and the Growth of Chinese Antiforeignism, 1860-1870 (Cambridge: Harvard University Press, 1963), pp. 72-73.

9. James R. Townsend, Political Participation in Communist China (Berkeley: University of California Press, 1967).

10. See J. J. M. de Groot, Sectarianism and Religious Persecution in China (Taipei: Ch'eng Wen Publishing Co., 1970), especially pp. 329-34, 387-405.

11. Ecclesiastical divisions of diocesan size in ascending rank: mission, independent mission, apostolic prefecture, apostolic vicariate, diocese, archdiocese. Technically speaking, the heads of the various divisions are: superior, superior, prefect apostolic, vicar apostolic, bishop, archbishop. When an apostolic vicariate becomes a diocese, the vicar apostolic becomes a bishop. This article will simplify by calling such men as de Besi who later became bishop "bishop" in future references.

12. Louis Hermand, S.J., Les étapes de la mission du Kiang-nan, 1842-1922 et de la mission de Nanking, 1922-1932 (Zicawei: Jesuites--Province de France, 1933), p. 15.

13. J. de La Serviere, S. J., Histoire de la mission du Kiangnan: Jesuites de la province de France (Paris) (1840-1899), 2 vols. (Shanghai: Catholic Mission Press, preface dated 1914), pp. 25-26n.

14. Ibid., p. 23.

15. Ibid., p. 24.

16. Hermand, Kiang-nan, p. 86.

17. Ibid., p. 47.

18. Remembering the old Jesuits with fondness, Kiangnan Christians had requested the return of the Society of Jesus.

They especially criticized the failure of the new missionaries to become proficient in Chinese and the study of
Chinese customs.

19. "As a result of the secular struggle of the Iberian
Peninsula against the Moslems, the Spanish Crown had been
invested with many powers in the religious sphere. Thus
it was that as early as 1493, one year after Columbus'
voyage, Pope Alexander VI established the line of demarca-
tion between Spain and Portugal, and conferred on the
Spanish kings the exclusive right (on their side of the
line) to take possession of and evangelize the newly conquered territories, and to exercise the right of patronage
over the churches to be established. In 1501 the Pope
accorded the tithes collected in America to the Spanish
Crown in perpetuity; in return, the Crown was charged with
the responsibility of founding and endowing the Real Patron-
ato." Francois Houtart and Emile Pin, The Church and the
Latin American Revolution (New York: Sheed and Ward,
1965), p. 6. In Portuguese this mandate was called the
Padroado.

20. La Serviere, Histoire, pp. 90-97.

21. Auguste M. Colombel, S.J., Histoire de la mission
du Kiangnan, 6 vols. (Shanghai: Mission Catholique, 1895-
1905), pp. 553-54. This handwritten manuscript is not
recommended to non-French scholars with weak eyes.

22. Ibid., p. 913.

23. Hsu Kuang-ch'i (1562-1633) was the most famous of
Ricci's converts. He eventually became Grand Secretary for
the Empire.

24. There is a Zicawei inset in the Shanghai ecclesiastical map accompanying Hermand, Kiang-nan. The site of the
cathedral was later moved to Tongkadou.

25. Jacques Leclercq, Thunder in the Distance (New York:
Sheed and Ward, 1958), pp. 55-56.

26. This was true of the most anti-clerical French
governments. French international influence was at stake,
not Catholic missionary zeal.

27. British Treaty of Tientsin, Article 8, cited by
Arne Sovik, "Church and State in Republican China" (Ph.D.
dissertation, Yale University, 1952), p. 44.

28. Ibid., p. 47.

29. Leclercq, Thunder, pp. 48-49.

30. Ibid., p. 49.

31. Sovik, "Church and State," pp. 141-42.

32. Leclercq, Thunder, pp. 210-13.

33. Costantini came as Apostolic Delegate, ecclesiastical representative of the Pope to the Catholic Church in China. Nuncio, on the other hand, is a political title referring to a diplomatic representative of the State of the Vatican. An Internuncio performs the same diplomatic functions, but holds a lesser diplomatic rank.

34. Leclercq, Thunder, pp. 243-44.

35. Sovik, "Church and State," p. 275.

36. Ibid., pp. 276-77.

37. Paul Yu-Pin, Eyes East (Patterson, N. J.: St. Anthony Guild Press, 1945), pp. 142-44.

38. Catholic commentators debate the political significance and intentions of Archbishop Riberi. Louis Wei Tsing-sing, Le Saint-Siege et la Chine de Pie XI a nos jours (Paris: Allais, 1971) faults Riberi for remaining at Nanking and failing to recognize the PRC. Bishop Walsh, in a letter to America, May 6, 1972, p. 484, and others, however, testify to the fact that Riberi sent an official request to the new government in which he proposed to come to Peking to present his credentials. Peking never replied and he could not obtain permission to travel to the capital. This is not surprising when it is noted that Peking also refused official contacts with the Buddhists at this time. A strong rejoinder to Wei's position is Fernando Mateos, S.J., "La Iglesia Catolica en China Comunista," Arbor (June 1972): 67-92.

39. The best study of the most significant local PRC-Catholic Church confrontation is Jean Lefeuvre, S.J., Shanghai: les enfants dans la ville (Paris: Casterman, 1956). The sixth edition was published in 1962 and continues the story after 1955. To make room, however, the author had to omit some very interesting sections on

Communist-Catholic relations from the earlier part of the
first edition. Both editions are invaluable to studying
this subject. For a general history of PRC-Church relations, see Richard C. Bush, Jr., Religion in Communist
China (Nashville, Tenn.: Abingdon Press, 1970). For documentation, see Donald E. MacInnis, Religion and Practice
in Communist China (New York: Macmillan, 1972).

40. Piero Gheddo, The Cross and the Bo Tree (New York:
Sheed and Ward, 1970). For Japan, see the modern classic
by Shusaku Endo, Silence (Tokyo: Charles E. Tuttle Co.,
1969).

41. Paul A. Varg, Missionaries, Chinese, and Diplomats
(Princeton: Princeton University Press, 1958), pp. 226-50
presents a whole chapter on "The Problem in Rural China,
1920-37." After citing Protestant emphasis on the cities,
he says, "The most important fact is that wherever Christian (Protestant) work was started in the rural villages
it tended to wither away." The Protestant individualism
that seemed so appealing to the new elite made penetration
at the local level impossible. "Christianity (Protestantism) made itself irrelevant by failing to include the
community, and, in turn the community never embraced the
esoteric Christian enterprise. The Christian convert,
left to pursue his own meaningless existence in a brutal
society, with no sustenance for his Christian life aside
from hymn singing and literal interpretation of Bible
texts, drifted away from the church."

42. Changhai is not an exception because most of the
Christian families came from the countryside. Hermand,
Kiang-nan, p. 12.

43. Term used by PRC Religious Affairs Bureau cadres.

44. The former Canton public security cadre I interviewed insisted again and again that there were no political
links between Catholics and heterodox sects. Interview,
Hong Kong, February 1975. The only charge of Catholic-
popular sect collusion I have found in the Communist press
is the claim that the Legion of Mary sheltered former sectarians. See, for example, Chieh fang jih pao /Liberation
Daily; CFJP/, October 12, 1951.

45. At the same time that the Shanghai municipal government was liquidating the heterodox sects in 1953, Shen
Chih-yuan entertained Catholic leaders and assured them

that the government considered Catholicism a great religion and not a secret superstition. Lefeuvre, Shanghai (1956), p. 249. Every Church source I interviewed testified to the distance between Catholicism and Chinese popular religion.

46. One Taiwan priest remarked that he heard his people say, "Just to smell temple incense makes me sick." When another priest proposed building a new church in temple style, his parishioners replied that they had renounced all that superstition and wanted to build a church in "universal Church style." At other places parishes have integrated popular religious usages. The point seems to be that Catholics on Taiwan see themselves belonging to a "modern" religion that is divorced from the traditional sociological religion. This surmise is substantiated by the fact that new urbanites show a shift to either non-belief or Christianity. See Wolfgang L. Grichting, The Value System in Taiwan 1970 (Taipei: Bethlehem Fathers, 1971), pp. 179-82.

47. The Taiwan Taoist priest and his entourage perform the chiao festival every sixty years to renew the community. Michael R. Saso, Taoism and the Rite of Cosmic Renewal (Pullman: Washington State University Press, 1972). Not to participate in or contribute money to community religious festivals is often perceived as an antisocial act. In former times the worshipers sometimes retaliated by burning down Christian churches. Pablo Fernandez, O.P., ed., One Hundred Years of Dominican Apostolate in Formosa (1859-1958) (Quezon City: Dominican Fathers, 1959), pp. 105-8. Even today, according to one of the Taiwan pastors, the hardest sacrifice one of his parishioners makes is not to participate in the annual Ma Tsu festival. This Catholic who is especially rich and therefore could afford to set off many firecrackers and gain much social prestige always leaves town at festival time. Donald R. DeGlopper, "Religion and Ritual in Lukang," in Arthur P. Wolf, ed., Religion and Ritual in Chinese Society (Stanford: Stanford University Press, 1974), p. 50, points out that the local elite manage the Ma Tsu temple in that city. In the competing Ma Tsu center of Peikang, the temple administers most of the land in that area and performs such public services as paving roads and putting in electric lights. The mayor has to be a temple man. Formerly the temple used its political influence to keep the national government from stationing troops in the area. Finally, government and temple reached a compromise which allowed the stationing of officers. Relations between the temple and the local Catholic Church are excellent, but being a Catholic in Peikang is like being a Moslem in Lourdes.

III – THE REACTION OF CHINESE INTELLECTUALS TOWARD RELIGION AND CHRISTIANITY IN THE EARLY TWENTIETH CENTURY

Yu-ming Shaw

I

Why should we try to find out the attitude of twentieth century Chinese intellectuals toward religion in general and toward Christianity in particular? Such an investigation is not only a worthy effort in the study of Chinese intellectual history, but is also important for our understanding of the reception of Christianity in China. In view of the fact that intellectuals throughout Chinese history--with the possible exception of recent years on mainland China--have been the guiding spirits for the Chinese nation and its people, their attitudes and opinions must have influenced the overall Chinese understanding of Christianity and its work in China.

Our present study is important also in terms of bridging a crucial gap in previous Western studies concerning Christianity in China in the twentieth century. Thanks to several illuminating studies, we know how Christianity was generally received in China during the nineteenth century.[1] We know, for example, that between 1860 and 1899 there were thousands of small incidents and some 240 overt riots or attacks on missionaries.[2] We also know that there were then very few Christians among Chinese intellectuals; that Chinese intellectuals were almost totally opposed to Christianity; and that their opposition was largely based on their faith in the Confucian tradition, their perception of a congruence of Western imperialism and Christian proselytization, and their belief in a necessary conflict between Christian practices and Chinese social customs. This is all well known, but the twentieth century still remains largely unstudied. While we know that Chinese anti-Christian activities in the early twentieth century were as prevalent as before, what were the attitudes of Chinese intellectuals toward Christianity and its work in China? Certainly the majority of them continued the opposition, but on what grounds? Conversely, were there defenders of the Christian faith among them? If so, what was the content of their defense? To answer these questions, we will have to make a detailed study of the writings of the Chinese intellectuals who have discussed these issues.

In this investigation I have found the extant studies made in the Western world not very satisfactory. These studies were largely based on Western sources, such as church records, missionary reminiscences, and those scholarly works in English that have a bearing on Christianity or Christian work in China.[3] The authors of these studies seldom consulted Chinese sources, especially those written by Chinese intellectuals and Chinese Christians. As a consequence, while we know much of the Western perspective of the Christian story in China, we are still very uninformed about how the Chinese felt. No transnational implantation, be it religious proselytization or otherwise, can succeed if the giver does not take into careful consideration the aspirations of the recipient, and no assessment of this implantation can be accurate if we ignore or remain ignorant of the perceptions and feelings of the recipient.

II

How can we find out the Chinese intellectuals' attitudes toward religion in general and Christianity in particular? With the lack of statistical surveys of the religious affiliation of these intellectuals and no other ready indicators of their religious opinions, the only way to arrive at some kind of approximation of their real position is to read through representative writings of some of the leading figures with the assumption that these intellectual leaders had exercised some sway over their followers. The Chinese intelligentsia has a traditional cohesiveness as a social group and a tendency to rely upon their intellectual leaders for leadership (as the seventy-two disciples always looked to Confucius for enlightenment, many twentieth century Chinese intellectuals also looked to their masters in the university circles of Peking and Shanghai for intellectual guidance).

Accepting the above assumptions, the following is a survey of the attitudes and opinions of eight leading Chinese intellectuals toward religion and/or Christianity: Liang Ch'i-ch'ao (Buddhist), Liang Shu-ming (or, Sou-ming) (Neo-Confucianist), Hu Shih (liberal), Ch'en Tu-hsiu (Marxist), Wu Chih-hui (anarchist), Yu Chia-chu (radical nationalist), Chao Tzu-ch'en (Christian liberal), and Wu Lei-ch'uan (Christian radical). Their selection is based on six criteria. First, they were important intellectual leaders of their day and commanded influence either among Chinese intellectuals as a whole or among their own ideological constituencies. They were chosen here not as authorities on religion, which most of them were not, but as very influential intellectuals of their day. Second, they represent diverse ideological positions, thus reflecting the general reality of the intellectual scene in early twentieth century China. Third, they gave detailed and coherent discussions of religion and Christianity in their writings, and in this way their opinions were more persuasive to their contemporaries than those of others. Fourth, their writings (or speeches) either appeared in their best known works or were delivered on important occasions when large audiences were present or national attention was focused on them. Fifth, in some cases, the reason for the exclusion of certain obvious leaders who also joined the discussion of religion and/or Christianity is that their ideas are already well represented by other intellectual leaders included in this survey.[4] Finally, those Chinese intellectuals who have expressed extensive views on religion and Christianity after the late 1930's are not treated in this survey for the simple reason that their views, as far as this author can ascertain, have not gone beyond either the scope or the depth of the views expressed earlier.[5] Therefore, I believe that the views of the intellectual leaders discussed in this survey cover a time span far beyond their own and may even reach to the present day.

III

Liang Ch'i-ch'ao

Among Chinese intellectuals who were Buddhists one of the
most influential was Liang Ch'i-ch'ao. His ideas on religion had undergone some changes between the late nineteenth
and the early twentieth century. Before 1902, he had promoted, together with his mentor K'ang Yu-wei, Confucianism
as a way to lift China and the East from its precarious
existence vis-a-vis the powerful West. After 1902, he
began to espouse Buddhism. Several articles written
around 1902 and 1903 reveal his thinking on religion and
Christianity.[6]

Liang believed that it was vital for a people or a nation
to possess religious thought or thinking (ssŭ-hsiang).
The benefits of such a possession were many: it could promote national and spiritual cohesiveness; it could bring
out hope in people's lives; it could liberate people from
mundane concerns and make them concentrate on noble endeavors; it could induce moral scruples and discipline;
and, finally, it would generate courage or a daring spirit
in life.[7]

But which religion was best for China? Liang's answer was
Buddhism, for it has these superior features: its faith
is derived from intellectual understanding and not from
blind acceptance; its goal is for universal, not just individual, perfection and salvation; its approach to life
was "into this world" and not other-worldly; its theory of
retribution, or the law of Karma, was a "self-sufficient"
theory in restraining man from evil; its allowance of an
equality between Buddhist disciples and Buddha was superior
to other religions. Lastly, Liang felt that it was a more
responsible religion than Christianity because it emphasized self-effort or self-help rather than external help.[8]
Liang's strong advocacy of Buddhism was largely a result
of his concern with the fate of China. He believed that
only through spiritual regeneration could national survival
and power be achieved.[9]

Liang's views on Christianity and its work in China were
not extensive. Obsessed with the superiority of Buddhism,
his understanding of Christianity was rather negative. In
the late 1890's Liang held the belief that the political
and humanistic achievements of the West had had very little

to do with its faith in Jesus or Christianity.[10] After the turn of the century, however, Liang began to accord much more importance to the Christian faith as a motive force in turning the West into a civilization of wealth and power. But, Liang still did not believe that Christianity could survive long in the West. Witnessing the decline of influence of the Catholic Church in its relations with political authorities and the separation of church and state in the West, Liang concluded that Christianity would continue to decline and, therefore, he questioned the wisdom for some of the Chinese in adopting such a religion.[11]

Even though Liang was not impressed with Christianity as a viable religion, he was very much taken by the achievements of the missionary work in China. Liang had a very meaningful intellectual fellowship with some Christian missionaries, such as Timothy Richard and Gilbert Reid, and accepted many of their ideas on reform and modernization.[12] He also admired and praised the missionary educational work in China.[13]

In Liang's analysis, there were two motives in Western mission work in China: one was to conduct genuine religious proselytization and the other was to use such work to expand Western interests at the expense of Chinese sovereignty. He also divided Chinese converts into two categories: those who were true believers and those who were using missionaries to gain personal benefits. While denouncing the missionaries' infringement of Chinese sovereign rights and those Chinese converts' engagement in personal aggrandizement, Liang, in the spirit of religious freedom, accepted missionary proselytization and the Chinese converts' right to adopt a foreign faith.[14]

Liang's stand on religion and Christianity never wavered after the early 1900's. Even in the heat of the anti-Christian movement of the 1920's, he still claimed that religion was a noble and vital force in any human society.. Instead of attacking Christianity, he called upon those Chinese religious detractors to focus their attack on those Buddhist and Taoist temples or sects that had become entirely superstitious and evil in their operations.[15]

Liang Shu-ming

In general, Neo-Confucianists opposed Christianity in moderate terms and their general argument was that Confucianism

was more suitable for China than any religion, whether
Christianity or Buddhism. This moderate attitude was in
sharp contrast with that of their predecessors in the nineteenth century. Except for Liang Shu-ming, most of the
leaders of Neo-Confucianism, such as Fung Yu-lan and Hsiung
Shih-li, did not engage in polemics over religion.

While Liang Ch'i-ch'ao took religion as a useful force for
personal and national progress, Liang Shu-ming considered
religion as the result of man's inevitable need for relief
from his ultimate anxieties. Liang Shu-ming defined religion by two principles: its essential concern was to comfort and soothe man's ultimate emotional anxieties, and
its foundation was its other-worldliness. The ultimate
human anxieties concern birth, old age, sickness, and
death. He believed that these anxieties could never be
totally alleviated by the progress of science; therefore,
man could only rest his hope on the world beyond. Furthermore, for a religion to survive permanently it not only
had to be able to satisfy man's emotional wants but also
had to agree with man's intellect. To maintain this balance of emotion and intellect was the secret of the permanence of a religion. In his judgment, Buddhism was the
only religion that maintains this balance.[16]

By these standards, Liang found that Confucianism was not
a religion because of its this-worldliness,[17] and that
Christianity would eventually be discarded because of its
supernaturalism, which was against the dictates of intellect
or reason. He predicted that Christian Christology and
soteriology would become bankrupt when human knowledge had
reached maturity through the advancement of epistemology
and metaphysics. Liang cited the emergence of Comte's
Positivism, Haeckel's Monism, and Eucken's Activism as
signs of the ongoing decline of Christianity.[18]

Strangely, though Liang's heart was for the other-worldly
Buddhism, his head was for Confucianism and Western civili-
zation. Liang's dominant concern in the 1920's was to save
China from internal chaos and foreign aggression. Since
Buddhism discouraged man's interest in earthly affairs,
Liang feared its adoption by the Chinese would cause them
to ignore the precarious Chinese situation and thus make
it deteriorate further. Therefore, he recommended to the
Chinese people that they appropriate the positive elements
in Western civilization and restore "true" Confucianism.[19]

In his analysis, Western civilization was characterized by

its emphasis on reason or intellect over the emotions, its
need to conquer nature rather than to harmonize with it,
and its interest in utilitarian pursuits rather than disin-
terested action.[20] Because of these characteristics, the
West had achieved tremendous material progress at the price
of spiritual emptiness. Since China was behind in material
progress but rich in spiritual resources, all those elements in Western civilization that would remedy Chinese
material deficiency should be adopted.[21] On the other
hand, the virtues of Confucianism were that it sought the
realization of Jen, which was the unity of man and Heaven
(t'ien) on this earth rather than in the world beyond; it
practiced the Golden Mean (chung-yung) and not extremism;
and it relied on intuition (chih-chueh) rather than on
speculations. Unfortunately, however, this "true" Confucianism had not been in existence for many years and what
had been practiced was a diluted version of Confucianism.
China should now try to restore this "true" Confucianism.[22]
In the future, because of man's need for the solution of
his ultimate anxieties, all human civilizations would go
in the direction of Indian civilization, which offers the
best spiritual solution.[23]

In the first half of the twentieth century Liang Shu-ming
was teaching in the most important academic centers in
China, such as Peking and Tsing Hua Universities. His
book, Tung-hsi wen-hua chi ch'i che-hsueh (The civilization and philosophies in the East and West) was one of the
best selling books among intellectuals in the twenties (it
went through eight editions in one decade).[24] His pessimism for the eventual decline of Christianity, his espousal
of Confucianism, and his prediction of the ultimate victory
of Buddhism over other religions must have dealt a serious
blow to the Christian effort to propagate their faith among
Chinese intellectuals and students.

Hu Shih

Among the leading Chinese liberals Hu Shih was one of the
very few to formulate and publicize his own "systematic
atheism."

Three months before the May Fourth Movement (1919) Hu Shih
published his article, "Immortality--My Religion," in Hsin
Ch'ing-nien (New youth). He claimed that there were only
two theories of immortality: the immortality of the human
soul as believed by the religious; and the immortality of

man's virtue (te), endeavor (kung) and utterance (yen) as
described in the classical commentary, Tso chuan. Hu refused to accept the first theory for he agreed with Fan
Chen's argument that the human soul cannot have a separate
existence from the body, and when the body dies, the soul
also vanishes. The second theory he accepted only with
reservations, for it contains three defective elements.
First, the high standards expected in this theory will
qualify only a very few superior men and will leave out
the large majority. Second, while it rewards those who
have achieved these standards, it does not punish those
who have failed, and thus it lacks prohibitive power.
Third, it offers no clear definition regarding these standards, so people will find it difficult to follow.[25]

Having attacked these two positions Hu offered his own
theory of "Social Immortality." Advancing from Leibnitz's
rationalism, which supposes that the ultimate constituents
of the universe are monads and they interact according to
the principle of a pre-established harmony, Hu asserted
that all the individual members of a society are mutually
influencing units; therefore their every action has consequences. No matter how trivial a contribution or a sin,
it will set off a continuous causal chain affecting everyone else. Because this chain is an endless one, it is
immortal. Hu explained that the superiority of his theory
over the other two lay in its applicability to all human
beings; in its restrained power because of its emphasis
on causes and effects; and in its comprehensive scope which
included all human acts--large or small, noble or evil.[26]

In 1922 Hu contributed to a Christian journal a short
article entitled, "Christianity and China." In his view,
every religion consists of, mainly, its ethical teachings,
its theological constructions, and its superstitions. In
Christianity, superstitions were the creations of ignorant
people of two thousand years ago, and as such should be
discarded. Its theological constructions are mostly wild
speculations of monks and scholastics in the Middle Ages,
and as such should also be thrown away. The moral teachings
of the social revolutionary and prophet Jesus are still
useful as long as reason has not yet assumed total control
of human behavior. In one stroke, Hu reduces all of Christianity into a religion of moral teachings and strips it
of all its theological and historical ingredients. As a
believer in religious freedom, Hu in this article also
advises his intellectual peers not to engage in blind opposition to Christianity but to try to tolerate and understand

it.[27]

In 1925 Hu discussed the major obstacles to Christian proselytization in China. The first was the new nationalistic
reaction against foreign imperialism in China, as shown in
the Chinese demands for the cancellation of the unequal
treaties. The second obstacle was the rise of rationalism
in China. Hu pointed out that the advent of Western
scientific thought in China had contributed to the revival
of Chinese traditional naturalistic philosophies, such as
Taoism and Neo-Confucianism of the Sung and Ming periods.
The third obstacle was the corruption within the Christian
Church in China. Hu pointed out that many pre-twentieth
century Western missionaries had been men of perseverance
and courage, such as Matteo Ricci and Robert Morrison, and
that they had had to struggle against many odds to spread
their faith. In contrast, the twentieth century missionaries were generally operating under much more favorable
circumstances and received less hostile public reaction.
For those teaching in mission schools, life was particularly easy. Hu believed that all these comforts had
generated corruption. Furthermore, the motives or reasons
for many of the twentieth century missionaries to come to
China were also not all purely religious; some were misfits
in their own countries, so they came to China to make a
living; some were in ill health, so they came to China for
rest and recuperation; some came for sightseeing or for fun;
and some even came for antique collecting. Hu believed
that the standards set up by Western mission boards in
selecting their missionaries were not as rigid as those
used by foreign kerosene or tobacco companies in choosing
their managers in the Chinese interior. Hu's central message in this article was clear: unless Christianity could
find ways to overcome these three obstacles, its future in
China would be doomed.[28]

Wu Chih-hui

While most of the Chinese liberals were critical of religion
in general and Christianity in particular, they did not reject religion entirely. Also, though these liberals were
all supporters of science, they did not consider science as
so omnipotent as to be able to solve all human problems.
But this slightly compromising attitude was not to be found
among anarchists such as Wu Chih-hui, Liu Shih-fu, or Ting
Wen-chiang. To them, religion was simply nonsense, a reflection of man's ignorance.[29]

Among these anarchists and worshippers of science probably
none was more famous or influential in the ordinary intellectual circles than Wu Chih-hui. Wu was a late Ch'ing
chu-jen, a Kuomintang stalwart, an anarchist, and most of
all, a philosophical materialist. His most detailed discussion of religion was made in his article, "The Problem
of Religion," published in 1908. In this article he discussed religion together with morality and socialism.
Arguing in a way similar to the Chinese traditional Con-
fucianists, he claimed that morality (or moral senses) was
an endowment that every living being was born with. Morality, like the physical world, progressed through time in
accordance with the degree of advancement in human knowl-
edge--the deeper the knowledge, the higher the morality.
In other words, morality also follows the law of evolution
and moves on a continuously upward curve. As for religion,
it was developed when human knowledge was shallow and
man's ability to master the world was weak. In such a
stage of human existence, religion fostered superstitions
and turned itself into a relationship between man and
ghosts. Once superstitions and other accompanying evils
emerged, religion became a stupefying force that blunted
man's inherited moral senses (or morality) and suffocated
the human mind. Therefore, religion, contrary to the
common assumption, not only cannot enhance human morality,
it actually retards it. Wu's solution for these unfortunate consequences of religion was simple: the substitution
of socialism (here he meant its anarchical kind) for religion. Wu believed that socialism was the most advanced
philosophy in the twentieth century and its development
closely coincided with the progress of human knowledge.
Socialism was better than religion for human welfare for
numerous reasons. First, since socialism was developed
when human knowledge had gained substantial progress, it
certainly would break down all the superstitions. Second,
it could promote man's morality because it would remove
all the evil practices (the creations of ignorant men and
superstitious religions) that had hindered the natural but
progressive flow of human morality. Therefore, religion
shrank man's morality but socialism would enlarge it. Third,
while religion accepted the status quo in the form of
tolerating differing social classes and worshipped ghosts
and gods, socialism championed human selflessness (or
equality) and universal love for all. In conclusion, Wu
affirmed that socialism was a philosophy that deals with
the reciprocal love between man and man, in contrast with
religion as a creed that controls the relationship between
man and ghosts.[30]

Proceeding from such an anti-religion bias and accepting the
Darwinian law of evolution, Wu naturally believed that
matter, and matter alone, was the ultimate ground of Being.
He explained this in the following way:

> Spirit is but a by-product of the formation of
> matter. With 110 pounds of pure water, 60 pounds
> of colloidal solution, 4 pounds 3 ounces of pro-
> tein, 4 pounds 5 ounces of cellulose, and 12 ounces
> of otein in a suitable combination, the result is
> an 147-pound "I." This formation of matter and
> substance goes under the name of "I," unwittingly
> follows the laws of this material world, . . .[31]

Wu never changed his basic ideas about religion, the world,
and the nature of human existence. In the famous debate
on science and the philosophy of life among many Chinese
intellectuals in 1923, Wu sided with Hu Shih and Ting Wen-
chiang and battled against Chang Chun-mai, Chang Tung-sun,
and Liang Ch'i-ch'ao, who emphasized a "philosophy of life"
(jen-sheng kuan) based on a consideration of ethics, religion, metaphysics, and the social sciences.[32] In a lengthy
essay, "A New Belief and Its Views of Man's Life and the
Universe" Wu attacked his opponents and also religion.
The following is very revealing of his intransigent attitude:

> . . .I actually despise that sort of philosophy
> which yields words and causes one great confusion.
> Such philosophies only succeed in using highly
> intoxicating verbiage to fool and flatter one
> another with magical and transcendental symbols
> and terms--Buddhism, Taoism, Confucianism, Greek
> philosophy, scholasticism, empiricism, rational-
> ism, criticism, or other "isms." All such efforts
> are but attempts to satisfy their original urge
> to find a suitable faith.[33]

Therefore, he advised man to eliminate God and to banish
the soul and spirit.

Whether Wu's ideas are representative of Scientism as he
himself claimed or of a teleological naturalism, is beyond
the scope of this discussion. The crucial importance of
his ideas was the devastating effect on religion or on
religious propagation. The harm was done; and probably
very few souls hesitating before the door of religion in
the 1920's and 1930's were not affected.

Ch'en Tu-hsiu

Among the Marxist opponents of religion none offered more extensive discussions than that of Ch'en Tu-hsiu. Though Ch'en was a firm believer in science, his attitude toward Christianity was rather ambivalent. He was against the establishment of Confucianism as a state religion and he generally considered religion a result of ignorance.[35] But, as far as his attitude toward the person of Jesus was concerned, he strangely turned into his supporter. The following is a detailing of the progression of his thinking on Jesus and Christianity.

In 1917 in a reply to a reader of his New Youth he said:

> The value of a religion should be judged as to the extent of its contribution to the welfare of the society. If we have to have a religion for our society, though I am not a Christian, from my conscience I dare say that to practice Christianity is far more useful than to practice Confucianism, for the former can contribute far more greatly to our social welfare. This is a true fact and I hope those stubborn traditionalists will not be alarmed by my words.[36]

In 1919 Ch'en was moved by the recent Korean independence movement and especially by the fact that many of its participants were Korean Christians. In his commentary on this movement he declared that from now on he dare not despise Christianity any more, though he lamented the passivity of the Chinese Christians toward larger political issues.[37]

While the above were his random commentaries, his most detailed discussion of Christianity was his article, "Christianity and The Chinese," published in 1920. Ch'en first pointed out that Christianity was a religion of love and had been one of the major sources of European civilization. Then he analyzed the causes for the Chinese rejection of such a religion of love. Contrary to other standard denunciations, such as the haughtiness of the missionaries and their reliance on treaty protection, he attributed Christian failure in China largely to the mistakes made by the Chinese people. These mistakes were: the existence of the "rice" Christians; Chinese cultural chauvinism; Chinese contempt for Jesus's early disciples for their lowly social status; disturbances developing because the Chinese were

hateful of the cowardly behavior of their officials in dealing with the foreigners and because Christian converts were
offended by the rigid cultural orthodoxy of the same officials; Chinese anger over the missionary intervention in
civil disputes, whether the missionary was protecting the
legitimate rights of his innocent converts or was covering
up for those misbehaving ones; the conflict between Christian doctrines and the Chinese worship of ancestors and
idols; the poor literary quality of the Chinese translation
of the Bible in comparison with the elegant Chinese classics;
and lastly, the Chinese fabrication of wild rumors regarding certain church practices due to their own ignorance.
As for the faults of the missionary, Ch'en blamed them only
for their meddling in Chinese civil disputes. Of course,
Ch'en also denounced the foreign governments for their use
of the missions as a means of aggression.[38]

Next, Ch'en discussed the personality of Jesus. He praised
Jesus for his substitutionary death; for his generosity in
forgiving almost all kinds of trespassers; and for his love
of all humanity. Jesus was the personification of all the
above virtues and these virtues were the essence of Christianity. Such a Christianity, Ch'en asserted, could never
be destroyed no matter how advanced science would become.[39]

Ch'en then criticized those Christians that had not yet
lived up to the requirements of Christianity. He blamed
Western Christians for their acceptance, and even support,
of their militarists and capitalists. Ch'en denounced
these Christians as the true corrupters of Christianity
and said that they might further destroy it completely.
Ch'en also criticized the Chinese Christians. He called
most of them "rice Christians" and scolded those who had
opposed Communism. To him, Christianity was the gospel of
the poor and Jesus was their friend.[40]

When the anti-Christian movement got under way in early
1922, the Anti-Christian Student Alliance published an
article by Ch'en. By this time Ch'en's attitude toward
Christianity had become more hostile. He now criticized
the contradiction between the concept of the omnipotence
of God and the reality of evil. Who had created this sinful world? If God was all good and omnipotent how could
he create such a world? Ch'en also doubted Jesus's virgin
birth, his miracles, and his resurrection, and believed
that no historical accounts and scientific proofs could
establish the validity of these alleged divine events.

But in this article Ch'en did not lose all of his earlier
enthusiasm for Christianity. He divided Christianity into
theology and its institutions; while he strongly objected
to the latter, his criticism of the former was not intense.
He still held that universal love and self-sacrifice were
the precious components of Christianity.[41]

Like most of the Chinese intellectuals, Ch'en was deeply
concerned with the question of how to find ways to save
China. Like Liang Ch'i-ch'ao and Sun Yat-sen,[42] he found
the Chinese, as a people, a loose or unorganized grouping;
therefore, a dynamic spiritual force had to be found to
unify them for national salvation. For this reason, Ch'en
looked at Christianity with favor for a while, but later
gave it up for Communism.

Yu Chia-chu

In addition to the anarchists and the Marxists, the other
group of Chinese intellectuals that was extremely anti-
religion and anti-Christian was the Young China Society
(Shao-nien Chung-kuo hsueh-hui). The Young China Society
was founded in July 1919, and its membership in the early
years included such noted personalities as Li Ta-chao,
Tseng Ch'i, Li Huang, and Mao Tse-tung. The avowed purpose of the Society was stated in the following way: "Our
association dedicates itself to social service under the
guidance of the scientific spirit in order to realize our
ideal of creating a Young China." Within a few years of
its founding a split developed among its members; some
left to found the Chinese Communist Party and some joined
the Kuomintang.[43] Since the Society was emulating the
Young Italy and the Young Turkey movements in Europe, radical nationalism became its political ideology. Moreover,
the radical aspect of its ideology could be seen from its
position on religion. Though not its foremost leader, Yu
Chia-chu was the only one in the Young China Society to
offer a systematic criticism of religion and Christianity.
He, therefore, deserves our examination.

Yu's ideas about religion and Christianity were expressed
in a lengthy article entitled "Christianity and Emotional
Life," published in the midst of the anti-religious movement of 1922. This article discussed three major questions: first, why should Christianity be the chief target
of the religious movement; second, the nature of religious
faith and the content and effects of religious emotions;

and third, how to build up a fulfilling life.

On the first question, Yu's main reason was that all of the other Chinese native religions either were not real religions or had become bankrupt. In this way, Christianity was the only viable religion left for attack. In his view, Confucianism was not a religion, for Confucius had never been enshrined as a deity and his teachings dealt mainly with earthly affairs and shied away from religious speculation. Buddhism emphasized the presence of the nature of Buddha in every living being and accepted the possibility that everyone could attain Buddhahood. Therefore, Buddhism was really not a religion (for it closed the gap between what was divine and what was secular) and was more or less a philosophy of self-cultivation. In addition to Confucianism and Buddhism, Yu also excluded other Chinese folk religions, such as the Eight Diagrams and the White Lotus, as being purely superstitious in nature. Because of this rejection of all of the Chinese native religions as religions, Yu came to the conclusion that only Christianity remained as a religion in China and should thus become the chief target in the anti-religious movement.

In his discussion of the nature of religious faith, Yu first challenged the existence of a divine Being or God. To him, the concept of God was simply the objectification or projection of the human mind. Quoting from Chang Pin-lin, a noted classical scholar and revolutionary, Yu asked whether there was a purpose in God's creation of man. If there was, man became a tool of God; if not, then creation was simply an act of God's mischief. Yu further asked whether God was all good and all powerful. If so, why is there so much evil in this world? If not, then God did not deserve to be taken as the supreme master of the world. Yu also found religious doctrines, such as retributive judgment and immortality, simply false promises to compensate for the injustice and ephemeral nature of human existence.

Yu then discussed the content and the effects of religious emotions or sentiments. Religious emotions consist of three elements: that of reverence, fear, and devotion. The emotion of reverence is a result of man's sense of his own inferiority and helplessness, and made man more willing to accept all of the seemingly inexplicable phenomena of the natural world as the working of God's hands. Thus man became less energetic in the exercise of his intelligence to understand these phenomena. The emotion of reverence

also tended to cause man to rely more on God than on himself
and made him become more fatalistic or deterministic in his
life outlook. The emotion of fear, as shown in the theories of heaven and hell and of the last judgment, was
really not a worthy emotion since it would only make people
unhappy and worried before they ever enjoy the fruits of
faith. Lastly, the emotion of devotion, as demonstrated
in prayers, was a ridiculous human feeling. In offering
prayers to God, who was a human creation, man was only
speaking to himself. In all of these disparaging words,
Yu ridiculed religious emotions as unprofitable and illog-
ical for man.

If religion was man's false imagination and religious emotions were self-delusions, then how was man going to
achieve a fulfilling life? The answer was to let reason
control man's emotions and to substitute self-cultivation
for religious help. Yu believed that only science
furthered rationality and man could gain emotional control
by having a deeper understanding of the operations of human
psychology. To develop a balanced frame of mind, Yu
advised that man should resort to Chinese traditional
practices, such as ts'un-yang (self-cultivation) and
sheng-ch'a (self-examination) on a daily basis. Through
constant training of one's mind and character, man could
live without the crutch of religion.

Throughout his article, Yu included Christianity in his
general criticism of religion, but in the end of his
article he singled out Christianity for special castiga-
tion, especially with regard to its theology and its
organized church activities. In contrast to religious
emotions, which were usually expressed in a spontaneous
way, Christian theology was a carefully constructed and
willfully preserved body of fallacy, which was nothing but
a crime against scientific truth. But worst of all were
the activities conducted by the organized Christian church.
Its priests openly and daily went out to seek followers
through propaganda and baptism. Because of their active
proselytization, they were worse than Chinese Buddhist
monks and Taoist priests who normally confined themselves
inside of their temples and would, at most, propagate
their faith through the writing of religious tracts. Therefore, at the end of his article, Yu called out that religious proselytization should be opposed and religions
totally destroyed.[44]

Yu's anti-religion propaganda did not cease with the

publication of this article; he was also one of the most
active campaigners for the so-called "restoration of the
right of education" movement in the mid-and-late 1920's
which aimed at the closing down of all mission schools
throughout China.[45]

Chao Tzu-ch'en

By the late 1930's the Chinese Christian community had grown
at least to a membership of about three to four million.[46]
From this large body many renowned Christian leaders
emerged. Among them, Wang Ming-tao, Chao Tzu-ch'en, Wu
Lei-ch'uan, Liu Ting-fang, Hsu Pao-ch'ien, and Wu Yao-tsung
were undoubtedly most influential. We will choose Chao
Tzu-ch'en and Wu Lei-ch'uan for the following discussion
because of the significance of their views and their influence among the Chinese Christian intellectuals.[47]

The Christian leaders or thinkers in the 1920's and 1930's
were faced with two major questions from their non-Christian
peers. From those who still cared to investigate Christianity but who were intellectually influenced by the contemporary emphases on science and reason, the basic issue
was how Christianity transcends superstition and corres-
ponds to the law of science and human reason. From those
who were most concerned with the problem of national salvation, the question was whether Christianity could meet
the political and social needs of China.

Chao Tzu-ch'en, who had received a B.A. from Soochow
University and an M.A. and B.D. from Vanderbilt University,
was Dean of the College of Arts and Sciences at Soochow
University from 1917 to 1925, and Dean of the School of
Religion at Yenching University from 1925 to the 1950's.
Because of his academic connections, he was "for almost
three decades a leading proponent of Christianity on
college campuses" and "one of the leading Christian intellectuals that China has had," and in 1948 was elected as
one of the six presidents of the World Council of Churches,
the highest religious post that had ever been held by a
Chinese Protestant leader.[48]

Before we introduce his replies to those questions posed by
his peers, we should first explain briefly his theological
thinking which was the foundation for his views on secular
issues.

Chao's theology in the 1920's and 1930's could be roughly termed as Modernism.[49] To Chao, Christianity was "a type of consciousness, a definite personal-social experience, and a new life that has its origin and realization in the person of Jesus Christ."[50] Jesus was only a man, though a perfect man who had a "profound awareness of God."[51] God revealed himself through Jesus but also through other sages, such as Confucius, Mo-tzu, Socrates, and Plato; therefore, Jesus was only one of many saviors.[52] Furthermore, since Jesus was only a man, Chao could not believe in such things as the virgin birth, miracles, the resurrection of Christ, and heaven and hell.[53] Furthermore, what was God? God was love: "God sent the savior (Jesus) into the world, to accomplish the great task of salvation through love and personality."[54]

Based on these liberal or modernistic theological views, Chao's answer to the first question--the relationship between Christianity and science or reason--was naturally an affirmation of the basic agreement of the two, for he said, "What is true in the realm of science cannot become falsehood in the realm of religion."[55] By claiming that Jesus was only a man and that those supernatural events recorded in the Bible were not to be believed, Chao really left very little ground in his theology for his anti-religious peers to attack him.

On the second question concerning Christianity's suitability in meeting China's political and social needs, Chao answered in the 1920's that Christianity could induce a spiritual regeneration and this regeneration was a prerequisite for the success of larger social and political changes, such as the betterment of people's lives, domestic political unity, and the expulsion of foreign imperialists from China.[56] In this respect, Chao's diagnosis of China's problems was basically the same as that of Hu Shih. In other words, foreign imperialism and the evil of capitalism were not as crucial as China's own spiritual and physical deficiencies.[57] Chao would have also agreed with Sun Yat-sen's analysis that China's weakness was largely a result of the corrupt personality of the Chinese and that only when this personality changed could China be saved.[58]

In the decade of the 1930's China's fate was even more precarious than before. Besides being burdened with her age-long problems of disorder, poverty, and corruption, the very survival of China was at stake because of the Japanese aggression since 1931. Under these conditions, the public outcry was for radical change in all areas.

Concerning this demand for radical political change, Chao's response was negative. He said in 1932 that:

> In these past thirty years, the people were first disappointed by the Constitutional Movement. Then they placed their hope in the revolution, and the revolution succeeded. But again they were disappointed by the attempt to return China to a monarchy. In the ensuing struggle, one faction triumphed one day, and the other factions claimed victory on other days. But it was the people's blood that was shed. After the Northern Expedition, it seemed as though the country was finally united, but the hope of the people was again crushed under the corrupt government.[59]

In 1935 Chao further declared that "I have decided to be revolutionary in spirit, and follow the course of gradual change in action."[60] Because of this negative attitude toward radical change, Chao in the 1920's and 1930's generally supported the existing Kuomintang government and refused to accept Communism, which he considered only as a "destructive force."[61]

If radical political change was not good for China, what should the Chinese Christians do to help China survive her national crisis? In 1932 Chao offered several kinds of work for them to do. First, they should try to bring Christianity into people's homes in order to raise a new generation of useful citizens for China. Second, they should carry out religious instruction among the masses so as to mould them into righteous and patriotic citizens. Third, they should inspire Chinese youth to engage in active social services and nation-building, such as the development of China's frontier regions, launching rural reconstruction projects, and making educational reforms.[62]

Chao's message with regard to social change and meeting the national crisis was certainly a logical development out of his Christian liberalism. While it might have been sound theology or useful advice, it was very doubtful that those non-Christian Chinese intellectuals in the 1930's were very impressed. Chao's methods were too gradual and most Chinese intellectuals were trying to find some more direct or even instant solution to the problems and dangers that China was confronted with at the time.

Wu Lei-ch'uan

If Chao's version of the Christian gospel sounded no clarion
call to the revolutionary youth and other concerned intellectuals, another Christian thinker, Wu Lei-ch'uan, had
formulated more convincing arguments. Wu Lei-ch'uan was
probably the most eclectic thinker among Chinese Christian
leaders. Before his conversion in 1915 he had been a Con-
fucianist carrying a <u>chin-shih</u> degree. A decade later, he
became the vice-president of Yenching University and was
promoted to the position of Chancellor in 1928. With no
knowledge of English, he could only study Christian theology
through reading the Bible and other Western works in translation. In the 1930's he made another surprising turn: he
adopted a radical and materialistic interpretation of history, religion, and revolution. Therefore, by the late
1930's, his brand of Christianity was a curious mixture of
Confucianism, Christianity and materialism. His intellectual favorites in the 1920's and 1930's were also a strange
amalgamation of personalities with differing ideological
positions: some Chinese neo-traditionalists, such as Wang
Hsin-ming and Ho Ping-sung; some Marxists, such as Ch'en
Tu-hsiu and Yeh Ch'ing; and some liberals, such as John
Dewey and Julius F. Hecker.[63]

To Wu, Jesus was not only a spiritual savior, a political
revolutionary, the greatest Jewish patriot, but also a
crusader against private property and the family system.
Therefore, since China was in need of spiritual, social,
and political changes, Jesus was just the right kind of
revolutionary leader for China to follow.[64] Like Christian
liberals in the West, Wu favored the establishment of the
Kingdom of God on this earth; and the way to establish it
was through revolution, for the gospel of Christianity was
a gospel of revolution.[65] Furthermore, he accepted the
materialistic interpretation of history, and declared that
man's misery was basically caused by an unhealthy and poor
material environment, and when this environment improved,
man's mind and behavior would also change for the better.[66]

Operating with these radical and materialistic notions,
Wu's suggested programs for China's salvation was naturally
one of radical change through revolution. In his most well-
known work--<u>Christianity and Chinese Culture</u> (Chi-tu chiao
<u>yu Chung-kuo wen-hua</u>)--published in 1936, he stated:

> The only aim of Christianity is to reconstruct
> society and to reconstruct society is what we

have normally called revolution . . . if we want
to reconstruct society we will have to seek political power, and to seek such a power we will have
to rely upon force. If we insist on avoiding the
tragedy of a revolutionary bloodbath, aren't we
going to turn our goal of societal reconstruction
into an empty dream?[67]

In order to carry out this social reconstruction Wu suggested China adopt collectivism and dictatorship.[68] He
eagerly called upon all Chinese Christians to dedicate
themselves to this task even at the cost of going through
a revolutionary bloodbath.[69] Wu's thought by the mid-
1930's had become more or less Marxist-oriented. As Chao
Tzu-ch'en correctly pointed out, Wu's thought consisted
of these elements: materialism, revolutionary change by
force, political dictatorship that fulfills modern needs,
religious sentimentality similar to that which existed
among the Soviet youth, and egalitarian socialism. He
added that Wu's thought was "close to Communism."[70]

Wu's concern in the 1930's was not only for the salvation
of China as a nation, but also for the revival of the Chinese people as a great race. For both tasks, Wu believed
that the Chinese Christian Church could make unique contributions. First, it could supply dynamic leaders.
Christians were followers of Jesus and since Jesus was such
a great man of personal sacrifice and of noble ideals, Chinese Christians could also become dynamic leaders. Second,
while national salvation was more or less a task directed
by the central political authority, as shown in the Chinese
government's resistance of Japanese aggression in the
1930's, the racial rejuvenation had to begin with the
transformation of Chinese society. In this latter task,
Chinese Christians, because of their Christian character
and dedication, could serve as yeast to leaven the whole
society and transform it into a society of great vitality.
Wu further affirmed that, in this task, Confucian teachings
would not do because of their elitist approach and feudal-
istic orientation.[71]

IV

A recent discussion of the Chinese anti-religious movement
of the 1920's concludes that, "By about 1927 the question
/of Christianity/ could be regarded as settled among most
Chinese intellectuals."[72] In light of our findings in the

above study, we can even say that as far as most of the
Chinese intellectuals were concerned, the general significance of religion was also a settled question.

From historical records we know the sequence of the demise
of a concern for religion in China: that K'ang Yu-wei
started to promote Confucianism as a state religion in the
1890's and failed;[73] that Ch'en Huang-chang tried to do
the same in the second decade of this century and met with
no success;[74] that the anti-religious and anti-Christian
movement of 1922 and the powerful anti-imperialist movement of 1925 both dealt a devastating blow to the Christian
movement;[75] and finally, that by the time the Northern
Expedition of the Kuomintang drew to a close in 1928,
religion and Christianity had simply become passé under
the tide of Chinese nationalism. Even to this day, the
majority of Chinese intellectuals still find religion in
general, and Christianity in particular, repulsive. There
is no doubt that the anti-religious legacy of the 1920's
still has its lingering effects on them.

There are many reasons for the failure of religion and
Christianity to capture the mind of Chinese intellectuals
in the early part of the twentieth century. One reason
is that the rise of scientism and the intrusion of Western
anti-religious currents into China after World War I had
emasculated any chance for religion. In the case of
Christianity, its seeming association with the hated
Western imperialism and its "strange" or "unscientific"
theology all made it unpalatable for patriotic and sensitive Chinese intellectuals. The anti-religious and anti-
Christian statements included in the present study all
attest to these facts.

But are there any other explanations or perspectives that
can be gleaned from the present study?

In our survey of the attitudes and opinions of Chinese intellectual leaders, their central concern was to save China
as a nation and race. Religion was almost always judged
on the chopping block of Nationalism. Thus, if it met
China's immediate needs, it would be retained; otherwise,
it was to be thrown away. Religion was not considered as
something that gives ultimate meaning to human existence
nor as providing spiritual food for daily sustenance.
When religion was valued only for its immediate utility in
secular pursuits, be it national salvation or the enshrine-
ment of science, it was profoundly misunderstood and

prematurely cast aside.

Under the pressure of the time, the Christian defenders, such as Chao Tzu-ch'en and Wu Lei-ch'uan, could not reverse this anti-religious and anti-Christian trend. Chao's argument for a peaceful reform through spiritual regeneration was simply too conservative in face of the national mood for radical change. But how about the more revolutionary or more "relevant" message that Wu Lei-ch'uan offered in the 1930's? Did it prick the ears of Chinese intellectuals at the time? As far as we know the intellectual history of the 1930's, the chief issue debated among Chinese intellectuals concerned the most effective means of repelling the Japanese and regenerating China, and their focus was on the choice between the Kuomintang type of authoritarianism, European fascism, and Communism.[76] Under the circumstances, religion and Christianity, together with liberalism and Neo-Confucianism, were all cast aside as either irrelevant or ineffectual.

In conclusion, religion was a dead issue in the minds of most of the Chinese intellectuals in the early decades of this century, and perhaps even until the present. Religion, especially Christianity, suffered that inevitable fate both because of the effective work of its detractors and because of the larger historical forces that were at work in China at the time.

NOTES

1. See Paul A. Cohen's <u>China and Christianity: The Missionary Movement and the Growth of Chinese Antiforeign-ism, 1860-1870</u> (Cambridge: Harvard University Press, 1963) and Lu Shih-ch'iang, <u>Chung-kuo kuan-shen fan-chiao chi yuan-yin</u> (The reasons for the Chinese officials and gentry to oppose Christianity) (Taipei, 1966).

2. John K. Fairbank et al., <u>East Asia: The Modern Transformation</u> (Boston: Houghton Mifflin Co., 1965), p. 334.

3. The most recent example of these studies is, John K. Fairbank, ed., <u>The Missionary Enterprise in China and America</u> (Cambridge: Harvard University Press, 1974).

4. These excluded leaders were, for example, Li Huang, Li Shih-tseng, Hsu Pao-ch'ien, and many others.

5. This is a general impression derived from some sampling of the publications issued after the 1930's.

6. Hao Chang, <u>Liang Ch'i-ch'ao and Intellectual Transition in China, 1890-1907</u> (Cambridge: Harvard University Press, 1971), Ch. 4 and 7.

7. Liang Ch'i-ch'ao, "Lun tsung-chiao-chia yu che-hsueh-chia chih ch'ang-tuan te-shih" (A comparison between the religionists and the philosophers) in <u>Yin-pin-shih ho-chi, wen-chi</u> (Collected works and essays from the Ice-drinker's Studio, collected essays) (Taipei, reprint, n.d.), ts'e 4, 9:44-50.

8. Liang Ch'i-ch'ao, "Lun Fo-chiao yu ch'un-chih chih kuan-hsi" (On the relationship between Buddhism and public uplifting), <u>Ibid.</u>, 10:45-52.

9. Hao Chang, <u>Liang Ch'i-ch'ao</u>.

10. Liang Ch'i-ch'ao, <u>Tu hsi-hsueh-shu fa</u> (Approaches to studying Western learning), in <u>Chih-hsueh ts'ung-shu ch'u-chi</u> (The first collection of the Chih-hsueh series) (Chih-hsueh Hui, 1896), p. 11a.

11. Liang Ch'i-ch'ao, "<u>Pao-chiao</u> fei so-i tsun K'ung lun" (To preserve a /narrow/ Confucianism is not the way

to exalt Confucius) in Yin-pin-shih ho-chi, wen-chi, t'se 4, 9:50-59.

12. Hao Chang, Liang Ch'i-ch'ao, pp. 70-72.

13. Liang Ch'i-ch'ao, Liang-jen-kung shu-tu (The correspondences of Liang Ch'i-ch'ao) (Shanghai, 1971), pp. 17-18.

14. Liang Ch'i-ch'ao, "Pao-chiao fei so-i tsun K'ung lun," p. 53.

15. Liang Ch'i-ch'ao, "P'ing fei tsung-chiao t'ung-meng" (Comment on the Anti-Religious Alliance), in Chang Ch'in-shih, ed., Kuo-nei chin shih-nien lai chih tsung-chiao ssu-ch'ao (The religious trend of the last ten years in China) (Peiping, 1927), pp. 270-71.

16. Liang Shu-ming, Tung-hsi wen-hua chi ch'i che-hsueh (The civilization and philosophies in the East and West) (Shanghai, 1934), pp. 90-112.

17. Ibid., pp. 121-22; 142-43; 210.

18. Ibid., pp. 79; 108-09.

19. Ibid., pp. 208-09.

20. Ibid., pp. 155; 199-205.

21. Ibid., pp. 202-14.

22. Ibid., pp. 125-45; 202.

23. Ibid., pp. 112-13.

24. Ibid., "Preface for the Eighth Edition," pp. 1-4.

25. Hu Shih, "Pu-hsiu--wo ti tsung-chiao," in Chang Chin-shih, Kuo-nei chin shih-nien lai chih tsung-chiao ssu-ch'ao, pp. 9-14.

26. Hu Shih, Ibid., pp. 15-22.

27. Hu Shih, "Chi-tu-chiao yu Chung-kuo," Sheng-ming (Life), 2,7 (March, 1922):3-4.

28. Hu Shih, "Chin-jih chiao-hui chiao-yu ti nan-kuan" (The difficulties in today's church education), Chung-hua Chi-tu-chiao chiao-yu chi-k'an (The educational quarterly of the Chinese Christian Church), I, 1 (March, 1925):7-13.

29. On Liu Shih-fu, see Yip, Ka-che, "The Anti-Christian Movement in China, 1922-1927, with Special Reference to the Experience of Protestant Missions," (Ph.D. dissertation, Columbia University, 1971), pp. 59-61. On Ting Wen-chiang, see Charlotte Furth, Ting Wen-chiang: Science and China's New Culture (Cambridge: Harvard University Press, 1970), Ch. 5.

30. Wu Chih-hui, "Tsung-chiao wen ti," in Wu Chih-hui hsueh-shu lun-chu (The scholarly writings of Wu Chih-hui) (Shanghai, 1926, 3rd edition), pp. 203-18.

31. Citation quoted from D. W. Y. Kwok, Scientism in Chinese Thought, 1900-1950 (New Haven: Yale University Press, 1965), pp. 41-42.

32. See Charlotte Furth, Ting Wen-chiang, Ch. 5.

33. D. W. Y. Kwok, Scientism, p. 52.

34. Charlotte Furth, op. cit., pp. 121-22.

35. Chow Tse-tsung, The May Fourth Movement: Intellectual Revolution in Modern China (Cambridge: Harvard University Press, 1964), pp. 320-21.

36. Hsin Ch'ing-nien, 3, 3 (1917): 284.

37. Ch'en Tu-hsiu, Tu-hsiu wen-ts'un (The collected essays of Ch'en Tu-hsiu) (Hong Kong, 1965), 2:608.

38. Ch'en Tu-hsiu, "Chi-tu-chiao yu Chung-kuo jen," Hsin Ch'ing-nien, 7, 3 (February, 1920):18.

39. Ibid., pp. 18-21.

40. Ibid., pp. 21-22.

41. Ch'en Tu-hsiu, "Chi-tu-chiao yu Chi-tu chiao-hui" (Christianity and the Christian Church), in Chang Chin-shih, Kuo-nei chin shih-nien lai, pp. 190-93.

42. There is an excellent analysis of Sun Yat-sen and his Christian modernism in Donald W. Treadgold, The West in Russia and China: Religious and Secular Thought in Modern Times (Cambridge University Press, 1973), 2:70-98.

43. Liu-hsia, ed., Shih-pa nien lai chih Chung-kuo Ch'ing-nien-tang (The eighteen years of the China Youth Party) (Chengtu, 1941), pp. 9-10.

44. Yu Chia-chu, "Chi-tu-chiao yu k'an-ch'ing sheng-huo," in Chang Chin-shih, Kuo-nei chin shih-nien lai, pp. 273-304.

45. See Jessie Lutz, China and the Christian Colleges, 1850-1950 (Ithaca, N. Y.: Cornell University Press, 1971), pp. 224, 227, 236-37, 241.

46. Prof. Kenneth S. Latourette estimated that by the end of the 1920's the Chinese Christian community numbered probably "between two and a half and three million baptized persons." (See his A History of Christian Missions in China /Reprint; New York: Russell and Russell, 1967/, p. 831.) Columbia Cary-Elwes, O.S.B. estimated in his China and the Cross (New York: P. J. Kennedy & Sons, 1956) that the number of Chinese Catholics alone was a little over three million in 1939 (p. 292). Therefore, including the Protestant population, China by the late 1930's must have had a Christian population numbering somewhere between three and four million, or even more.

47. Wang Ming-tao was not well-known in the intellectual circles, so he does not fall into the scope of this study; Liu Ting-fang and Hsu Pao-ch'ien were on the faculty of Yenching University and their views were not essentially different from that of Chao Tzu-ch'en's. Wu Yao-tsung's ideas were basically an extension of that of Wu Lei-ch'uan, and he did not become a religious leader until in the late 1940's and 1950's, a period not emphasized in the present study.

48. L. M. Ng, "Christianity and Social Change: The Case in China, 1920-1950" (Ph.D. dissertation, Princeton Theological Seminary, 1971), pp. 96-97.

49. On Modernism, the most recent scholarship is one by Prof. William R. Hutchison, The Modernist Impulse in American Protestantism (Cambridge: Harvard University Press, 1976).

50. Quoted in L. M. Ng, op. cit., p. 180.

51. Ibid., p. 106.

52. Ibid., pp. 106-07.

53. Ihid., p. 125.

54. Ibid., p. 107.

55. Ibid., p. 125.

56. Ibid., pp. 112-13.

57. On Hu Shih's ideas in this regard, see Jerome B. Grieder, Hu Shih and the Chinese Renaissance: Liberalism in the Chinese Revolution, 1917-1937 (Cambridge: Harvard University Press, 1970).

58. For Sun Yat-sen's ideas, see his "Kuo-min yao-i jen-ko chiu-kuo" (Citizens should save the nation by having a /sound/ character), in Tsung-li ch'uan-chi (The collected works of Tsung-li), Hu-Han-min, ed. (Shanghai, 1923), 2:289-302.

59. Quoted in L. M. Ng, op., cit., pp. 145-46.

60. Ibid., p. 147.

61. Ibid., pp. 143-44.

62. Chao Tzu-ch'en, "Tsung-chiao chiao-yu che ying ju-ho ying-fu kuo nan" (What should the religious educators do to meet the national crisis), Cheng-li yu sheng-ming (Truth and life), 6, 6 (1 April, 1932):1-8.

63. Wu Lei-ch'uan, Chi-tu-chiao yu Chung-kuo wen-hua, 3rd edition (Shanghai, 1948), pp. 15-8, 142-44, 249, 282-87, 275-82.

64. Wu Lei-ch'uan, "Lun Chung-kuo Chi-tu-t'u tui-yu kuo-chia ying-fu ti tse-jen" (On the responsibilities of the Chinese Christians toward their nation," Sheng-ming (Life), 5, 5 (February, 1925):5-7; also "Chi-tu-chiao ti hsin-li chien-she" (On the psychological reconstruction of the Christian Church), Chen-li yu sheng-ming, 8, 1 (15 March, 1934):6-9.

65. Wu Lei-ch'uan, "Chi-tu-chiao yu ko-ming" (Chris-

tianity and revolution), Chen-li yu sheng-ming, 5, 4 (January, 1931): 1-5.

66. Ibid., pp. 4-5.

67. Wu Lei-ch'uan, Chi-tu-chiao yu Chung-kuo wen-hua, p. 291.

68. Ibid., pp. 290-93.

69. Ibid.

70. Chao Tzu-ch'en, "'Yeh-su wei Chi-tu': P'ing Wu Lei-ch'uan hsien-sheng chi Chi-tu-chiao yu Chung-kuo wen-hua" ('Jesus as Christ': On Mr. Wu Lei-ch'uan's Christianity and Chinese Culture), Chen-li yu sheng-ming, 10, 7 (December 15, 1936), p. 426. A more complete and very penetrating analysis of Wu's transformation from a social reformer to a Marxist revolutionary thinker is made by Philip West in "Christianity and Nationalism: The Career of Wu Lei-ch'uan at Yenching University," in The Missionary Enterprise in China and America, ed., John K. Fairbank (Cambridge: Harvard University Press, 1974), pp. 240-46.

71. Wu Lei-ch'uan, op. cit., p. 297.

72. Donald W. Treadgold, The West in Russia and China, 2: 147.

73. Hao Chang, Liang Ch'i-ch'ao, Ch. 4.

74. Chow Tse-tsung, The May Fourth Movement, pp. 291-92.

75. Ka-che Yip, "The Anti-Christian Movement."

76. Lloyd E. Eastman, The Abortive Revolution: China under Nationalist Rule, 1927-1937 (Cambridge: Harvard University Press, 1974), pp. Ch. 4.

IV – THE PROBLEM OF CHRISTIANITY IN NON-WESTERN CULTURES: THE CASE OF CHINA

Donald W. Treadgold

A Soviet colleague recently told an American, "All of your scholars who study the USSR hate the Soviet Union. All of your scholars who study China love China." Despite the fact that the statement is too sweeping, there is some basis for the assertion, though it might be more accurate to say that U.S. Soviet specialists seem more inclined to distinguish between the Russians, Ukrainians, and other peoples of the Soviet Union on the one hand and the Soviet government on the other, than do many U.S. China specialists between the people and the government they study. Here is not the place to explain the difference and how it came about. One may argue that scholars ought to approach the people they study with sympathy--or love, if you like. But their professional obligation is to conduct their studies as objectively and dispassionately as possible; misplaced passion may lead to distortion.

* * *

"Jesus was born in the reign of Han Ai-ti . . . he was killed on a cross for man's sins. . . ." So wrote the K'ang-hsi emperor, reporting not his own beliefs but those of a Chinese Christian. The emperor added that "/the Christians/ had meetings in which slaves and masters, men

and women, mixed together and drank some holy substance."
Most impressive is the fact that the emperor draws up a
statement regarding the three crucial issues of the Rites
Controversy and in his own words confirms the Peking
Fathers' position in every detail as being based on the
facts of contemporary Chinese culture. After Rome's envoy
Maigrot exposed his defective knowledge--better to say,
ignorance--of things Chinese in a famous interview with
the same emperor in 1705, the ruler writes that Maigrot
"fled the country when he could not get his way, a sinner
against the Catholic teaching and a rebel to China" (my
italics).[1] Obviously 250 years ago Christianity was, in
China, and to the emperor himself, a respectable belief,
one worthy of serious consideration. The Jesuits who
followed the teachings of Matteo Ricci were welcome; their
opponents were not, and were in fact expelled from China;
the Peking Fathers were specifically permitted to remain
if they would reaffirm the Ricci position. Ultimately
they could not do so, because their vow of obedience to
the papacy prevented them, not because the Chinese were
indifferent or hostile.

Christian and non-Christian scholars and non-scholars need
to reevaluate and reconsider the whole story of Christianity in China. Those who counsel the Church now to take
some action in regard to China based only on the circumstances of this moment, imperfectly understood at that,
risk making themselves ridiculous in a few more decades,
years, or even months.

A full understanding of this story can be based only on
comparative studies. The way China has responded to Christianity needs to be examined in connection with responses
to Buddhism, Islam, and to a lesser extent Judaism, which
also came to China as foreign faiths. In addition, it
needs study in comparison with the reception of the post-
Christian secular ideologies of the West, including liberalism, non-Communist socialism, and the Communism under which
China lives today. Other non-Western areas can be fruit-
fully studied with respect to the similarities and differences in the manner they received foreign religions,
including secular faiths. All of these problems require
formidable linguistic equipment, profoundly diverse kinds
of knowledge of differing cultures and religions, and hard
work. Having examined the papers of the Bastad and Louvain
conferences on the subject of "Christianity and the New
China," I regret to report that much of that work remains
to be done.[2] Marshall Hodgson, in his seminal posthumous

work, The Venture of Islam, in three volumes, declares, "a serious exploration of any one religious tradition in its several dimensions could consume more than one lifetime, and it is not to be expected that many persons can genuinely explore two."[3] All of us should take such cautions seriously. When confronted with a difficult but vital task, however, the best thing to do is to begin, and hope that some useful contribution may result.

Let me offer for consideration several propositions regarding the way in which some Christians have drawn faulty conclusions, over the past several centuries, in assessing the relationship between China and Christianity. Since I have in the past shared some of these errors, at least in part, I cannot expect instant agreement from everyone at this point, and I am conscious of the fact that I may now be mistaken about some of what I believe to be mistakes. My aim is not to reproach any individual, or to propose lines of division between people alleged to be always right and those always wrong. I seek to encourage the sort of re-examination of fundamental problems on the basis of evidence out of which more accurate conclusions might emerge.

Mistake No. 1: China could not be Christianized without abandoning her own ancient cultural traditions. This mistake had several aspects. First, it was not empirically true. On Fr. Ricci's death, in 1610, there were perhaps 2500 Christians in China; a century later, at the time of the climax of the Rites Controversy, there may have been a hundred times that many, or 250,000; but most important, they included substantial numbers of the ruling class and thus the prospects for further growth were bright. Second, there is good authority for the view that there was no reason stemming from orthodox Christian theology to demand that China's cultural traditions be abandoned, and much reason to insist that they be preserved. One may cite two remarks in that connection, the first from Clement of Alexandria, one of the ante-Nicene Fathers: "To us he gave the New Testament; those of the Judeans and Hellenes are the Old ones." Clement was preoccupied with the problem of Christianizing Greeks, the missionary task that comes closest to that of China in Christian history, since the Greeks had a highly developed culture to start with, as the Chinese did. The Jesuits found in the Chinese classics material as worthy to be termed "Old Testament" as in the figurative sense Clement of Alexandria used that phrase in connection with Greek literature. The other remark comes from a great writer who is still alive, Father Georges

Florovsky: "Traditions are kept and even cherished, but they are drawn into the process of Christian re-interpretation."[4]

It was precisely the problem of Christian re-interpretation that arose in China. Ricci and his successors faced it squarely. Their solution may not have been perfect, but it had two merits which in retrospect appear monumental. The solution did not compromise with the essentials of orthodox theology, so that no Chinese Christian had to experience the condescension that would be evident if he was told, you are not capable of what we Westerners can do; its other merit was to assume that virtue was to be found in Chinese culture failing evidence to the contrary.

This may be the point to remind ourselves that the Church from the very start faced and rejected the view that Christianization meant adopting the culture of any given people. At the Council of Jerusalem in 50 A.D. the issue arose regarding the Jews, and it was to reappear many times. Christianity has never been and is not culture-bound; unfortunately, many professed Christians have been, and undoubtedly will be. In its ability to cross cultural boundaries, of course, Christianity is not unique: to cite the two leading examples, Buddhism spread from India to China, Japan, and Indo-China; Islam spread from Arabia to the Maghreb on the west and to Indonesia on the east. And, to anticipate some comments on the secular faiths, Communism is not culture-bound, having spread as a ruling system from Poland to Vietnam, and as a belief much farther.

Mistake No. 1 was made by Clement XI and forces around him in his papacy and not only his. The Counter-reformation proved ambivalent: one hand reached with all the best intellectual resources of the time round the entire world and the other hand cut off the fingers of the first at the crucial instant. The mistake was repeated by the pietists of the nineteenth century, who hated all things Roman Catholic, let alone "papistical," and yet obstinately adhered to the very position taken in the papal decree Ex illa die of 1715. In both the seventeenth century and the nineteenth century there were those who saw the mistake, but in the former it was virtually the entire Jesuit order, though they had to repress their insight, while in the nineteenth the dissident pietists, who found their way back to the Ricci solution through trial and error, could be counted on the fingers of one hand--James Legge, Timothy Richard, and two or three others.[5] In regard to the brutal

way that those who sought to avoid the error were silenced,
there was nothing to choose from between the Catholics and
Protestants who were in the dominant position in each case.

Mistake No. 2: It is not entirely unrelated to the first,
but the focus is different. The mistake is that Chinese
might individually or in small numbers be interested in
Christianity, but never en masse. Dr. Hu Shih used to josh
his American friends--many of them at least nominal Chris-
tians--by alleging that generations of Christian missionaries were frustrated, ultimately by the fact that the
Chinese would not take seriously a sense of sin. Dr. Hu
was one of the greatest twentieth-century Chinese, whose
friendship I cherished, but the remark all too clearly
reflected the fact that it was the crippled pietist version
of Christianity which prevailed in the China of his youth.
That version, of course, stressed individual conversion,
so that when Timothy Richard declared that what was needed
was not that but instead "conversion by the million," no
one really heard him, let alone paid any attention to him.
Here a gigantic paradox looms: it was pietism which produced the ideology of the movement which was the greatest
Christian success of all Chinese history, though a fleet-
ing success and perhaps shallowly based. That was the
T'ai-p'ing rebellion, which nearly toppled the Ch'ing
dynasty at just the moment when in the judgment of many
its cyclical time had run out and it was ripe for overthrow. In Chinese history many rebel bands and armies had
been rather easily dispersed when confronted with forces
that obviously meant business; therefore, we should remember the 100,000 T'ai-p'ing Christians who were massacred
when Tseng Kuo-fan captured Nanking in 1864; not one
surrendered.

Mistake No. 3: Christianity never had any significant influence in Chinese culture or politics. Here let us leave
aside the question of the contributions to science and the
arts in the form of writings and masterpieces created by
individual Westerners in China or Chinese Christians, preserved and used for decades or centuries after the lifetimes
concerned. What I have in mind is several contentions that
it may be best to regard as hypotheses pending further
investigation, but potentially of great interest. First
is the opinion of Fr. Henri Bernard and H. G. Creel that
the Jesuits may have influenced both the Tung-lin school
of the late Ming and the "Han learning" school of the
Ch'ing in criticizing Sung neo-Confucianism as being, in
part, of Buddhist inspiration, and in seeking to look at

the Confucian texts afresh. If Bernard and Creel are right, the manner in which Ricci and others sought to approach the question of the compatibility of pristine Confucianism with Christianity affected the whole subsequent course of Chinese philosophical development. Second is the view of Chen Chi-yun that missionary influences on K'ang Yu-wei and Liang Ch'i-ch'ao "have been ignored or even expressly denied," but were crucial. If that can be fully demonstrated, not only what I have termed the syncretist school of K'ang-Liang and others but also the Hundred Days' reform of 1898 and other political aspects of the last years of the Ch'ing dynasty may require reevaluation. Third is my own view, supported by a good deal of evidence, that Sun Yat-sen owes much of his intellectual formation, before he became first president of the Republic and down to his last months as leader of the revived Kuomintang, to modernist Christianity. Other examples may be given.[6]

Mistake No. 4: China was never in modern times (a reservation that takes care of Buddhism) significantly influenced by any outside sources, and all fundamental changes in China are to be explained as indigenous. A wide range of observers, I regret to say, regard eighteenth- and nineteenth-century Western imperialism of China and elsewhere merely from the moral point of view and, from that point of view, as something totally evil. The economic, political, and generally institutional effects of imperialism, positive and negative, have been studied by some scholars, but much public discourse on the subject assumes that it was nothing but a kind of plague from which China suffered for a time and then got well. Karl Marx knew better, and paid tribute to the manner in which the British in India carried out the only revolution ever carried through up till that point against the Asiatic mode of production and its resultant despotic institutions. "England," he wrote, "has to fulfil a double mission in India: one destructive, and the other regenerating--the annihilation of old Asiatic society, and the laying the material foundations of Western society in Asia."[7] From that point of view, there was too little British imperialism in China, not too much. But it is not necessary to accept the conclusion of Marx or anyone else; it is necessary to regard imperialism as an historical problem, and not a story of simple good and evil in Manichean style, or perhaps more familiarly, like that of a Hollywood B movie. One effect of imperialism was that a whole generation of young Chinese was educated in American and other Western universities or mission schools in China. They are far

from being all dead at this time, and many are in mainland
China. Chiang K'ai-shek, indeed, was a Christian, and Mao
Tse-tung was, emphatically, not. (To hear a number of
professed Christians talk today, an outsider might conclude
that it was the other way round, but that is not my point
at the moment.) But both were extensively exposed to
Western education. Frederic Wakeman's book, History and
Will, makes that clear enough, in great detail, regarding
Mao.[8]

Mistake No. 5: The Peoples Republic of China (PRC) was
somehow the product of an indigenous revolution and an indigenous ideology, as contrasted with Christianity which
is foreign. It is almost incredible to me that professed
Christians should speak in such a manner, which indicates
a kind of Selbsthass, a feeling of repentance not for any
particular misdeed or misdeeds but simply for being a
Christian. What are the facts? There have been Christians
in China uninterruptedly since 1582, and with interruptions
at least since 635. There have been Communists in China
since 1921. Who are the newcomers?

The Chinese Communist Party was a creation of a mission
sent to China from the new Far Eastern Secretariat of the
Comintern in the spring of 1920, led by Grigorii Voitin-
sky, who like many of his Western predecessor-missionaries
knew no Chinese and had to operate through an interpreter,
but did so very successfully. His meetings with Chinese
radicals from which the Chinese Communist Party emerged
were held in the comfortable house of Ch'en Tu-hsiu in the
French Concession of Shanghai, an imperialist setting if
there ever was one. Marxism-Leninism has been the basis
of the CCP from its founding to the present moment, and
the portraits of Marx, Engels, Lenin, and Stalin, which
adorn every important public building and many unimportant
ones in the PRC today preserve one more Russian Communist
prophet than the present Soviet leadership does. "Maoism"
is a Western term, never used in China, where the proper
phrase is "Marxism-Leninism and the thought of Mao Tse-
tung." This is not the place for a full analysis of the
specific characteristics of Chinese Communism, or an examination of the question of who in the world may have the
best claim to be truly Marxist-Leninist. On that question,
however, there is no doubt whatever that the leaders of
the PRC advance the claim to be the true inheritors, not
of Confucius or the Chinese tradition, which they have
sought to exterminate, but of Marx and Lenin.

Mistake No. 6: In order to be up-to-date, the Church in China must try to harmonize its views with Chinese Communist ideology. One should begin the consideration of this problem by a brief overview of the relations between PRC government and the Christian churches in China. During the last months of the Civil War and the first months after the proclamation of the PRC on October 1, 1949, a fair amount of optimism was expressed by various Western missionaries and Chinese Christians regarding the possibilities for Christianity to survive in China. A group of Protestant Christians met with Premier Chou En-lai in May 1950 and formulated a "Christian Manifesto," which dealt mainly not with Christianity but with imperialism and the alleged need for Chinese Christian persons and institutions to fight it, and sketched a path for development of a "self-governing, self-supporting, self-propagating" church, a movement termed Three-Self by Protestants and Three Autonomies by Catholics. A biennial meeting of the National Christian Council was held in Shanghai in October 1950 which adopted the Manifesto. The upshot was the departure of virtually all foreign missionaries from China within months. No one was permitted to mention the fact that foreign missionaries themselves had a history of centuries in attempting to work toward churches governed, supported, and propagated by Chinese and had made considerable headway in so doing, despite their shortcomings and failures. The campaigns of the government--the Land Reform, the three-Anti and five-Anti campaigns in particular--resulted in closing a number of churches, but some were permitted to reopen and in the middle 1950's the Protestant churches were beleaguered but not crushed. The regime had found a number of collaborators among Protestant leaders, notably Y. T. Wu, but there were a few courageous evangelicals who refused to collaborate, such as Wang Ming-tao. Wang went on preaching to ever-growing crowds until his arrest--along with that of his wife and about 18 students--in August 1955. Among the charges against him were such allegedly treasonable statements of his as "Love your enemies." About a year later he signed a confession and was released, but it appears that he recanted and was jailed again. His was merely the best-known of several such cases. During these years of persecution a number of foreign Christians visited China and reported that all was well with the Chinese churches. There was evidently increasing pressure on Protestants until the early 1960's, but there is no doubt about what happened after 1965-66 as the Great Proletarian Cultural Revolution got under way. Many Christian clergy and lay people were martyred,

tortured, imprisoned, and placed in concentration camps.
Some of these reports are difficult to verify, but some
are well attested, such as the pillaging of a Roman
Catholic school in Peking for foreign children during which
eight aged European nuns were forced to run a gauntlet of
bamboo sticks, then deported to Hong Kong where one woman
85 years old died the day after arrival. The Protestant
churches were driven entirely underground.

The Catholics at the beginning resisted much more effectively than the Protestants, and the first few months or
years witnessed growth not decline. The Legion of Mary,
organized in China only in 1948, continued to spread until
1951. Archbishop Antonio Riberi, the Vatican's nuncio,
rallied the resisters until May 1951, when he was placed
under house arrest and then in September expelled from
China. When asked to condemn Riberi, Father John Tung
declared publicly that next would be a request to condemn
the pope, and next Christ himself. "If I strangle the
voice of my conscience, deny my God, leave the church and
cheat the government, I am nothing more than an opportunist
and a coward. . . ."[9] He was arrested, and fourteen years
later was reported to be still alive and in good spirits
in a concentration camp. The witness of Father Tung,
writes Richard Bush, is worthy of comparison with Justin
Martyr and other Christian leaders of the suffering church
of the first and second centuries. However, the PRC overcame such resistance, first by promoting the so-called
Patriotic Church, without much success until 1955, but
then it managed to organize a National Patriotic Catholic
Association in July 1957. The papacy issued three ency-
clicals from 1952 to 1958 urging resistance to invalid
elections of bishops. In 1960 Bishops Kung Pin-mei and
James E. Walsh were arrested, and the battle was over.
Just before Pope Paul VI visited Asia and Australia in
1970, Walsh was released, and as a result the pope made a
brief visit to Hong Kong. There seems little doubt that
the Vatican is willing to take another tack; there is no
indication whatever that the PRC is willing to permit the
resumption of Roman Catholic worship.

For all practical purposes the Church in China has ceased
to exist. My own observation, confirmed by the best Hong
Kong sources, is that one Christian church only continues
to operate regularly, St. Mary's in Peking, which serves
Roman Catholic diplomats and a handful of ancient Chinese.
That is, to use the Soviet term, there is a single "working
church" in the whole of China. (If there are in fact at

the moment a couple of others somewhere, that does not
affect my point.) My Chinese guides told me that there
is freedom to believe, freedom not to believe, and freedom
to propagate atheism--the precise provisions, by the way,
of the Soviet Constitution. But in answer to the question, does religious belief in fact survive, they frankly
replied in the negative, and made no attempt to allege
that organized religion survives in China. Any foreign
Christian must regard with the utmost sympathy the predic-
ament of the Chinese Christian today, for there is ample
evidence that Christian believers do survive, though they
have no opportunity to worship openly. In fact, one
Chinese Christian layman was arrested not long ago for
merely praying with a dying friend. But sympathy for the
Chinese Christian is far from the same as advice to him
to become a Communist.

There is ample experience on which to draw in assessing
the possibility that the church may co-exist with Communism. The Roman Catholic church in Poland survives
despite its difficulties, but it has two advantages absent
in neighboring countries: it includes almost 100% of the
population within the boundaries of the new Poland, and
its leaders cooperated with the Gomulka regime in holding
the country back from armed revolt in 1956. The Eastern
Orthodox churches in Romania, Bulgaria, and the Serb part
of Yugoslavia and the Roman Catholic churches of Czecho-
slovakia, Hungary, and the Croat part of Yugoslavia, survive but with much greater problems. The Russian Orthodox
church, too deeply rooted in the Russian tradition to be
exterminated, has survived 60 years of Communist rule in
Russia. Its hierarchs have, of course, had to pay the price
of the grudging and severely limited toleration extended
it by the regime; that price is to be willing to echo the
foreign-policy pronouncements of the Soviet rulers. But
lamentable as the plight of the church is in the USSR,
there has been no attempt to rewrite or revise Christian
theology, and the Patriarchate of Moscow is known for its
steadfast adherence to Eastern Orthodox tradition. The
line is often difficult to draw between the Christian
obligation to be good citizens and submit to the powers
that be, to the extent they do not demand for Caesar what
is God's alone, and Christian collaboration with governments
dedicated to the destruction of not only the church but
also Christianity and all religion. The foreign Christian
ought at least refrain from adding to the confusion of the
suffering men and women who try to follow Christ in today's
China.

Mistake No. 7: Despite all its executions, concentration camps, and repression of free thought, the PRC represents something like the march of God on earth. Since the last phrase is Hegel's, I may cite Eric Voegelin's remark about Hegel's reaction to the imperial events of his own time connected with the French Revolution and Napoleon, which, he declares, induced anxiety in Hegel provoking apocalyptic symbolism. Voegelin writes ironically, "such disorder cannot be admitted to be the misery it is; the God who permits it must, in this devious way, pursue an ultimate purpose of order. . . ."[10] He is clearly warning against the most serious error a Christian historian, or a Christian interested in secular affairs past and present, can make (the fact that Voegelin is not a Christian need not detain us here): the error of confusing sacred and profane history, of divinizing human events, including the most calamitous and brutal actions of man.

Sheila Johnson[11] and others have already cautioned us lest we go through with regard to China the same process of hailing the victory of Communism in Russia--whether like Lincoln Steffens ("I have seen the future and it works") or Anna Louise Strong, a fellow Seattleite of mine who after suffering under Stalin in Moscow decided that Peking was better, and may symbolize the beginning of comparable reactions to the PRC by outside visitors. There always will be people for whom the fact that railroads run on time or the garbage is swept up overshadows and justifies the incarceration of multitudes and the extinction of freedom. The most important point to make here, however, is that whether one sympathizes with totalitarian regimes or not, one cannot take what one sees and hears within their borders at face value.

I recognize authenticity in the following statement, made by an anonymous Chinese Christian, not a refugee, but one who left China after 1970: "In recent years, some Western scholars have tended to describe people in Communist China as a kind of 'New Man,' with newly acquired qualities of devoted service and self-sacrifice, faithfully following Chairman Mao's moral exhortations in pursuit of lofty social goals. This, however, is mainly the view of deluded observers from outside."[12] The visitor, safely equipped with a valid foreign passport, who enters such a country expecting soon to leave it, asks people what they really think, and expects that they will tell him, needs more experience with and study of such systems, to put it mildly.

A noted German writes that in China and other areas

> the secular government is a theocracy, the ruler
> is also high priest or God, the constitution of
> the state and its legislation are also religion,
> and the religious and moral injunctions, or rather
> customs, are also state and judicial laws. In the
> splendor of this whole, the individual is sub-
> merged without rights.[13]

The writer might be a contemporary, but he is not; he is
Hegel again, writing of the Chinese and other Oriental
empires. In the respects Hegel mentions, and others, the
Chinese Empire and the PRC are similar. There are, to be
sure, important differences. Over two millenia, the Chinese Empire punished and executed many people brutally,
exiled enemies, and silenced criticism; but in less than
thirty years the PRC has been responsible for the deaths
of millions, probably 30 million at least;[14] today has
perhaps 40 million in concentration camps; has purged
people from the very highest positions, including the
chairman of the republic, to the lowest, so that even adherence to the party cannot guarantee security. (If some-
one, incidentally, is critical of my estimates of victims,
he should remember that under Stalin such reports were
often dismissed by sympathizers as exaggerated, but that
the truth has proven to be not only quite as bad, but even
worse, than those so-called unverified reports of yester-
year.) Why Communism should be hailed as "liberation" by
anyone except Communists is a question I have never been
able to answer. Christians of the past had no difficulty
in discerning the evil effects of despotism; has the process of spiritual and intellectual decay in the West
advanced so far that they have lost the power of discernment today?

There is much else that could be said on every mistake I
have argued that Christians have made during the past four
centuries in regard to China. Not all will agree with my
arguments. For those who believe that some kind of synthesis between Christianity and Chinese Marxism is possible,
I recommend Dale Vree's recent book, On Synthesizing
Marxism and Christianity, in which he comes to a clear
conclusion: it is only possible to synthesize the two,
provided the Christianity in question is heretical and the
Marxism in question is revisionist.[15] I shall not try to
summarize his excellent and clear case here. For those,
Christian or not, who want nothing to do with Marxism--as

distinguished from recognizing the truth in the analysis of
certain problems to be found in Marx, Engels, and other
Marxists--the task of studying Christianity in China is
made easier, for there is no need to convert the story of
human suffering into Heilsgeschichte. One may simply try
to understand what happened.

But on one point I feel confident in urging caution. G. K.
Chesterton writes, "the Church is the only thing that saves
us from the degrading slavery of becoming children of our
times." The perspective of the Church, and indeed the perspective of any decent historian, should not be the passing
moment, for the very good reason that the moment will pass.
Nothing is as dead today as yesterday's burning relevance
or newest fashion. At the time of the Revolution of 1917
a host of Christian clergy in the West decided that Russian Orthodoxy deserved to be buried by the Communists,
and that it was in fact on the verge of being buried, since
no one was in the churches except old women--those remarkable old women who are still there and so must today be
nearing 140 or 150 years of age. As the Russian church
was written off, providential designs were found in Russian Communism. Those delusions are today hard to fathom,
but they were widespread. Today some of the most vigorous
voices in all Christianity come from the spokesmen of resurgent faith in the USSR, who have only contempt for
those foreign churchmen who sought to cuddle up to the
Soviet regime in one way or other. They are also defenders of a revived Russian cultural tradition, and not even
Christianity in its Russian Orthodox form is the same
thing, for Christianity always speaks to all mankind as it
may also deal with the individual or the group.

After examining carefully the situation of all religions in
China today, Richard C. Bush, Jr., declares that "almost
anyone who speaks about Chinese history observes that Chinese tradition, culture, philosophy . . . in spite of invasions by barbarians, Manchus, Japanese, or the West,
always manages to reassert itself."[16] For the moment,
Bush notes, Confucius's temple and tomb are defaced. If
the Red Guards did not succeed in "/wiping/ out completely
the old ideologies, culture, customs, and habits accumulated over thousands of years"[17] as they were assigned to
do during the Great Proletarian Cultural Revolution, there
should be no mistake about the Communist wish to do so.
In the era of the new Ch'in Shih-huang, and the new burning
of books and burial of scholars, who will keep the Chinese
tradition alive, who will one day reconstruct New Texts

and rediscover Old Texts? Probably not the Buddhists nor
the Muslims nor the Taoists. Who then? Quite possibly,
Christians. Matteo Ricci once set himself the task of
identifying the message of the Confucius who believed the
cosmos to be a moral order with which man should seek
harmony, and who forged an ethical system permeated by
the notion of individual responsibility. Ricci sought to
uncover this message in its earliest form--as yet uncor-
rupted by the annexation of certain Confucian ideas by the
Chinese Empire for the purposes of what James Legge called
"imperial Confucianism" and by the ambiguities of Sung
Neo-Confucianism. So in the twentieth century may Chinese
Christians be found who will cherish and keep alive the
humane impulses of Chinese civilization until the time
comes once again when they may be partly tolerated or even
honored on the mainland.

Mao Tse-tung said more than once that the Chinese people
are "poor and blank." In the past most of them were poor;
today virtually all of them are not merely poor, but equal
in their poverty, if that is an improvement. But they
were never blank, never tabulae rasae for tyrants to write
on them what they wished. They are still bearers of a
great tradition, and with the help of Christians that
tradition may survive. A Chinese Solzhenitsyn may lie
ahead, mutatis mutandis, and perhaps many such people.
They may or may not appear as Christians, but whoever they
are, the ideal of liberation from fear and oppression, not
unrelated to the true freedom which is in Christ, should
inspire Christians to stand by their side.

NOTES

1. Jonathan Spence, Emperor of China: Self-Portrait of K'ang-hsi (Alfred Knopf, New York, 1974), pp. 79, 80, 84.

2. Christianity and the New China (Ecclesia Publications, South Pasadena, California, 1976).

3. Marshall Hodgson, The Venture of Islam. 3 vols. (University of Chicago Press, 1974), Vol. 1, p. 29.

4. Georges Florovsky, Christianity and Culture. Vol. 2 of Collected Works (Nordland, Belmont, Massachusetts, 1974), p. 123.

5. I discuss the details in The West in Russia and China. 2 vols. (Cambridge University Press, 1973), Vol. I, China, 1582-1949.

6. Ibid., pp. 32-33; p. 223, fn. 25; Chapter 3.

7. Marx in his article in the New York Daily Tribune of June 25, 1853, called what the British had done "the only social revolution ever heard of in Asia." The quotation in the text comes from his July 22, 1853 article.

8. Frederic Wakeman, Jr., History and Will: Philosophical Perspectives of Mao Tse-tung's Thought (University of California Press, Berkeley and Los Angeles, 1973).

9. Richard C. Bush, Jr., Religion in Communist China (Abingdon Press, Nashville and New York, 1970), pp. 111-12.

10. Eric Voegelin, Order in History. Vol. 4, The Ecumenic Age (Louisiana State University Press, Baton Rouge), p. 329.

11. Sheila K. Johnson, "To China, With Love," Commentary, June 1973.

12. Christianity and the New China, Vol. 2, p. 45.

13. G. F. Hegel, Grundlinien der Philosophie des Rechts, Vol. 2 of Studienausgabe (Frankfurt, 1968), pp. 319-20.

14. In 1959 a New York Times editorial estimated that

30 million people had been exterminated in the first
decade of Communist rule alone; in 1969 Radio Moscow
estimated 26.4 million killed from 1949 to 1965. See
"The Human Cost of Communism in China," Committee Print
for the U.S. Senate Committee on the Judiciary, Washington,
1971, esp. table on p. 16 and accompanying analysis of
references. Current classified documents not accessible
to me doubtless provide a firmer basis for estimates than
can be found elsewhere.

15. Dale Vree, On Synthesizing Marxism and Christianity (John Wiley & Sons, New York, 1976), esp. pp. viii-xii.

16. Bush, Religion in Communist China, p. 380.

17. Peking Radio, August 23, 1966.

PART THREE

CHINA AND GOD'S PRESENCE
IN HISTORY:
THEOLOGICAL REFLECTIONS

INTRODUCTION

James D. Whitehead

Five quite different theological reflections comprise the
final section of Cnina and Christianity. Lawrence Burkholder, in the introductory essay, suggests that the
striking events in China in the past three decades may
provide a mirror for Christian self-reflection. Such a
mirror may not only assist reflection, but also illumi-
nate our own (as Christians) actions for social justice,
and our life styles of simplicity or excessive consumption.

Two theologically relevant facets of Maoism that fascinate
Burkholder are the kairos-like timing of Mao's coming to
power--in the midst of a collapse of traditional China and
a revolutionary, even eschatological sense of expecta-
tion--and Maoism's all-encompassing management of Chinese
life which gives it the appearance of a "secular Marxist
counterpart to the (historical) Corpus Christianum."

This essay is followed by two reflections in conflict.
Raymond Whitehead, in his "Christ, Salvation and Maoism,"
argues from a Liberation Theology point of view for a
bolder recognition of the good being achieved in the new
China. Whitehead suggests that since God works through
specific historical forces--and the Old Testament attests
to such workings--Christians can affirm the human liberation

occurring in China as a religious event. This essay concludes by urging the Christian Churches to repent of their
historical imperialism in China and to practice the kind
of justice and social concern in their own lives that will
attract those involved in the Maoist development of China.

Charles West, in his theological reflection on China, argues
against an identification of the work of the Lord with a
specific historical movement: "No power, of status quo or
revolution, is as such God's saving or liberating instru-
ment." If we are careful to distinguish God's purposes
from those ambiguous programs of any historical movement,
West suggests that we can then discover in Maoist ideology
motifs which may allow for a dialogue with Christians. One
such motif is that of the "continuing revolution" with its
implied openness to change, self-critique and influence
from outside its own belief structure.

The fourth reflection in part three occurred on the second
day of the Notre Dame Conference in a panel discussion of
"China and God's Presence in History." Five theologians,
joined by other participants of the conference, explored
the central ambiguity and confusion of contemporary China
and Christian faith: the ambiguity surrounding what, in
fact, is happening in China today (especially in terms of
individual freedom and social coercion); and the confusion
for Christians that the enormous changes in China toward
equality and the relief of poverty are occurring without
them. Debate focused on the meaning of "salvation,"
"God's judgment in history," as well as the response that
the Christian Churches are called to make to contemporary
China.

Part three concludes with the theological reflection
offered by Joseph Spae in "The Notre Dame Conference: A
Prospective Evaluation." Following a brief and clear summary of the major points pursued at the conference, Spae
reminds the reader of the urgency of a truly ecumenical
response of the Christian Churches to China. In the context of the Notre Dame conference, this urgency especially
concerns the involvement of the American Catholic Church
and its scholars in this dialogue between a nation which
comprises one-fourth of the world's population and a
religious tradition which makes up another one-fourth of
this world.

Throughout these five reflections it becomes quite clear
that a revolution in Christian missiological thought

induces a crisis in ecclesiology. In all these reflections the central point repeatedly returned to concerns the meaning and purpose of the Church: who are we and what are we to be for China? Charles West offers one definition which expresses the conviction of many about a less dichotomous and more intimate relationship between Church and world: "The Church is the place where the world in all its variety, its conflicts, its pride and its need, is concentrated in the presence of God and works out its relationship with him."

I – RETHINKING CHRISTIAN LIFE AND MISSION IN LIGHT OF THE CHINESE EXPERIENCE

Lawrence J. Burkholder

If we as Christians are intrigued by the New China, it is quite unlikely that we have been moved initially by the "thoughts of Mao" or by esoteric elements in Chinese revolutionary philosophy. Rather, it is the other way around. We have been led to examine the mystical and moral dimensions of the revolution by objective events in Chinese revolutionary history. The New China has brought order and styles of personal and communal life that have enabled the nation to make striking, albeit uneven, progress toward solving some of its great historical problems. China emerges nearly thirty years after the revolution as an alternative for developing nations and as a mirror by which Christians may review their life and mission.

The extent to which the New China has succeeded as a social system and as a moral influence is, of course, debated. We must acknowledge at the outset that China is ambiguous. The story of the New China includes many negative chapters--the heavy cost of human life, trying periods of chaos, rash economic miscalculations, wrenching social convulsions, wearisome propaganda, arbitrary restrictions on intellectuals, painful suppression of traditional religions, and unresolved ideological conflicts. Nevertheless, some of us who recall the Old China from personal experience respond with enthusiasm and gratitude for the achievements of the past thirty years while we await freer access to the people and further indications of the direction of the revolution.

It is important how we approach China. We cannot approach China piecemeal if we wish to understand its meaning. It is important to see China as a whole and against its historical and philosophical backgrounds. In this connection, we must recognize that China cannot be understood simply by applying Western tools of social analysis. For China is a "unitive" society and as such it resists functional analysis based upon divisions of society that have developed in the West. For the same reason we cannot isolate and lift out aspects of Chinese life in neglect of the total social system.

For the sake of overall perspective, here are some of the outstanding achievements of the New China:

1. A productive, non-inflationary economy, relying on domestic sources of energy and raw materials providing sustenance and full employment for nearly a quarter of the human race.
2. An egalitarian social system doing away with personal wealth and abject poverty.
3. Revolutionary consciousness of the masses and a sense of national pride and identity.
4. Personal and public morality, low crime rate, sex probity, elimination of prostitution, venereal disease and illicit use of drugs.
5. A strong sense of national destiny combining realism and utopian hope.
6. An ethic of selfless service.
7. Progress toward universal primary education, increase in literacy, advancement in technical education and mass indoctrination.
8. Socialized medicine incorporating preventive principles adapted to the needs of a developing nation.
9. An alternative model for developing nations.

The achievements of the past thirty years contain a number of unusual if not mysterious elements. One of them concerns the question of how it has been possible for the revolution to influence so many people so deeply. To be

sure, sinologists debate how much of the Old China lies
under the surface of the New China. Nevertheless, the
revolution has swept the nation and has altered the circumstances of some 800 million people. That a revolution
as radical as China's could happen is to this writer an
historical enigma.

There are of course explanations for the breadth and the
depth of the revolution--traditional Chinese collectivism,
grinding poverty, the power and the discipline of the
army, the coincidence of selfless devotion with the revolution and self-interest and the cult of Mao.

But in addition to these plausible explanations there is
a mystery analogous to what Christians call the "kairos"
or "appointed time." By the appointed time we mean the
strange and unpredictable configuration of events within
which Mao appeared. Mao appeared with the collapse of
traditional China among circumstances which bring to mind
the coming of Christianity with the decline of classical
antiquity. In both instances, radical eschatological
revolutionary movements replaced dying traditions with
class systems that failed to meet the spiritual and
physical needs of the people.

Another unpredictable factor is the personality of Mao--
in particular, his confidence in the power of ideology
and will. Mao approached ideology with an unusual gift
for generalization. Ideology of course presumes the art
of simplification according to which the universal is
thought to be epitomized in the most significant particular. For Mao, reality was epitomized in the peasant.
From his intimate knowledge of rural life, he generalized
to the needs of the nation as a whole--not entirely
strange in view of the composition of China's population.
As an ideologist, he resisted complexity and ignored
differences, shades and nuances by boldly lifting the
rudimentary elements of China to universal significance--
food, rivers, mountains, pigs, manure, suffering, struggle,
fate. It would seem to take an activist with the imagination of a nineteenth century idealistic philosopher to
envisage the possibility of understanding, ordering,
educating, and transforming so large and complex a nation
as China. In this respect, it is easier to think of Mao
in connection with nineteenth century philosophy than as
a product of twentieth century science and technology.

With respect to his concept of will, he may have surpassed

all earthly leaders by his paradoxical expectations of rebellion and conformism. When faced by such "mountains" as feudalism and imperialism, he was confident that the goals of the revolution would be assured by willful defiance. He appealed to the transcending will when confronted by such intractable historical contradictions as spirit and bureaucracy, freedom and fate, passion and intellect, agriculture and industry, revolutionary and capitalist tendencies, and even old age. According to Lucian Pye:

> For him the dialectic of history was less the clash of class interests than the contradiction between the spirit of revolutionary progress and tendencies toward selfishness and status. . . . Mao transformed Communist ideology into a morality play between forces of good and evil in which there is a constant danger that evil will seduce even the most virtuous from the straight and narrow path of revolutionary dedication.[1]

But if Mao recognized the omnipresence of sin, he refused to be aligned with an institutionally oriented revolution of bureaucracies and armies. Mao's "voluntarism," culminating in the cultural revolution, looked not only nor primarily toward changes in the class system but to the conversion of the masses on a national scale.

Another closely related mystery is the morality of China. Undoubtedly this introduces controversial questions. To what extent have the Chinese been "transformed"? How deep is Chinese revolutionary morality? To what extent has it been internalized? There are no scientific ways to know the answer to these questions. However, the evidence gathered by visitors is enough to substantiate the claim that the socialization process has been remarkably effective. Some 400 million young people born since the beginning of the Revolution have been taught that the purpose of life is to "serve the people" within a society structured to make service possible without contradiction. The secret of Chinese success in transforming people is, at least in part, the coincidence of self-giving and self-interest implicit in a system within which the preponderance of one's personal needs are met socially instead of individually.

The extent to which the thoughts of the Chinese are pure and their wills directed toward "serving the people" may be only slightly more intriguing than the assumption that

the masses could be changed. Confidence in popular moral
renewal would seem to defy much of historical experience
and the broad consensus of the philosophers and theologians
who have impressed upon Western culture such ideas as
"original sin" (Augustine), "radical evil" (Kant), "sickness unto death" (Kierkegaard) and "ambiguity" (Niebuhr).
Mao's confidence in the moral possibilities of man may be
more Chinese than Promethean and more Confucian than
Marxist.

Under what terms may the New China help us to rethink the
Christian life and mission? I would propose that Christians would do well to test their life styles, social
attitudes, and the social systems within which they live
and witness by a broad and in-depth comparison with Chinese experience. This is not to say that we thereby defer
to modern China in a way which would compromise our commitment to Jesus as Lord. Rather, we would look to China
as a reference from which we would see ourselves in relation to Christ and the Christian faith. Frankly, China
is not our model. China may serve as something of a
"model" for the nations but as a "mirror" for Christians.
The distinction between a model and a mirror does not
imply an arbitrary spirit of orthodoxy, but an assumption,
based upon considerable evidence, that much of what
strikes us as being good in China is similar to what may
be found implicit within Christian thought or explicit
within Christian history. Such an approach does not dispute the impact of actuality in the Chinese situation.

This approach enables one to benefit from looking at China
without having to see through China. That is to say, we
need not wait until the inscrutable aspects of Chinese
life are removed in order to profit by Chinese experience.
China may help us to know as Christians what we should be
or do before we are really sure that the New China is what
it seems to be. If the following description of China's
achievements turns out to be more ideal than real, it may,
nevertheless, serve as a basis for rethinking the Christian life.

I would propose five closely related structural principles
in China's system which the church should examine. These
are indicative not only of China's political order but its
system of values and moral commitment. They are (1) survival, (2) egalitarianism, (3) simplicity, (4) service,
and (5) eschatology. These will be described briefly and
followed by some suggestions as to how Christians may
respond.

It may seem fortuitous for a former relief administrator
to propose that the primary reason for the revolution in
the first place and the most determinative principle
affecting Chinese life and organization is survival. When
one considers Chinese history and recalls traditional
promises for reform through more equitable distribution
of land, lower taxes, flood control, and reforestation,
one realizes that the meaning of China's historic struggles
is basically the survival of its people. When one considers from a logistical point of view what is implied by
the support of some 800 million people, it would appear no
less than miraculous that the Chinese people are eating
and evidently eating fairly well. Some of us who recall
the thin bodies of Chinese refugees, their sallow com-
plexions, infectious sores, and cracked, bleeding feet are
grateful that not only some but _all_ Chinese now have rice
allotments, vegetables, and an occasional chicken or duck.
This fact goes a long way in counterbalancing negative
aspects of Chinese national life such as limits upon individual freedom and thought control.

Reference to the fact that the Chinese are eating may seem
slightly out of character with a conference devoted to the
"religious dimension." However, emphasis upon food may be
more in character with the history of China and the spirit
of revolutionary politics than vague references to a
religious quality in Maoism. That all shall eat is the
foundational moral commitment of revolutionary China.
The nation is designed first of all to sustain life. The
fact that China has had the courage and the imagination
to choose its priorities and its instrumentalities so that
all shall work, eat and be clothed is to China's indis-
putable honor, the envy of developing nations, and the
embarrassment of affluent nations. Parenthetically, it
may be pointed out that China has virtually removed itself
from international aid for some thirty years--a consideration of vital significance in view of world food short-
ages and inflationary pressures.

Integral to China's survival ethic is its policy of full
employment (including the employment of women). It is
ironic that the only developing nation in the world with
full employment is also the largest and most populous.
Full employment is not accidental. It is planned as a
human right. The purpose of full employment is not only
to maximize production but to bestow upon all the people
a sense of identity and participation in the life of the
community. Furthermore, full employment is correlated

with a pension system without insidious distinctions between those who work and those who do not. The Chinese
economy itself may be described as a vast support system
oriented toward essential commodities rather than money
and toward production rather than toward the exchange of
goods. It is a controlled economy with prices that are
set within a broad range of social and market considerations

Closely associated with the principle of survival is the
principle of egalitarianism. Egalitarianism may be seen
as a theoretical implication of Marxism but its application and interpretation frequently follow lines of practical necessity in view of China's problems of scarcity.
As such, egalitarianism functions as a moral principle.
If, indeed, necessity has provided the occasion for
egalitarianism, one may find many parallels in this
respect in the Christian tradition from Pentecost to
modern intentional communities, according to which the
practice of the "community goods" arose out of emergency
situations only to be followed by doctrines of "love
communism."

Be that as it may, China's egalitarianism is a practice
with radical social and psychological implications. The
leveling of doctors and nurses, managers and workers,
officers and soldiers is intended to reinforce a national
ethos of comradeship and challenges tendencies toward
pride and privilege. The egalitarian spirit is the
essence of the revolutionary spirit as interpreted by
Mao. It was in quest of the spirit of the Long March
and Yenan, in which the extremities of guerrilla warfare
issued in the experience of mutuality, that Mao launched
the Cultural Revolution. Mao trusted that out of the
confusion ("the more the better") the revolutionary
spirit would become diffused throughout the nation.

Another structural principle is the principle of simplicity. By simplicity we do not mean a particular style of
life only, but also a design for society as a whole.
China is organized consciously around what it can do
without as well as what can be done with what it has.
A presupposition of Chinese life is that of living within
one's means. This expresses itself in international relations, on all levels of government, in communes and
family life. The line between necessity and luxury is
drawn sharply in accordance with the resources of the
nation. The absence of private cars, private estates,

night clubs, jewelry and dogs accounts for the absence of
bare feet. China is a "garbage-less" society and a
society without advertising agents, sports heroes, movie
stars. Simplicity is emphasized as an implication of
wholesomeness, good taste and propriety.

Simplicity of life is one of the reasons why China has had
little or no inflation. The rate of inflation is just
below Switzerland's 1 per cent! It is ironical that the
only non-inflationary economy in the world is that of a
developing nation with tremendous population pressures.
The coincidence of China's "poverty" and her economic
independence is anomalous. It results from passionate
self-reliance and the spirit of austerity.

It should also be pointed out that China is a disciplined
society. Discipline consists of the claims of the community upon the individual. The loci of discipline are
the neighborhood, the commune, the school, the place of
work, or the bureau, depending upon one's position.
Theoretically, everyone lives under a discipline as if
recruited into a military force. One of the most important implications of discipline is what it means psychologically for individual initiative and responsibility.
To be sure, communal discipline is the end of individualism. There is no place within the New China for individual gain, self-fulfillment, career planning, independent
wealth, private enterprise and competitive struggle,
except to the extent that these may be compatible with
social purposes or when, by some quirk or looseness
within the system, they creep in inadvertently. As a
result of the claims of community, China seeks to produce
a "new socialized man." China is an immense crucible in
which contradictory claims of individuality and sociality
are being tested. At this stage of the revolution the
outcome would seem to be uncertain.

Another principle of social organization in China is the
ethic of "service." "Serving the people" is the essence
of Maoist morality, the motivating power of the nation,
and the measure of right and wrong. By a multitude of
ingenious ways--plays, songs, dances, myths, art, slogans,
propaganda--the ethic of selfless service is impressed on
the people. Never in the history of mankind have so many
people been impressed by and organized around the principle of service. In character with China's unitive
tendencies, "serving the people" does not consist of isolated acts on the perimeter of life. Rather, the service

motive is supposed to be "diffused" throughout life in a manner characteristic of religion within traditional Chinese culture. Life is conceived as a form of service. What matters more than the importance of the act is the motive of "serving the people."

What the Chinese have attempted to do by a radical socialist structure is to reduce the tension between personal virtue and social policy. The purpose of the Revolution would seem to be to remove whatever truth there may be implicit in that maxim of "moral man and immoral society." Obviously, they have not completely succeeded in making goodness "work," but underneath the revolution, as interpreted and guided by Mao, lies the assumption that personal goodness and power are not as inimical as they are frequently held to be in the West. Or, "among the Chinese virtue leads to power and the purpose of power is to spread virtue."[2]

Finally, the New China is formed by an eschatological view of history. Chinese eschatology, to borrow from theological terminology, sees history as meaningful. As such, it is thought to be moving toward the end which is implicit in the nature of things. This is not the occasion to elaborate on such questions as the Chinese version of Marxist utopianism, the concrete implications of the dream for social harmony and its proximity in time. Suffice it to say that for some fifty years the leaders of the P.R.C. have been motivated by a hope which has now spread to the populace, however fragmentarily and obscurely. The Chinese leaders have believed that the meaning of history is being accomplished through them. Every achievement testifies to the inevitability of pure Communism after periods of socialist "struggle." Every failure witnesses to the elusiveness of the goal, giving rise to the doctrine of "continuous revolution."

Chinese eschatology injects an element of hope into Chinese life which otherwise may be characterized by monotony and struggle. Young people in particular find in the Communist view of history reason for choosing the "correct line" and thinking "correct thoughts." It has "liberated" many of them from a psychology of cyclical recurrences and has added a dimension of movement to their consciousness. In addition to the motif of morality, the motif of progress as represented by the omnipresence of production figures, reveals a national experience of hope for a stronger nation, a better life, and eventually utopia.

Broadly speaking, Chinese Communism and Christianity have
views of history which have much in common. Both see
history eschatologically as a process of liberation.
Both despair of classical conservative social organization because they fail to provide justice and peace.[3]
"Shalom, Shalom, but there is no Shalom." Both see man
as sinful and yet renewable.

> Behold the days are coming, says the Lord, when
> I will make a new covenant with the house of
> Israel, not like the covenant which I made with
> their fathers. . . . But this is the covenant
> which I will make with the house of Israel. . . .
> I will write my law upon their hearts. (Jeremiah
> 31:31)

Similarities between Marxist expectations and Christian
faith have long been noted. However, the similarities
between Maoist thought and New Testament Christianity in
particular are especially intriguing. Both emphasize
ethics rather than metaphysics, history rather than
transcendence, radical discontinuity rather than evolutionary change and charismatic order rather than institutional power. One can observe tensions between New
Testament Christianity and later forms similar to
tensions between Maoist and "revisionist" forms of Communism. The term "revision" functions in the Maoist
vocabulary as the term "compromise" functions in the
Christian vocabulary. It may be noted in passing that
Chinese Communism, like primitive Christianity, is a
young movement. It will be interesting to observe
whether China will be forced to make concessions to time
and complexity similar to those made by Christianity or
whether China's adjustments may be of a different kind,
reflecting the influence of Chinese culture.

If indeed Christians may benefit by the experience of
China, it is essential to emphasize the differences between Christianity as a religion and China as a nation.
The differences between their realities, their instrumentalities, powers, and methods are instructive for
Christians as they seek to understand their obligations
and possibilities. Possibly, the most important point
of this study concerns the nature of Christianity when
seen against the reality of the New China. That is to
say, what does it mean to come to terms with the fact
that Christianity is a religion and the church is a
spiritual community and the power of the church is the

power of the Spirit? Sometimes comparisons are made in which Christianity is by implication held to be continuous with China or somehow the church is identified with democratic nations and therefore judged by the same criteria. The pathos of Christian life and mission lies in the fact that both the church and China are committed to certain similar goals and yet China is a nation with all that that means and the church is a spiritual community with all that that means.[4]

If only China were a nation in the modern democratic sense, the contrast between China and the church would be relatively simple. However, the contrast is complicated by the fact that China is more than a nation. It is an all-embracing moral and spiritual establishment as well. By analogy it is both church and state. It is analogous to the church in the sense that it addresses itself to questions of ultimate significance and it regulates the behavior of its people with moral authority never dreamed of by the most zealous of popes. The Chinese government in its many forms and numerous manifestations is the one and only authority on everything that matters. In this respect, it is totalitarian. The government of China promotes a metaphysical view of reality, a system of morality, an interpretation of religion and filial obligation, attitudes toward sex, marriage, work and death. The authority of the nation pervades the entire texture of life. It defines the truth in psychology, the nature of man, and the social good. It seeks to remake the human subject according to its image of a "new man." Many of its practices resemble cultic rituals and it fosters a moralistic, quasi-religious ethos.

China impresses this Western observer as an anthropocentric counterpart to ancient theocracies. Possibly the term "anthropocracy" would be allowed for what the Chinese call the "dictatorship of the people." Structurally, it has more in common with medieval Christendom and Calvin's Geneva than with modern pluralistic states. It is no less conformist and intolerant. It seeks to revolutionize society for the people as Geneva sought to reform society for the glory of God. From the standpoint of the history of political and cultural organizations, it is antiquarian.

Furthermore, China is a relatively undifferentiated society, an organic whole under the domination of an all-pervasive, many-leveled political presence. It may be referred to as a "unitive" society in the sense that all

segments are integrated for revolutionary purposes. Its
unity is perfected beyond that of medieval Christendom,
for in Christendom at least a distinction between the
spiritual and the earthly powers persisted for more than
a thousand years. China has one arm--not two, played
against each other as in Western Europe. The meaning of
the New China lies in its passion for unity--absolute
unity according to which all competing ideas and powers,
be they Confucian, Christian, capitalistic or whatever,
are systematically removed. Anything that threatens the
unity of China is revisionist and must be eliminated,
according to Maoist thought.

To be sure, China is surprisingly decentralized. But its
decentralization does not imply genuine independence.
Decentralization is the ingenious way by which the political blanket adjusts to the contours of Chinese society.
And although China includes major divisions such as economics, education, agriculture, industry and the military,
all function as within a political lump. Politics pervades all of life. Everything melts into politics--
economics, the military, education, agriculture, art,
literature, family. A division between public and private sectors no longer exists. The private sector in
Chinese life has been abolished.

The fact that the church and China are committed to
similar purposes and yet are fundamentally different
realities means that they can be considered on the same
continuum only if we know what we are doing. It cannot
be assumed that what is possible for one is possible for
the other and what is appropriate for one is appropriate
for the other. The church cannot do all that China is
doing. Discussions about the meaning of China for the
churches reach their most poignant levels when focused on
the question of whether in the long run humanity will be
"saved" through the instrumentality of a unitive social
order--Christian, Maoist, whatever--or by the instrumentality of spiritual community within the context of an
open society, or neither.

I would propose that our response as Christians should be
as follows: (1) We must inquire anew as to what it means
to be a Christian in the context of an open society. (2)
We must establish new forms of voluntary, disciplined
community in response to loneliness and loss of identity.
(3) We must identify emotionally and politically with the
poor and oppressed.

The whole question of what it means to be a Christian brings
to the fore the meaning of discipleship for our time. Obviously, the distance is great between the apocalyptically
oriented call to discipleship as recorded in the Gospels
and the call to participate faithfully in the modern world.
Legalistic responses to the Sermon on the Mount are inappropriate. Rather, what is needed is a sense of what is
appropriate in light of the obvious excesses of an indulgent
age and the deeper problems facing the world. If indeed
we are living in a world of limited resources, Christians
may parallel the Chinese in search for simpler ways of
living. If, indeed, modern society is excessively caught
up in greedy pursuit of money, Christians may make life
choices in which material gain is subordinated to other
values. If western societies find it difficult to corre-
late discipline with freedom, Christians must join the
Chinese in the practice of discipline appropriate to their
situation. It is time for Christians to break dramatically
with the decadent aspects of western culture, such as un-
bridled individualism, extreme selfishness, sexual immoral-
ity, indulgent waste, and class privilege--not as moralistic Savonarolas but as those who have come to realize that
the future holds these excesses in judgment for their
'unreality." The Christian life must be defined in terms
of the possibilities of humanization given the limits of
the earth, man and society. They must witness to the fact
that simple disciplined living is living according to the
realities of a finite world and elemental values.

Christians must oppose by word and example the disparity
between the salaries of corporation executives, some who
make in excess of $400,000 per year, and people who live on
or below the poverty level. They must protest the cult of
television personalities, sports heroes and celebrities who
symbolize an "ideal" life style far beyond the reach of
most people--an ideal which contributes to general dissatisfaction and crime.

What Christians must do is to adopt patterns of life which
will embody on a voluntary basis many of the values implicit within China's unitive society. Unless Christians
in general, or at least a significant minority, adopt
styles of life which cut across the accepted patterns of
western affluent decadence, the tendency of the Chinese
and many in developing nations to identify Christianity
with the sins of western society cannot be gainsaid. Only
a rigorous, concrete program of non-conformism will enable
Christianity to be distinguished from the excesses of

capitalism and liberalism.

It is obvious that Christians will not reform society, let alone bring in the Kingdom, simply by adopting sane, sacrificial patterns of life on an individual basis. It would appear to most of us, and especially to structure-minded socialists, that personal discipleship cannot be substituted for structural change. However, to call for social change apart from personal struggle with sin, selfishness, unreality, and indulgence is dishonest and the chances of social change are vastly increased by a committed people.

The task of living a simple life that transcends the inequities, individualism and decadence of affluent societies is in many respects more difficult than to live according to prescription in a Chinese commune. For, while it is theoretically possible to choose freely one's life style in liberal societies, social pressures are so subtle and so powerful that few people are successful in transcending them. To be a disciple in affluent western societies, one must not only be able to "discern the spirits," i.e., the underlying commitments of the age, but to struggle individually against evils that are structured within the fabric of society. The unselfish spirit of the committed disciple is bound to confront a general ethos and an economic system which are ambiguous.

Radical discipleship, however, is not intended to be the lonely struggles of isolated moral heroes. It is intended to be communal experience. The disciple is a member of a fellowship from which he receives spiritual support, understanding, and a sense of identity. New Testament Christianity knows nothing about the spirit of individualism which has come to characterize western culture and which characterizes many institutional churches as well. Discipleship by definition is communal.

It may take such a massive phenomenon as the New China within which some 800 million people live communally to alert Christians to the fact that their faith presupposes community as well. To be sure, communal forms may vary. They have varied historically from the most rigorous, egalitarian groups to natural communities such as villages, valleys and city neighborhoods where interaction is less intentional. We are learning both from our theology and from experience that man is intended to share his life with others. The widespread problem of loss of identity, alienation, and loneliness bespeaks a lack of community in western culture.

The challenge implicit within Chinese communal organization
is for the church to discover new forms of fellowship that
combine the discipline of the group with the freedom of
open societies. The most significant development in this
respect is the discussion which is taking place broadly
within ecumenical circles regarding the nature of the
church. It is increasingly recognized that the church is
not intended to be primarily a hierarchy or an institution
but a fellowship (<u>koinonia</u>) of the people of God. The
church is "life together" within the Spirit.

Of course the theological definition of the church as a
"fellowship of the spirit" leads to practical questions
about congregational structures which make fellowship a
reality. Surely the Chinese would regard the character of
fellowship within the congregation a far cry from comradeship in a commune or in a "neighborhood." We would hold,
however, that non-congregational life should be free to
reflect individuality. Congregations should tolerate at
least some differences of wealth or social position, not
to speak of philosophical and political differences, among
their members. At any rate, churches, renewed and re-
structured for fellowship, may be in a position to provide
many communal services in a context of pluralistic freedom
which more than mitigates the isolation of western man.

But what about Christian communism? There is in the history of Christianity a long tradition of radical community
in the form of "love communism." According to Ernst
Troeltsch, love communism is

> one of the permanent results of the teaching of
> Jesus. When . . . men tried to construct a purely
> abstract theory out of Jesus' exhortations on
> social questions--that is, when men tried to re-
> duce the absolute readiness of love to sacrifice
> into a theory--this always led quite logically to
> a fresh attempt to realize the communism of love.[5]

However, Troeltsch points out that love communism has never
been accepted by the church at large as a permanent possibility. It has been left to certain monastic orders and
small groups. The reasons for the refusal of the Christian
church to insist upon love communism as a general policy
are not only selfish individualism but also the conflict
between the voluntary character of Christian love and the

revolutionary compulsion which would be necessary for its establishment and maintenance.

The New China may be accepted as a challenge by the churches to continue the search for forms of fellowship of many kinds and on a vast scale within modern pluralistic societies, thus replacing natural communities of simpler times and ameliorating the alienation of modern industrial civilization. Such a search would result in the dramatic reorganization of church life with important social and doctrinal implications. Sacramental institutions would increasingly become havens for masses of people who are wounded and lonely and oppressed by modern life.

Finally, China reminds the church of the urgent need for social justice. Modern China represents, albeit ambiguously, one of the most significant single events of liberation in history. Since the Biblical message is the promise of justice through the coming of the Kingdom, the church must at least appreciate the central purposes of the Chinese revolution despite reservations which it may have about violent revolution. Understandably the church looks to China today with a measure of awe against its own background of 1900 years of missionary activity which resulted in Christendom and continued into this century through the modern missionary movement. When one reflects upon the fact that the church has survived the centuries and has tamed many a "barbaric" tribe and cruel heart and has helped to humanize Western civilization, one may be impressed by the mysterious and gracious power of God that has accompanied its amazing history. However, one is impressed at the same time by the fact that revolutionary China has achieved as it were, with a single stroke, release of millions from oppression and has established an order which is supporting life. At the moment the church would seem to be the weaker in the process of liberation.

Nevertheless, the churches must seek justice for the poor in all parts of the world insofar as it has the power and the wisdom to do so. In order to do this, the churches must move on three fronts: (1) the task of theological formulation: The church must learn from a theological perspective that salvation is this-worldly as well as otherworldly, and that the central message of the Bible is the coming of the Kingdom as a political reality. This means that the Gospel must be seen as one of deliverance and the Christian hope as a hope for a just social order. This is not to deny the importance of "religious" experience.

Rather, it places religious experience, including sacramental life, in a social context.

(2) Also, the church must continue to search for ways by
which it may identify with human suffering. The middle-
class status of the church in the West makes genuine identification with suffering people of the world problematic,
to say the least. However, mission, if it means anything,
implies radical renunciation of privilege in an attitude
of repentance. The major stumbling block to genuine identification with the victims of injustice are habits of
privilege and affluence and not physical distance nor the
problems of missionary visas nor the dangers of patron-
izing attitudes of "service." The church will have become
authentically missionary when its reputation among the
poor will have become one of unqualified support for the
oppressed. So far, that has not happened.

(3) A third task of the church is to explore the relation
between its hope for the kingdom and political ideology.
The church today is quite properly reluctant to commit
itself to a particular ideology. Ideologies of necessity
oversimplify and reflect a limited and often parochial
set of circumstances. However, it is obvious that the
church cannot speak to historical situations without a
measure of consistency and without some presuppositions.
The church is bound to reflect preferences and when these
are followed to their roots they suggest at least a bias.
Consequently, it is the responsibility of the church to
study the great options of our time such as liberalism,
democracy, capitalism, socialism, communism, gradualism,
revolution. They should be debated in relation to concrete historical problems without accepting any of them as
"christian."

Reluctance upon the part of the church to identify explicitly with particular ideologies results not only from
the limits of ideology as such but also from the present
situation of the church vis-a-vis political power. The
church is no longer in the business of helping to establish
and defend political orders, at least, not as in former
times. That great historical development of over a thousand years in forming Christian civilization has come to
an end. The church no longer is in league with its princes;
it no longer has armies and it no longer compels obedience.
The period of triumphalism is past. The Renaissance, the
left wing of the Reformation, democracy and modernity have
placed the church in an entirely different position from

the one it occupied for most of its history. It now occupies the humble position of a minority with only the authority which issues from its authenticity. It is a community among other religious and secular communities amid the pluralism of the modern democratic state. This means that the churches are no longer required by force of administration to formulate "Christian" political policies. There are no Christian nations any more.

Late nineteenth and early twentieth century liberalism represents the final expression of a comprehensive vision of Christian society. The modern missionary movement as represented particularly by the major denominations of Protestantism tied the Gospel to a liberal interpretation of society and politics. Many missionaries to China during the early part of this century carried in their conceptual steamer trunks hope for the immanent coming of the Kingdom of God. This hope was a far cry from the apocalypticism of the Gospels. It was hope for a Christianized world organized around liberal conceptions of evolutionary development through science, medicine, John Dewey's educational philosophy, democratic institutions, and Christian politicians. But confidence in a Christian world order came to a thunderous close with World War II and we have yet to work through its implications.

Today there is no living, concrete expectation for the Christianization of the world, except possibly among certain evangelicals with whom the vision of John R. Mott remains ironically alive. Hence, there is no comprehensive social policy. This means that the role of the church is now limited to acts of mercy, prophetic criticism of secular movements, the encouragement of proper attitudes toward specific historical problems such as racial injustice and discussions about revolutionary movements for liberation.

By the same token, the church has no concrete vision of the Kingdom of God. This also disappeared with World War II. Whereas the Kingdom of God was once visualized, however dimly, in connection with liberal modernity, now the church is impressed by dangers of identifying any historical development with the coming of the Kingdom of God. Hence, the church speaks prophetically to specific problems. For example, in the context of liberal democracies, it calls for justice for the underprivileged and in the context of Chinese Communism, it may call, if given an opportunity, for greater freedom for the individual. It would commend the democracies for human rights and commend Chinese Communism for equality and sobriety without identifying in an absolute sense with liberal or Communist ideologies as such.

This brings us then to the point of Maoist Communism. Roughly speaking, Mao has attempted to do in China what the church tried to do in Christendom--to transform man and society totally through the application of all instruments of change and control available. Christendom was an attempt to make the Kingdom of God an historical reality through human instrumentality. The approach was total-- through missionary witness, preaching, morality plays, by teaching barbarians the Ten Commandments and the Lord's Prayer, by parochial organization, by the just price, Christian jurisprudence, intolerance, and the use of armed forces. The end result was intended to be "Christian society" preparatory to the Kingdom of God in its fullness.

Similarly, Mao conquered China by a total approach--the use of armed revolutionary force, radical structural changes, voluntarism, myth, education, the destruction of enemies, and eschatological passion. All these influences were brought together in a unitive society which is tighter in organization and more powerful than medieval emperors could have imagined. The New China impresses some of us from the West as the secular Marxist counterpart to the Corpus Christianum. The New China combines, as it were, the rigor of the sect with the totality of Christian civilization. The church, having been stripped of its temporal power, has, in effect, deferred to Chinese Communists who are taking up the task of bringing in the "Kingdom," by the application of every conceivable means.

What Christians can learn from China about themselves is their comparative loss of temporal power. What Americans especially need to learn is that the church today "has no abiding place" in the world. Christians are increasingly strangers and pilgrims. Imagine the position of the foreign missionary today. If he can get a visa to a foreign country, he becomes a guest of the country; he has no political power though he may have political sympathies which he must express discreetly, if at all. He may carry some prestige, but if so, it emanates from his nationality rather than from his religion. He may exercise some institutional power, but this is precarious in the face of policies of nationalization. The only power that the missionary has is the power of authenticity, the "power" of the servant, the power derived from memories of the cross and the

Resurrection and the power of the Gospel and the Holy Spirit. The challenge to missionaries today is to exercise power through weakness. Never again shall the church attempt to control history. It shall not define the Kingdom of God in political detail. It shall not align itself with any ideology even though it may speak to concrete situations. It shall not engage in violent revolutionary activity. The church simply cannot trust itself with power. It too would become an oppressor as indeed it did for much of its history.

Radical Christianity, therefore, takes the role of the servant wherever there is suffering. The church labors for justice but it looks to the Spirit to bring in the Kingdom as the Spirit wills. The church will not "seize the Kingdom by force" even though the cries of the oppressed tempt the church to join the "zealots." The coming of the Kingdom belongs to the mystery of God. Confidence in the coming of the Kingdom in the face of weakness and disappointment is the essence of New Testament faith, already a struggle for the disciples of Jesus (Mark 13:3).

With respect to communication with China the church should take advantage of any opportunities it may have. There would appear to be little or no basis for communication from the standpoint of the Chinese, given their memories of imperialism and their attitudes toward religion. Communication in the near future will probably occur, if at all, incidentally and largely accidentally in connection with cultural and scientific exchange. China feels no need to communicate with Christians as Christians. Furthermore, it is not clear at this time what Christians would say were they to communicate with the Chinese. Generally speaking, the Chinese have the moral advantage on the basis of objective behavior and the Chinese are not interested in discussing metaphysics or the Lordship of Christ.

I would suggest, however, that the Chinese situation may not be as fixed as it may appear. The internal life of China is bound to churn in light of ideological tensions and its probable passage to an increasingly technologically oriented society. It would seem that there may be developments in China which would parallel Western experience in which the church has been a major participant. Possibly these would provide some basis for discussion. I refer, for example, to a process of cultural differentiation accompanying modernity. Will China be able to maintain its unitive character in the face of modernity? Does not the experience of Western nations, as well as Japan, suggest the possibility of conflict between the Maoist dream of unity and technology with its sophistication, creativity, individuality, and international cross-fertilization? No ideology has demonstrated its power to cope successfully with modernity. It threatens Marxist ideology, and it may dissolve Maoist ideology unless there is something in Chinese culture which is of a tougher quality. That has yet to be seen.

This is not to suggest that China would see in Christian experience much help in coping with strains of incipient pluralism. Discussion would bring to China only discouraging news since Christianity has given up its ideal of cultural unity. One may speculate that when China recognizes the passing of the Maoist dream it will take recourse in as many "non-contradictory contradictions" as possible and when these fail, China may draw on the Confucian tradition.

It would also appear that China's apparent decisions to develop in the direction of an industrial power commensurate to its size and supply of natural resources will require movement in the direction of a bureaucratically controlled economy along with the routinization of the charisma and the transfer of power by constitutional law. But such a scenario assumes that Western methods of social analysis apply to China. This cannot be predicted with certainty.

Along with problems of cultural differentiation, it may also become evident to the Chinese that the doctrine of "continuous struggle" may try the human spirit more than it can bear. Sometime China may search for sources of consolation in the face of disappointment. As a young movement, Chinese Communism presently experiences the thrill of revolutionary change. But China is also aware of the elusiveness of historical fulfillment. One may be certain that time will set in motion introspective awareness of failure. Disappointment may not necessarily be related to China's success or failure as such. It is the experience of all idealistic movements.

One may question whether Maoist ideology includes resources sufficient to meet the need of more brooding, less revolutionary, generations to come. It may be pointed out that it was in response to moral failure and eschatological

disappointment that doctrines of grace and the sacerdotal
system developed among Christians. Some theologians see
this as an unfortunate development away from Kingdom interpretations of the Gospel but even when Christianity was
most successful in conquering the known world for Christ,
it had to be reassured through channels of grace. Will
China look for sources of grace in the face of waning confidence in the possibility of total transformation?

Another possible area for discussion may be the question of
transcendence. It would appear to some of us who are
admittedly biased by our Western experience that China's
approach to transcendent reality may not be adequate in the
long run. I refer to her reluctance to enter into philosophical discussions about life and death except along
Marxist lines. China's flat and dull naturalistic explanation of things strikes one as inadequately representative
of human experience. To be sure, it is claimed that China
is so preoccupied with practical problems of life that she
does not have time to think about the dimensions of
mystery. She is, of course, currently fascinated by human
transcendence as experienced in community. But certainly
there is more to it than that. Reluctance to talk about
existential experience, quite apart from Chinese reserve,
would seem to be largely ideological. One may wonder
whether a social order which already shows signs of flat-
ness and monotony, despite the beauty and mystery of rural
life, will become intolerably dull with the grayness of
industrial development. Will the time come when that
aspect of human nature which once expressed itself in
diffused and institutional religion finds expression in
the New China? If so, Christians may be in a position to
speak with the Chinese, assuming that in the meantime
Christians have not totally succumbed to the West's own
secular denial of the Spirit!

Furthermore, is it possible that China may look for a
transcendent ground for moral experience? The ethic of
"serving the people" may have needed no more justification
than hardship itself in the early stages of revolution.
But as time passes and presumably standards of living rise,
will there need to be a basis for altruism beyond what is
manifest in the immediate situation--especially if one's
comrade may not always commend himself as especially
worthy of sacrifice? In other words, are not some people
bound to ask why one should prefer another to oneself?
Apart from a conception of a God who loves the unworthy
and expects His frail children to do the same, the answer

may not be self-evident.

The deliverance of the Chinese from the evils of imperialism and the feudal system together with the transformation
of the masses must be accepted as a mystery in the providence of God. God may be heard speaking through China
about the need for deliverance and about the possibility
of massive renewal The call to the church is to repent
for its indifference in the face of injustice and its un-
critical attitude toward decadence. China challenges the
church to find ways within the context of liberal societies
to be effective as an agent of deliverance and renewal
despite its loss of temporal power. The way ahead is not
yet clear but the church will discover the way through
repentance, cross-bearing, and the unpredictable manifestations of the Spirit. Only through radical renewal will
the church be saved from the judgment which is bound to
come upon Western societies for their abuse of freedom.
China too stands under the judgment of God and especially
its idolatrous absolutization of "the people." History
contains enough ambiguity to remind us all--Chinese and
Western Christians--that the strenuous efforts of 1900
years of Christian mission and thirty years of Maoist
revolution have at best brought forth "signs" of the Kingdom. Both Christians and Maoist-Marxists live by faith.
Christians especially live by grace.

NOTES

1. Lucian W. Pye, China, An Introduction (Boston: Little, Brown and Company, 1972), p. 214.

2. Ibid., p. 331.

3. Obviously, the diversity, within Christianity, of views on eschatology, liberation and social organization represents interpretations of New Testament theology rather than the consensus of the church.

4. When references to the "church" are made, the author has in mind generally the Catholic and Protestant traditions as they developed in Western Europe and America. This is a limitation. However, it is necessary because he feels less than qualified to speak from a broader frame of reference on the basis of personal experience.

5. Ernst Troeltsch, The Social Teachings of the Christian Churches (New York: Harper Torchbooks, 1960), Vol. I, p. 63.

II – CHRIST, SALVATION AND MAOISM

Raymond L. Whitehead

Introduction: Why Consider Maoism?

Maoism and developments in the People's Republic of China capture the imagination of many people, not a small number of Christians included. The novelty of Chinese revolutionary thought should not, however, mislead us into thinking that any totally new questions are raised for missiology by the Chinese experience. Non-Christian culture, Marxism, atheism, violent social struggle, secularity, collectivism are all encountered in other contexts, as well as in China.

Yet China still commands our attention because of the overwhelming impact of the Chinese experience. The sheer size of China is a factor. It has been pointed out that the population of China constitutes about a quarter of the human race and Christians another quarter, with minimal overlap between these two.[1] This means that the interaction of Christian thought and Chinese thought involves half the world's people.

In addition, and of much greater importance than the size of China, is the breadth and depth of the Chinese revolution. All aspects of life in China--cultural, religious,

political, economic, social--were severely altered by the
Maoist victory when the country was catapulted from a semi-
feudal and semi-colonial condition toward a modern, revolu-
tionized state.

Another factor which presses China onto our consciousness
is the recollection of the extensive missionary enterprise
there and its sudden demise. China was one of our largest
"missions fields." At the peak of mission efforts in China,
major health and educational institutions were Christian-
run, leaders such as Sun Yat-sen and Chiang Kai-shek were
baptized believers. Hope burned that China would become
Christianized. The complete end of the foreign mission
establishment came with the outbreak of the Korean War.
This was a reversal of the greatest magnitude.

We still have not completely overcome the shock of this
change of fortunes, although the diatribes which the Maoist
victory elicited from the Christian press have gradually
abated. It was "only yesterday" that we read passages
like the following in a 1953 editorial in the Christian
Herald:

> Red lies, red murder, red rape, red slavery and
> red atheism are over half the world today. . . .
> In the United States there are a few . . . 'red
> deans,' red educators, red labor leaders, red
> politicians and red journalists.[2]

The editor criticized Protestant leaders who urged recognition of Red China while the Panmunjom armistice talks
were underway in Korea.

> They /missing American missionaries/ are dead,
> and they were marched, or starved, or shot, or
> tortured to death. Look again at the pictures
> of our American soldiers wired together, executed
> and dumped into mass burials.
> We must sit now in armistice talks with the evil
> men who have done this, but shall we make them
> presently or ever our chosen comrades? Shall we
> give them the honored places of that most loyal
> ally, Nationalist China? . . . Specifically, shall
> we who worship the 'One God and His Christ' support
> a co-equal compact with this government /Red China/
> which is infinitely worse than infidel?
> No!
> The United States must fight this infamy to the

last, and then at last, use the vote.[3]

<u>The Christian Century</u>, a decade later, editorialized on what they saw as Mao's desire for a war against "the white race":

> His /Mao's/ call for worldwide racial war reflects a degree of hatred and desperation which can only be described as psychotic. . . . Mao and the other leaders of China have been isolated so long and so completely that they have lost touch with the realities of the modern world.[4]

It is good to remember that views such as these form a part of our recent past, and represent emotions which are not far below the surface for many of us. This complicates the task of discussing "Christ, Salvation and Maoism." There is a level at which Christ is felt to bring salvation from evils such as Maoism. My own view is quite different, as will become clear below.

I have to admit that I am both enticed and put off by the title, "Christ, Salvation and Maoism." It seems like a topic impossible either to deal with or to ignore. I will first set out the terms of the discussion in a very sketchy way, simply to let the reader know my general position. Then I will proceed with a series of propositions. I feel it is more useful to make some clear, if perhaps controversial, statements about this topic than to attempt a systematic analysis. I am not opposed to a rigorous approach, or to what Europeans still quaintly refer to as "scientific theology." A problem with "rigor," however, is that it also means an inability to respond to stimuli. China floods us with new stimuli. <u>What I am presenting is a working paper, to be used as the basis of discussion, and not a finished document</u>.

The terms "Christ," "Salvation," and "Maoism" arouse emotions which may not be the same for all of us. In <u>Christ and Culture</u>, H. Richard Niebuhr listed several ways in which Christ is understood by various theologians—the liberals emphasize the virtue of love; the eschatologists that of hope; the existentialists that of radical obedience; traditional Protestants that of faith; monastics that of humility. Niebuhr felt that these virtues had to be taken into account in order to understand the teachings of Jesus. He felt that single-hearted trust in God underlay them all.[5] This seems like a useful enough summary for our purposes here, remembering in our definition also that Christ is seen as the Word which was in the beginning, as agent of creation as well as redemption.

Salvation is a process of liberation from the powers of evil; it is both past and present and future; both personal and corporate; it is found within the Judeo-Christian tradition and community, and beyond it as well. Salvation has to do with political, economic, and social structures, and the struggle to overcome all forms of oppression within these structures. Salvation is the movement of communities toward peace and justice; it is continuing growth in freedom and joy. Christians do not own the salvation process, and the Church is not the only locus of salvation, although the Christian may interpret all action toward salvation as the saving work of Christ.

Maoism is a term not used in China. Chinese use the term "Marxism-Leninism-Mao Zedong Thought."[6] "Maoism" is a convenient abbreviated form as long as its meaning is agreed upon. There are various groups outside of China which refer to themselves as Maoist. When I use the term, unless otherwise stated, it refers to Chinese citizens who are followers of "Marxism-Leninism-Mao Zedong Thought."

It is impossible to give a brief definition of Maoism. I would point out three dimensions which are crucial for an understanding of Mao's thought.

(1) Struggle and contradiction are basic and permanent characteristics of the natural order and of human societies and individuals. Revolution is permanent. This is in distinction from views which make harmony and stability basic.
(2) In human struggle there are moral factors at work, issues of justice and dignity. In Maoism it is believed that justice will triumph over its enemies.
(3) Central to Maoism is a vision of the future where fullness and dignity of human life is shared by all. Maoism is future-oriented. There is a paradox in Mao's thought in that he both affirmed that revolution was permanent and also looked to a future society without exploitation.[7]

In dealing with Maoism our starting point is not so much Mao's philosophy, as the realities of Chinese society. What kind of society has resulted from Mao's revolution? Here we are into the crucial and complex question of assessment. How do we assess what has taken place in

China? One cause of anti-China diatribes in Christian
writing is the, perhaps subconscious, realization that if
genuine liberation and human development is taking place
in Mao's China, then our theological security is threat-
ened. "What does it mean," asks C. S. Song, "when atheistic Communist regimes . . . act as liberators from poverty,
starvation, social injustices and human indignity?" It
requires a change in our theology of mission. "An understanding of Christian mission in terms of evangelizing and
converting the pagans and bringing them into the fold of
the church is irrelevant in the context of modern China."[8]

We are still subjected to Anti-China diatribes from those
who seem to be dependent on Western political, philosophical, and religious traditions for their security, as well
as from those whose identity is tied to pre-revolutionary
China. These predictable negative assessments do little
to improve our understanding of China or to enable us to
confront the serious missiological questions which China
raises.

We are confronted with a dilemma. In order to see the
implications of China for theology we need to see China
clearly. But to see China clearly we have to have moved
to a more open theological stance.

This is a dilemma which cannot be resolved here. My own
position, the basis of which is stated in other writings,[9]
is that the main thrust of the Chinese revolution has been
a movement toward genuine liberation, greater justice, and
a revitalized common morality. In this movement there have
been mistakes and mistreatment of people. There are unresolved problems, and the future cannot be predicted. On
the whole, so far, the record is favorable, even exciting.

A series of propositions follows from and gives rise to
this assessment.

Proposition I: Salvation is to be Found in Maoist China.

There is a level on which this proposition cannot be refuted
within Christian theology. Since Creation and Redemption
are not totally separate, since God is the God of all Creation, then China cannot be left out of God's Providence.
In this sense, White South Africa, the ruling classes of
Chile and south Korea and North America, and all kinds of
persons and groups are not totally separated from God's

saving work.

The point here is different. It is based on an assessment
of China which says that in the Maoist revolution to a
significant extent justice is done and the broken are
healed. Insofar as this is true, what Christians call
God's saving power is there.

There are those who claim to disagree with this position on
theological grounds. Charles West has said that it is
idolatrous to identify God's salvation with any particular
human movement.[10] On these grounds the biblical writers
are idolatrous. The liberation of the people of Israel
from bondage in Egypt, a violent event in which Pharaoh's
army was drowned, is interpreted by the biblical writers
and remembered by the people, as God's saving act. It is
a prototype of Salvation referred to again and again in
the entire Judeo-Christian tradition. If a secular historian had been there she may have recorded the event in
different terms from Miriam with her timbrels and dancing
(Ex. 15:20-21). The people saw the event as God's saving
act:

> I will sing to the Lord, for he has triumphed gloriously;
>   the horse and his rider he has thrown into the sea.
> The Lord is my strength and my song,
>   and he has become my salvation;
> this is my God, and I will praise him,
>   my father's God, and I will exalt him.
> The Lord is a man of war; the Lord is his name.
>
> Pharaoh's chariots and his host he cast into the sea;
>   And his picked officers are sunk in the Red Sea.
> The floods cover them;
>   they went down into the depths like a stone.
> Thy right hand, O Lord, glorious in power,
>   thy right hand, O Lord, shatters the enemy.
>   (Exodus 15:1-6)

The biblical writers take the risk of identifying political
events with Salvation History. Examples from the prophetic
literature are numerous. References to the agents of salvation being outside the faith community, like Cyrus, are
not infrequent. C. S. Song pointed this out and said,
"Unless we, like second Isaiah, . . . begin to see those
alien to our faith as making a contribution to the development of human community, as agents of God, our reading of
history will be onesided, and for that reason, poor and

inaccurate."[11]

The principle here is more important than just the question of Maoism. We are called constantly to make decisions about political issues. To simply identify as God's will the causes we discern to be correct would be an error. Nevertheless, it is wrong also to say that such issues and decisions have nothing to do with salvation.

The Japanese scholar, Kazuhiko Sumiya, has compared the Long March of Mao's army with the Exodus.[12] He has done this within the framework of the sociology of religion and not theology. Nevertheless, as a Christian scholar he has suggested a role for the Chinese revolution which goes beyond the minor concession that it may have done some good.

There are no theological grounds on which the Long March and the Chinese revolution should necessarily be excluded from Salvation History. The fact that these events took place outside Judeo-Christian institutional life is hardly relevant, although it bothers many people. Jonathan Chao, responding to Charles West's paper referred to above, praised West for "dismantling the false interpretive structures of the so-called liberation theologians who equate Maoist liberation history with the redeeming work of Christ. He calls such theological betrayal 'idolatry'."[13] What about the so-called evangelical theologians who equate other human movements, such as evangelism campaigns, with the redeeming work of Christ? If the one approach is idolatrous, so is the other. In my opinion, neither is necessarily idolatrous. They become so only if they interpret a particular movement as exclusively, absolutely, and purely, the saving work of God.

The church, with all its service and evangelism programs, is not the exclusive or highest or necessary locus of salvation. "Extra ecclesiam nulla salus" is an unimaginative misinterpretation of the biblical message. One has only to open one's eyes to see signs of what Christians call God's grace, love, saving power, mercy in places beyond the reach of gospel-laden balloons and gospel-laden radio waves. When Christians close their eyes to the human struggles for liberation, cultural dignity, political participation, economic justice, and concentrate on verbal "evangelism," it is not surprising that some are led to wonder if it might not be truer to say, "intra ecclesiam nulla salus."

The God of Israel is a God who acts. Does Yahweh act only through the Judeo-Christian communities? No.

"Are you not like the Ethiopians to me,
O people of Israel?" says the Lord.
"Did I not bring up Israel from the land of
    Egypt,
and the Philistine from Caphtor
and the Syrians from Kir?"
                        (Amos 9:7)

The Judeo-Christian tradition has always discovered salvific meaning in diverse human movements. There are no
theological or biblical grounds for denying the possibility of salvific meaning in the Chinese revolution. The
problem becomes one, then, of our very human and imperfect
assessment of the political, cultural and social factors
at work in that movement.

I would contend that this problem underlies Charles West's
theological reflections on China, although he does not make
it explicit. It is not so much a question of whether or
not we can see God's saving work in human movements, but
in which movements.

Charles West writes:

    . . . (T)he Christian is committed from the roots
    of Biblical reality to a different picture of
    human nature than we see developing in China and
    in Marxism. For the Christian human beings are
    created and called in a relationship: the limit
    of the other person. Human life is not realized
    in collective units but in the exploration and
    cultivation of relationships, respect for differ-
    ences, and mutual change. . . . The imposition
    of any collective vision on these relationships
    dehumanizes and enslaves real people. This is no
    less true in the apparently idyllic conditions of
    China than elsewhere.[14]

We have here, then, an evaluation of culture and values in
China and a comparison of these with West's interpretation
of biblical values. One can ask, however, whether the
anti-community bias in West's view is biblical or cultural.
The covenant community and "corporate personality" in the
Hebrew scriptures, and the "body of Christ" in Christian
writings, suggest a biblical "imposition" of a collective
vision. Does the communal vision in China dehumanize and
enslave any more than the fragmented individualism of the
Western world? In any event, we have to do here with
political questions which can never be separated from

theological and missiological issues.

Whether the Long March, the Chinese revolution and Maoism
can be affirmed within a Christian understanding of Salvation History is a political problem, a problem of assessment. Johannes Aargaard has written, rightly, I feel:

> Salvation today--in China? No need for the ques-
> tion mark. The kingdom of God--in China? How can
> it be questioned? But the church and missions in
> China? That is quite another matter, not unimpor-
> tant, but not that important. A Norwegian old
> missionary lady once said, "Mao has done much harm
> to the church in China, but he has done much good
> for China and China is more important for God than
> the Church in China." This is a true insight. God
> saves the world and the church is meant to be an
> instrument of that salvation. But if it has become
> a bad instrument, it will be cast away. As an in-
> strument it has no value in itself. And God can
> find new instruments of His salvation. That is
> not only so in China.[15]

Proposition II: Faith, hope, love, struggle and sacrifice
are not absent among the Chinese, even though they (almost
universally) are not Christians.

Sacrifice and struggle are clearly present in the revolutionary movement in China. Some of Mao's important essays
are in praise of those who made sacrifices for the revolution. "Serve the People" was a speech Mao gave in a
memorial service for a common soldier, in which Mao said
"when we die for the people it is a worthy death."[16]
Another essay, "In Memory of Norman Bethune," praised the
famous Canadian doctor who gave his life helping the
Chinese wounded.[17]

Nor is love absent in Maoism (although it is important to
see this in relationship to the revolutionary struggle for
justice).[18] Mao, in "Serve the People" said, "all people
in the revolutionary ranks must care for each other, must
love and help each other."[19] One can see the expression of
love in the quality of human relationships in China today.
Joseph Needham has said that in China the second great
commandment, love of neighbor, is practiced more fully than
in countries where Christianity is strong.[20]

Hope is seen in the optimism with which Chinese are

transforming their land. I mentioned above that Maoism is future oriented. It is hopeful about what can be achieved by people working cooperatively, who remain vigilant against new forms of selfishness which may arise.[21]

What about faith in a non-Christian setting such as China? If we use faith as did the Jesus of the Synoptics, then there is no problem. The word faith does not appear in John's Gospel, and only once in the Johannine letters. (In John the word "belief" is of central importance.) In the Synoptics, Jesus spoke of faith most often in dealing with outsiders. The Roman centurion was said to have greater faith than could be found in Israel (Mt. 8:10, Lk. 7:9). Jesus noted the faith of a Samaritan leper (Lk. 17:11-19) and of a Canaanite woman (Mt. 15:21-28). He spoke of the faith of those whom he healed—the paralytic and the blind—who had little chance of knowing and believing the teachings of Jesus.

Faith in this sense might be seen as a basic trust, which is not exclusively tied to any one belief system or religious tradition. Such faith can be found in Maoism—a sense of trust, of being part of an historical movement toward justice, peace, and human fulfillment. There is a confidence in Maoism that the people will triumph because their cause is just. This suggests a latent faith that at the core of the universe there is justice. This faith is pervasive and underlies much of what is said and done by Maoists.

Proposition III: Maoist atheism does not exclude the spiritual dimension of life.

One finds in Chinese life under Maoism a quality which can only be described as spiritual. Flat-headed secularism in the West often lacks both appreciation of the depth of life and commitment beyond selfish interests. In the professedly secular and atheistic society of Maoist China, one finds both.

Commitment can be seen in the willingness of people to live simply for the sake of the larger community. This life style was set during the long years of revolutionary war when harsh conditions were suffered by all those in the struggle. The deep and genuine mourning at the deaths of Zhou Enlai (Chou En-lai) and Mao Zedong resulted to a degree from respect for the simple and dedicated lives these men had led. They were tempered by long years of living in frequent danger under inhospitable conditions.

There is also in China, a sense of the depth and mystery of life. The emphasis on community life rather than self-ish individualism, leads to this spiritual quality. Introducing the communal dimension immediately takes life beyond the narrowness of self. One story might illustrate this. Traveling in China I visited a hospital where I witnessed operations which used acupuncture anaesthesia, the patient being thus awake throughout. In conversation afterward I asked the doctors about the anxiety of a patient facing surgery awake. One doctor explained that prior to the operation doctors, patient and technicians discussed together the role of each, the problems which might be encountered, and how they would be faced. We then go on, he said, to discuss with the patient the meaning of life and why a person wants to be healed. Further questioning led to the statement that Maoists believe a person should want to be healed in order to serve the people. Health, then, is not simply an individual concern, but is a corporate question. Meaning is found by living as a contributing member of the community.

A quality of human understanding came through in this discussion which I find deeply spiritual, and which I find missing in the individualism of Western secular humanism. This communally-based "secular spirituality" is felt by many visitors to China, and causes confusion since it does not fit into our established categories. The editor of the journal Humanist in Canada pointed to this problem. He wrote of a Catholic priest, who on a visit to China, was puzzled because the Chinese seemed to be producing a healthy and virtuous people without the aid of religion. The humanist editor himself, however, was surprised by the religious dimension of Maoism:

> So a Christian and a Humanist visit China. Both are baffled--the Christian because he finds the Chinese living good lives without what he calls religion, the Humanist because he finds that to do so the Chinese seem to need what he calls religion![22]

Mao's poetry captures some of the feeling of depth and mystery in life. Mao's first wife was killed by the Kuomintang (Nationalists) in the 1930's. In 1957 Mao wrote about his "Poplar" (the meaning of his departed wife's name) and a friend's "willow."

I lost my proud Poplar and you your Willow,
Poplar and Willow soar to the Ninth Heaven.
Wu Kang, asked what he can give,
Serves them a laurel brew.

The lonely moon goddess spreads her ample sleeves
To dance for these loyal souls in infinite space.
Earth suddenly reports the tiger subdued,
Tears of joy pour forth falling as mighty rain.[23]

"The tiger subdued" refers to liberation and the defeat of
Chiang Kai-shek. There is a symbolic representation here
of the martyred loved ones sharing in the rejoicing.

Two films have been shown in Toronto recently, one on the
mourning for Zhou Enlai, the other on the mourning for
Chairman Mao. The Zhou film begins and ends with scenes
of clouds and mountains and sea, and the suggestion of
his continuing presence. The Mao film is similar and
included the following song:

Oh, Chairman Mao,
Your footprints are everywhere in our motherland,
Your voice constantly resounds in our hearts.
You visited our tea plantations,
You came to our cotton fields.
Wherever you went, there joy is engraved in our
    memories.
You haven't left us,
You are still at our side.
In the morning sunlight,
We see you walking toward us with firm strides.[24]

"Secular spirituality," it seems to me, describes the
"religious" feeling which underlies these lines, even
though, intellectually, Maoists reject religion.

Proposition IV: The professed atheism of
Maoism should not exercise us unduly.

The problem here is that of the transcendent, of what
Christians refer to as God, Yahweh, Theos, or some reference point beyond the mundane and merely human. A confusion in the discussion of China arises when it is said
that Maoists are trying to transform society and persons
"by human means alone," in distinction from Christians
and others who want to transform the world with divine

guidance and intervention. The confusion is in the assumption that to profess atheism is to exclude God's power.
The immanence of the Spirit in human life and history, of
which Christians speak, is not confined to those who
verbally affirm it. The Christian who says that the power
of God is active in the world is making an interpretive
statement about human individuals and communities. Not
to make that statement, or to deny that statement, does
not of itself change the reality which the Christian describes. To say that the Chinese are transforming society
"by human means alone" is not consistent with a theological understanding of the power of God in the world.

Getting too exercised about the atheism of Maoists is con-
fusing on another level as well. It tends to put the
Christian on the side of theists. In the parable of the
Last Judgment, the saved were those who acted justly. No
reference was made to their particular beliefs about the
transcendent. As Gutierrez and Bonino have pointed out,
Jeremiah implies that to act justly is to know Yahweh.[25]
Atheists who act justly can be said to "know Yahweh."
Christians should not put themselves on the side of
theists over-against atheists, but on the side of justice
over-against those who oppress. This will affect our
priorities in mission.

There are two further points on the question of atheism
in China which must be made. The Maoists are attempting
to overcome the inertia of peasants and workers in order
to change those things which can be changed. By getting
people to build dykes and irrigation systems rather than
to pray that gods or spirits will control flood and drought,
the Chinese are encouraging people to act rationally.
People are thus taught to be innovative and to dare to
resist superstition or defeatism. The Christian can only
rejoice in this development.

A last point is that the Chinese do have an implied "transcendent" of sorts. They talk of the inevitable laws of
history which operate regardless of human will. These
laws move peoples toward liberation and fulfillment. In
a sense the Maoists live with the same necessary paradoxes
as the Christian--a person is morally responsible, yet
there are forces at work over which one does not have
control.

Proposition V: Christians from the West should
resist the urge to evangelize China.

I say Western Christians because I feel it is not my place
to tell non-Western Christians that it is wrong to pursue
evangelistic activities in relation to China if they wish
to do so.   I would raise questions for such persons, if
asked.

There are two reasons why we should resist the urge to
evangelize China.   One is relative to our particular historical situation.   The other is a more general theological consideration.

We are not at the point in history when speaking the word
of the Gospel to China is appropriate.   "There is a time
to keep silence and a time to speak" (Ecclesiastes 3:7).
Keeping silence is not just a negative act.   It can be
self-critical listening, a time of seeking to understand.
The inappropriateness of preaching to China at this point
is not just a matter of chance but is the result of our
own actions in the past.   There is little we can say now
about Christianity that will not be misunderstood.   The
more we appear to be preparing for Christian onslaught on
China, the more we delay the time when any meaningful
communication can take place.

China brings us to an impasse.   There is no way honest,
humble communication can take place now.   We are forced
to choose either silence or dishonest techniques.   We are
uncomfortable with silence, but it may be good for us.

The second reason for resisting the urge to evangelize
China is a deeper theological consideration.   The Christian
who approaches China does not have any exclusive, ultimate, absolute truths to proclaim to the Chinese people.
Christians may point to an absolute they see in the Christ
experience, but our words will always be relative to our
culture, class, ethnic background, and level of faith and
understanding.[26]   It is our lack of self-awareness on this
point, our inability to see our Christian formulations in
all their relativity which caused many of our difficulties with China in the first place.

Does this approach mean that there is nothing the Christian
can do in relation to China but listen and reflect?   No.
It means that we must live and act in such a way that we
will be known by our deeds, our fruits.   Patriotic Chinese

friends in Hong Kong (loyal to Peking) only became interested in the discussion of Christianity when the topic
turned to Christian involvement in the struggles for
justice and liberation. There was curiosity about "Maoist
Christians" in the Philippines, church opposition to the
American war in Vietnam, Christian support for Black
liberation movements in southern Africa. Curiosity is
aroused because, to them, Christians in these situations
seemed to be acting "out of character." Was it possible
that the church was not totally on the side of colonialism
and imperialism?

Christians involved in "politics" may not talk so much
about evangelism, but their deeds preserve or create the
possibility of the word being spoken. Bishop Winter of
Namibia, in a talk in Toronto last year, said that however one may feel about the World Council of Churches'
grants to Black liberation movements, it was this act
which saved the church in southern Africa. To have made
the grants in order to save the church would have been
dishonest (seeking to save its life and thereby losing
it). But the act, done out of conviction, showed that
the church has some commitment to justice and human dignity. Without this, Black people would have given up on
the Church.

Is contributing to Black liberation movements evangelism?
Yes. It is a matter of the fruits of the Christian life
by which we are known.

Such support is not necessary in China now. It is too
late for that. The question Chinese people have every
right to ask, however, is where Christians stand in relation to the struggles for liberation and human dignity in
the world today. Not only where we stand, but what we do.
If our action as Christians are such that it makes the
Chinese curious, that it suggests we are willing to
struggle for human goals, then the possibility of communication will arise.

Is such action enough? What about preaching the gospel
to the nations? In an unpublished paper, "Mandate for
Mission: A Meditation on the Great Commission," Len
Keighley showed how this text (Matthew 28:18-20) has been
distorted in recent times by taking it out of context.[27]
The Great Commission must be seen in relation to the
parable of the Last Judgment in Matthew 25, where those
who are saved are rewarded for their action of justice

and mercy, and are not even aware of verbal formulas of salvation.

Keighley argued that a narrow interpretation of the Great Commission prevents us from "discerning God's initiative in the world around us."

> In the past we would have been very unlikely to entertain the thought, as some of us do today, that, in much we see happening in modern China, God may well be at work creating a 'new humanity' and true community.[28]

The meaning of "teaching them to observe all things I have commanded you" (Matthew 28:20) is explained in terms of love and justice.

> The emphasis is not, our long tradition to the contrary, on profession of faith, conversion and incorporation into the church, but on human values, love for God and man, values of the kingdom yet to come. . . . (H)ow easy it is to narrow down the great commission, and in fact to misinterpret it, if we fail to put it into the context of the whole Bible, or at the very least, into that of Jesus' own life and teachings among men.[29]

The proposition was that Western Christians should resist the urge to evangelize China. To try to evangelize China, given the meaning that "evangelism" has assumed and the techniques it has incorporated, would be a distortion of our Christian faith. Attempts now to evangelize China in traditional ways can only be counter-productive, given the history of relationships between China and Western Christianity. Our impasse in China, however, is also an opportunity to look again at what we mean by evangelism and to move beyond the narrow-mindedness which this term has acquired.

<u>Proposition VI: Salvation is not complete in Maoism, nor in the church and therefore Maoist-Christian dialogue is useful</u>.

Any idealisation of China and Maoism is incorrect, not only from the Christian point of view but also from the Maoist as well. The Chinese would be the first to grant that contradictions, class struggle, corruption, crime,

selfishness, laziness and pride continue in China.
Christians should not be the last to admit that these
problems and more continue in the church.

Not only do problems continue, but there is also an incom-
pleteness about Christian theology and Maoist thought.
Neither is a neat system of dogmas (although some in each
camp would make them that), rather each is open to the
future and seeks truth in particular historical situations.

Is dialogue possible? Not very easily. Christians are
not, for the most part, ready to learn from Maoism. This
is as serious a problem as the fact that Maoists are not
really interested in what Christians have to say.

What was said above about evangelism should not be over-
looked here. Christians will be looked upon by Maoists
in terms of what the Christians do about the problems of
oppression in the world. If Christians are involved in
the struggles for liberation, then the way may be opened
for meaningful dialogue.

A tacit dialogue is already possible. Christians can look
at what Maoists do and say. In a sense, this paper is an
act of tacit dialogue. Other aspects of this tacit dialogue could include looking seriously at Chinese charges
of cultural imperialism in the mission endeavors of the
past, re-evaluating Christian identification with bourgeois
individualism, and pondering the medical and educational
reforms in China in the light of Christian work in these
areas.

Proposition VII: The Churches of the West should make a
statement of repentance for their involvement in structures of imperialism in China prior to Liberation.

Making such a statement should not become, nor be seen as,
a guilt-trip. There is no sense wallowing in guilt of the
past. Repentance is an acknowledgment of guilt in which
forgiveness is already present. It is a turning away from
wrong action and turning toward right behavior. It takes
a degree of maturity to recognize the mistakes of the past
and deal with them. There are indications that Christians
in China feel that Western Christians have never adequately
recognized the imperialist dimensions of the missionary
enterprise in China. If we are concerned about dialogue,

if we are concerned about genuine communication, if we are concerned about truth and justice, then a formal act of repentance by those churches which had mission work in China in the past would be the logical next step.

Some Concluding Comments.

In a sense my conclusions are contained in the propositions which are listed in the paper. I would ask, in the light of what has been said, how do we look to the future of China and Christianity? What might the situation be a century from now? What would we like it to be?

Charles West has said, "China needs the Christian church in its midst, not to add a dimension beyond society to its experience but to confront the theory and practice of its whole common life with their judge and their redeemer." Is this what Christians desire to see in China? The growth and expansion of the church so that it can be the medium of judgment and redemption for Chinese society? How many Christians in how many provinces are required for such a task? Historically, how often has the church played that role well, even when it has been powerful? And what will be the medium of judgment and redemption which keeps the church purified?

Or is it hoped that the so-called doors will open and the opportunity will present itself for outsiders, Western or other, again to enter China to win individual souls for Christ, to pick up the Nineteenth Century mission where it was so rudely interrupted?

Do we hope to see the collapse of the Maoist regime, "red murder and red rape" avenged? Or do we look for the "democratisation" of the Maoist system? Or for the introduction of liberal humanism, a little bit of bourgeois selfishness, with elections every four or five years?

What do I, as a Christian, hope for in China in the next hundred years? Certainly continued progress in areas such as food production, health care, education, industrial organization with worker participation, development of people's culture and art; in other words, development along the revolutionary path China has been taking.

I hope also for spiritual growth in China. I have the same hope for Western society. I do not expect spiritual development in China to come from Christian mission or evangelistic assaults. What I hope for in China and in ourselves is mutuality, a willingness to learn from each other and dialogue in the context of struggle for justice and for a more human future.

NOTES

1. Pro Mundi Vita, "China and the Churches in the Making of One World," in Christianity and the New China (Pasadena: Ecclesia Press, 1976), II, pp. 5-6.

2. Christian Herald, Vol. 76, No. 5, May 1953, p. 16.

3. Christian Herald, Vol. 76, No. 10, October 1953, p. 16.

4. Christian Century, Vol. 79, No. 48, November 28, 1962, p. 1439.

5. H. Richard Niebuhr, Christ and Culture (New York: Harper, 1951), pp. 15-27.

6. I use the Pinyin romanization (Mao Zedong instead of Mao Tse-tung, Zhou Enlai instead of Chou En-lai). See the Glossary in my book, Love and Struggle in Mao's Thought (Maryknoll, New York: Orbis Books, 1977), pp. 155-61.

7. For a fuller treatment of these themes see Love and Struggle in Mao's Thought, pp. 15-21.

8. C. S. Song, "From Israel to Asia: A Theological Leap," in Mission Trends No. 3, ed. Gerald H. Anderson and Thomas F. Stransky (Toronto: Paulist Press, 1976), p. 220.

9. See, for example, Love and Struggle in Mao's Thought, and Committee of Concerned Asian Scholars, China! Inside the People's Republic (New York: Bantam, 1972). The latter was written by several people and there are points with which I would disagree, but I stand by the main thrust of that document.

10. Charles C. West, "Some Theological Reflections on China," China Notes, Vol. XIV, No. 4, Fall, 1976, p. 39.

11. C. S. Song, op. cit., p. 217.

12. Kazuhiko Sumiya, "The Long March and the Exodus: 'The Thought of Mao Tse-tung' and the Contemporary Significance of 'Emissary Prophecy'" in China and Ourselves (Boston: Beacon Press, 1969), eds., Douglass and Terrill.

13. Jonathan Chao, "Responses," China Notes, Vol. XIV, No. 4, Fall, 1976, p. 40.

14. West, op. cit., p. 40.

15. Johannes Aagaard, "Salvation Today--In China?", unpublished paper, no date, mimeographed, probably 1972 or 1973, possibly available from Lutheran World Federation, Department of Studies, Geneva.

16. Mao Tse-tung, Selected Readings (single volume), (Peking: Foreign Languages Press, 1971), pp. 310-311.

17. Ibid., pp. 179-81.

18. See Love and Struggle in Mao's Thought.

19. Loc. cit.

20. Joseph Needham, "Christian Hope and Social Evolution," China Notes, Vol. XII, No. 2, Spring, 1974, p. 18.

21. Love and Struggle in Mao's Thought, pp. 19-21.

22. Humanist in Canada, November, 1976, p. 2.

23. Mao Tse-tung, Poems (Peking: Foreign Languages Press, 1976), p. 33.

24. Translation of sound track accompanying the film Eternal Glory to the Great Leader and Teacher Chairman Mao, mimeographed, p. 23.

25. Jose Miguez Bonino, Christians and Marxists (Grand Rapids, Michigan: Wm. Eerdmans, 1976), pp. 31-38; and Gustavo Gutierrez, A Theology of Liberation (Maryknoll, New York: Orbis Books, 1973), pp. 194ff.

26. H. Richard Niebuhr, op. cit., pp. 234-41.

27. Len Keighley, "Mandate for Mission: A Meditation on the Great Commission," mimeographed, Ecumenical Forum of Canada Occasional Paper, Fall 1975.

28. Ibid., p. 4.

29. Ibid., p. 5.

III – THEOLOGICAL REFLECTION ON CHINA

Charles C. West

An author can only be profoundly grateful when his writing receives as much intelligent critical attention as did the first installment of these reflections.[1] This essay is an effort to continue the discussion with these critics in relation to two issues which were not raised in the earlier paper but which are basic to our subject: (1) What is the theological meaning of Maoism for human history: not just China's history, but that which we all share? (2) What is the place of the Christian Church in that history of which Maoist China is a part?

I. What Does Maoism Mean For Our Christian Understanding Of Human History?

Philip Wickeri, in his critique of the first part of this paper, expresses most sharply a dissatisfaction with my implicit answer to this question, which is certainly shared by many. To "endure the tension between judgment and grace" in a historical movement sounds to him like holding onto the status quo. Instead, he seeks a "messianic word in our situation" which will enable us to participate in the, penultimate to be sure, solving of social contradictions, finding in movements that do this an action of God which is not complete but liberating and

good as far as it goes. Ray Whitehead, in his Bastad
paper, expresses a similar conviction with relation to
China. He draws, rightly, on Gustavo Gutierrez' Theology
of Liberation for theological support: "Salvation, or
liberation, is not final and complete in China, or in any
Christian community, or in any community. Are not all
liberation experiences relative within a process of permanent revolution?"[2] The Chinese revolution, however,
like others, is part of the salvific work of Christ. This
includes even the moments in that revolution that seem to
contradict Christ's own teaching and example, such as
cultivation of hatred for those who opposed the revolution
and rejection of grace and reconciliation prior to the
conquest of power by the revolution's promoters. He calls
for "a theology of struggle" which "will allow room for a
creative hatred or animosity"[3] as a strange work of love
(Tillich's phrase). The cross and resurrection of Christ
are "a sign of hope and struggle, of resurrection and in-
surrection."[4] Grace is the sustaining power of God
through this struggle, expressed in confidence in its
success. This kind of dynamic, Whitehead believes, was
at work under Mao's leadership in China.

Other writers carry the theme further. Parig Digan quotes
Joseph Needham:

> The Chinese society of the present day...is, I
> think, further on the way to the true society
> of mankind, the Kingdom of God if you like, than
> our own. I think China is the only truly Chris-
> tian country in the world in the present day, in
> spite of its absolute rejection of all religion....
> Where is Christ to be found?.... Where the good
> are and where good things are being done.... That
> means appreciating what is happening in China at
> the present day.[5]

Digan will not go so far. But he does suggest (1) that
if ours is a history of salvation, the work of the Communist revolution in China must be seen as in some sense
"a work of God, a work of Christ, and even a work of the
Church,"[6] and (2) that the kerygmatic message of the
church has become so mixed with western worldly power in
the past that the church's mission must be expressed "more
in terms of leavening the world than of churching the
people" today.[7]

All of these witnesses want to say yes to God in history

by an active participation in its creative movements which
bring liberty to the oppressed and justice to society.
Who could disagree? But what does it mean to say yes to
God in such a history and how does this relate to affirming the powers and ideologies that have put themselves in
charge of the struggle? Where do we go, to discover what
God may be doing to save people yesterday, today, and to-
morrow? If I must disagree with the theology of history
these expressions reflect, it is primarily because I find
in the Bible a different pattern of interaction between
God's salvation and human struggle than this. I find there
the story of a people--Israel first, then the church--
called not to wield great power, or to sanctify the power
of others, but to live as servants and witnesses of the
power of God that transforms both them and the world.
The people of God in the Biblical history were oppressed
and struggled against it. Often they hated their enemies,
as the Psalms show. But:

a. It was God who fought for them, and his victory
prevailed. When they depended on their own strength they
were defeated. When they sought victory according to
their own interests and ideologies they were corrected.
It was God's plan, not their liberation struggle, that
was realized, reaching out to embrace all peoples.

b. God called his people into a covenant with himself.
This relationship is the starting point, not the goal of
liberation. Gutierrez has his theology backwards. One
who is free in Christ participates in the reality of the
risen lord of the world, even while oppressed by the
powers of the world. The struggle for social liberation
is a consequence of this and is controlled both in its
method and goals by the God who has revealed himself in
Christ. When it happens the other way around, the result
is only the substitution of a new tyranny, on the other
side of the revolution, for the old.

c. The God who called his people in the Bible into
covenant also called them to repentance, that is, to continual self-transformation by his Spirit guided by his
law, so that they would be more faithful servants and
witnesses of him. In both the Old Testament and the New--
and not least among the crowd that followed Moses out of
Egypt--the enemies of God are within as well as without.
The Psalms over and over again ask for liberation from an
unrighteousness in the world and in the self. Whether
this openness to repentance and reform is effectively
present is the test of the trustworthiness of any earthly

power, conservative or revolutionary.

    d. The goal of the Kingdom of God is his peace which comes through the grace by which he forgives transgressors and reconciles them to one another and to himself. This is the dominant theme of history, not the struggle of people for liberation conceived in terms of their own ideologies. The entire power struggle needs to be understood in this context. Because this is so, no power, of status quo or revolution, is as such God's saving or liberating instrument. The best any police force--or any guerrilla band--can do is neutralize brutal counterforce so as to make the development of meaningful covenant relations, undergirded by grace and forgiveness and the mutual affirmation we call justice, more possible. Here is where real change in society takes place. Revolution by coercive power may be necessary, like war, sometimes, as an <u>ultima ratio</u>. But nothing in the Bible allows us to call it a means of grace.

If this is so, and if the Biblical history is the key to understanding the realities of our history, I think it means three things: (1) To make Christ known, by words and by the style of our obedience, is the first task of the church for the sake of the world anywhere, any time. (2) The church is called to affirm the powers of this world and help them to perform their legitimate tasks of promoting peace and justice in society. Because of Christ's risen power, it starts with a positive, supporting attitude toward them. (3) By this very token, the church will undermine the ideological claims of these powers to be more than their task requires, or to be purer than human powers can be. Part of its task will be to debunk the rationalizations of the holders of power, to remind them of limits, and to support effective limiting counterpower, where it can. Another part will be to serve as advocate for those whom power oppresses and exploits, wherever they are, and whatever the regime under which they suffer.

With this as background, what can be said about China? I suggest four things.

First, China is unique in the radicality with which it has grasped the problem and promise of universal history in the twentieth century. In this sense it is the world's most drastic response to 2,000 years of the Christian mission. Parig Digan is certainly right in saying that

the work of the church has had a hand in making China what
it is today, not so much through the direct influence of
its mission there, as by the sense of historicity which
it imparted to the whole impact of the western world on
China, including imperial industry, commerce, military
might on the one side, and political-social ideas, both
liberal and Marxist, on the other. Historians would be
hard put to find another example at any time of a great
civilization sweeping away, even savagely repudiating, its
entire culture, on behalf of a modern foreign ideology
adapted only in practical emphases to its new society.
But this is what has happened in China. A special cultural history, with its emphasis on the past, has been
surrendered for an ideology that purports to explain all
of history in every place in terms which are a secularized
reflection of the Christian themes of creation, the fall,
redemption and the coming of the Kingdom.

China has in short been historicized and ecumenized. It
has happened in Marxist terms. The promise and command
of God have been appropriated as the power of the people
and the laws of historical development. But in the long
run these will not be an adequate vehicle. The power of
God has been humanized into the power of the Party. But
this power is morally and spiritually ambiguous. The
question is bound to arise, as it has already in other
Marxist-dominated countries: where is the historical
power that transcends the human with its inhumanities?
Where lies hope? In this positive and negative sense
Communist revolution in China is an episode in the _missio
dei_.

Second, the events of twentieth-century China are without
doubt a judgment of God on an ambiguously missionary church
which failed to grasp the divine promise for a revolutionary situation. This is not to say that Christian missions
in China were in no sense servants of God's mission. It
is only to say that a dimension of the Gospel was missing
or distorted in those missions: the dimension of social
judgment and promise for a country that desperately needed
models to cope with the new powers that were both transforming and disrupting her life. The fault lay in the
sending churches themselves. The nineteenth century was
a time of culture--Christianity on the one hand, which had
too much confidence in the benevolence of imperial power,
and of evangelical dualism on the other, that could not
understand the promise of God for the world. In neither
case did a style of interaction between church and the

powers of the world arise which might have generated an effective Christian critique of power and Christian social movement. So the Gospel message so faithfully preached and the many service projects conducted with so much love and sacrifice lacked a context in the discern-ment of the signs of the times. It left the Christian churches exposed, along with other Chinese, to Communist power and ideology

Third, there are characteristics of Communist Chinese rule about which any observer of China must say, they express the God-ordained task of government better than most pre-vious regimes. Efficiency in meeting human need is one of the most obvious. There may be starvation still in China, as some observers maintain and distribution of food and basic necessities may not be completely equal. But com-pared with the glaring inequities of the past, the demands of distributive justice are, on the whole, much more satisfied. A spirit of equality and of public service undercutting corruption and private ambitions is another example. Even taken at a discount for propaganda, the Chinese achievement here is impressive.

Potentially most important, however, because it repre-sents a real advance in Marxist theory, is the concept of continuing revolution. It is also the most ambiguous. It is the means whereby people examine themselves, each other and their government, in the light of the purposes and values they share. It also is the means whereby ideological conformity is enforced right down to the private thoughts of the peasant and worker. It is poten-tially a way of openness to the other and this is its theological importance. No matter that God is not men-tioned in the first instance. When the powers in charge of society allow challenge and dissent, they are beginning to acknowledge that they are only powers for a function and not gods. Can China institutionalize what no other Communist government has been able to allow? Can the ideological terms which limit the idea of continuing revo-lution be burst so that freedom of religion, freedom to relate to the past, and freedom to communicate with people of other ideologies and societies will be restored? The evidence does not invite a positive answer so far, but one can hope.

Finally, if one wants to search out the Christian meaning of Maoism for history, one must go to the people who are living that history at the most exposed point, to the

Christians in China today. I mean all the Christians:
the K. H. Tings, Y. T. Wus and others who have tried to
lead the ever dwindling organized church along a path of
cooperation with the government, the resisters who harbor
their faith and their fellowship as secretly as they can,
the old pastors and priests who still try to minister, and
the young who hear afresh by word of mouth about Christ
and his church. We know too little about these people,
though we have evidence enough that they exist. As Christians they are clearly outside the plan and purpose of
Communist China. Doubtless they have little time and
few resources to develop a sophisticated encounter with
Maoist ideology or a Christian social ethic of their own.
They live, they suffer, they serve, they witness. They
are carrying the seed of China's future more directly than
anyone in government. It is they who, in the long run,
will judge whether any insights we have about the Christian meaning of current Chinese history are valid.

II. What Is The Place Of The Christian Church In That
History Of Which Maoist China Is A Part?

There are some, like Needham above, who feel that Maoist
society has taken the place of the church, so we no longer
need it. Digan, as we have seen, suggests a suspension
of church-building activities in favor of leavening
society. K. H. Ting, in the most recent interview with
him, pictures a dwindling church in a happy society where
people can get help in suffering from the government and
don't find personal disharmonies a great problem any
more. He would not be surprised to see Christianity die
out when the present generation passes, though he thinks
there will always be a few people who will find in Christianity answers to the ultimate questions of life.
Donald MacInnis gathers these thoughts together with the
comment:

The indigenous Christians, and those in the West,
if they are to serve as the salt and leaven of
society, must practice that kind of self-giving
and responsiveness to divine grace that will lead
to the rediscovery of the church's "ultimate
identity precisely in that divine self-emptying
through which it...first came into existence.
It is only in such a perspective, in such a
church, in such a world--all three being still

in the making--that the legacy of Christendom
and the century of Mao Tse-tung can ever be seen
as reconcilable."[8]

The problem with all of these expressions is not in what
they affirm but in what they deny. It is right that the
church should empty itself and take the form of a servant,
that it should not be self-centered, that its one reason
for existence should be the revelation it gives and not
other benefits. But this is a second fact about the
church, not the first. Does one detect in each of these
expressions a certain embarrassment about the first fact?
The church exists because Jesus Christ is the risen lord
of the world, the judge and redeemer of Mao Tse-tung and
his communists as well as of Christians. The church is
the place where this Christ is known and confessed by
sinful people who are healed and directed by his word and
sacrament. There may be all kinds of other influences in
the church as well: triumphalism, imperialism, cultural
pride, exploitation, fanaticism, even hatred. But in the
church Christ himself defeats these enemies, brings about
repentance and new life. He is the major actor there.
There is no non-confessing church therefore. A body of
Christians that only repents, or that only serves, and
does not consciously refer the world to its lord, is not
a church, but something less.

The first task of the church therefore is to be indeed
the church, as the Oxford Conference put it so many years
ago. This means, I think, two things, which interact
with each other.

     a. The church is not to be conformed to the world, not
even Mao's world, beautiful as it is in some people's eyes.
It is not to take its standards of judgment from there.
It is rather to be conformed to Christ as he confronts
the world and transforms it. The church lives in the
wonderful reality of Christ, works out from there the
implications of that reality for all the society, and
looks forward to the coming of his kingdom. We Christians
of the western world have not taken this calling seriously
enough. We have been too worldly and have covered our
worldliness with gospel words. The other part of the
world has spotted this and called us hypocrites. They
were right but they didn't know the half of it. It is not
by the standard of Marxist ideology or Maoist revolution
that we were wrong, but by the standard of our missionary
calling itself to share the being of Christ in and for the

world. The way of repentance is not to identify with any
human movement but to rediscover the calling and identity
we have been given and thus both to serve and to proclaim.

b. The church is the world before God. All of us are
part of the world--Americans, Chinese, businessmen, revo-
lutionaries, clergy, laity and the rest. The church is
the place where the world in all its variety, its conflicts, its pride and its need, is concentrated in the
presence of God and works out its relationship with him.
We are all in this together. We need each other's counsel, prayers, and sometimes critique if we are to discover
the ways of God with our various but interlocking spheres.
This is the only reason for Christians concerning themselves with mission in other lands and cultures than their
own. Dr. Chao Tien-en, in a comment on my earlier paper,
put it thusly:

> It seems that the Christian doctrines of man, of
> history, and of culture are basic theological
> foundations necessary for authentic theological
> reflection on China, or any human movement. But
> why China? Is there any theological justification
> for this selection? The meaning and justification
> must be found within the realm of missiological
> concerns. Otherwise I strongly object to such
> objectification and theologization of my people.[9]

Only, then, as we submit ourselves to God in the church,
and to our fellow Christians in the Lord, does any of us
have any business concerning ourselves with the missio
dei in another land. Because the promise of God is ecumenical however--more ecumenical still than imperialism
or the socialist revolution--we must discern it together,
for us all.

The church, then, is that part of the world which knows
itself in the presence of God, is judged and redeemed and
conformed to Christ by God in all of its common life. It
knows that this is happening to and for the whole world
as well. Therefore, the church will be evangelistic in
its service to the world's needs. It will witness to
Christ's reconciliation in its participation in the
world's struggle for social justice. It will commend
Christ to others in its repentance for worldly sins. It
will not separate itself in a religious sphere concerned
only with ultimate questions. Neither will it lose itself in some human power movement, Maoist, imperialist,

technocratic or otherwise. If it is faithful it will
always be somewhat uncomfortable to the powers that be,
just in the way it serves, proclaims, celebrates and is.
Out of this tension comes a transforming influence in
society that no revolution can offer, and a humanizing
vision that no humanist ideology can give to itself.
This is the calling of the church in China--and in the
United States.

NOTES

1. See "Some Theological Reflections on China," in China Notes (publication of The National Council of Churches), volume 14, No. 4 (Fall, 1976), pp. 37-42. (This second installment originally appeared as "Theological Reflection on China - II," in the Spring, 1977 issue of China Notes, pp. 16-18.)

2. Christianity and the New China, South Pasadena, California: Ecclesia Publications, 1976, volume 1, p. 73.

3. Ibid., p. 80.

4. Ibid., p. 83.

5. China Notes, Spring 1974.

6. China and the Churches, Pro Mundi Vita, 1975, p. 23.

7. Ibid., p. 20.

8. "The People's Republic of China--Challenges to Contemporary Missiology." Unpublished manuscript, p. 27. The quote within the quote is from the French Catholic journal Fides, April 4, 1973.

9. China Notes, Fall 1976, p. 41.

IV – CHINA AND GOD'S PRESENCE IN HISTORY: A PANEL DISCUSSION

On the second day of the Notre Dame Conference a panel of Theologians gathered to reflect on how the events of the past thirty years in China may relate to the purposes of God in human history and what such relations might teach us about the mission of the Christian Church in China.
The panel was composed of Professor Charles West (Princeton); Professor Langdon Gilkey (Chicago); Dr. Raymond Whitehead (Canadian China Program); Rev. Joseph Spae (Pro Mundi Vita; Brussels); and Dr. Lawrence Burkholder (president of Goshen College, Goshen, Indiana).

(The following account represents an edited and slightly compressed version of the panel discussion.)

(Charles West introduced the discussion by outlining the three major questions under consideration:)
First, the question: how are the events in China during the past thirty years related to the purposes of God in human history? I think that's a general question which has popped up in dozens of ways in the last two or three days, and has to do with our theological understanding of

human history and our understanding of the direction which
human history has taken in Chinese culture both before and
after the victory of Maoism. The question of the salvific
implications of that is one part of it, and the question of how
or in what way we can speak of divine judgment at work in
these events is the second, and third, the question of
grace.

Secondly, and related to this: what is the importance, if
any, of the mission of the Church in China today? I put
it that way without raising yet the question (underneath
that would be the question of mission from outside or
mission from within) of what form it should take.

Here, three sub-questions suggest themselves: (1) How
important is it to make known the Christian message in The
People's Republic of China, and is the question evangelism?
If the answer to this is yes, then we can ask: how? (2)
What is the relation, if any, of the religious dimensions
of Chinese Marxism, or Maoism, to the Christian message,
and what should be the form of the cultural covenant (I
take that phrase from Langdon Gilkey's opening lecture)
with the Chinese people? You will remember that the
analogy that he drew was the cultural covenant with Hellenism in the early centuries of the existence of the Church,
and suggests this might be a model for it. How does the
Christian message relate to the religious or transcendent
dimensions or the open dimensions of Chinese Marxism, if
there are any? (3) What is the importance of the Church
in Chinese society and of Church-building, if any?

These I take to be the basic questions which have been concerning us here. Another, ancillary question concerns
certain themes in Chinese Marxism: the role of struggle
and of continuing revolution in Chinese Marxism; the question of how we evaluate that theologically; how we evaluate
the issues of personal freedom versus collective justice--
these are the terms which just indicate a range of problems.

How do we understand theologically this range of questions
which have to do with evaluating individual liberties and
social justice and the interaction between? Finally, how
do we evaluate the spirit of self-sacrifice for the people
and the political force which sustains it in Communist
China? These themes are not necessarily related to one
another, but they are themes which also came up. So with
that agenda, I invite the members of the panel to plunge
in at any point where they find they would like to take off.

(Ray Whitehead responded to the first question, concerning the recent history of China and the salvific purposes of God:)
I personally am very careful to use the word salvation in connection with China in a very, very guarded way. In fact, I just don't use it at all. I don't use it because it's a big thing, as one of my colleagues here said, and it raises problems which are of a speculative nature; I love to speculate on theological things and indeed, a lot of speculation has gone on in the history of the Church, as you well know, as to whether it is possible for people outside the Church, outside the Christian tradition, to be saved. There are indications in the Church Fathers, and in fact, in the New Testament (specifically, Colossians) of a positive answer to this question. I have a theology which says it is indeed possible that God may be saving people out there, and I've said that in some very evangelical circles. But to say that it is happening, is to me, at this point, presumptuous. It is speculative, to be sure, and to say it with certainty is presumptuous. It is presumptuous because to say who is saved is a pretty adventurous thing in any case, anywhere. It's up to God.

Secondly, there are just so many ambiguous elements in China that it becomes extremely uncertain, and it raises a red flag in a lot of circles.

(This issue of salvation and how to judge who is saved opened up a number of other questions, both practical and historical:)
Archie Crouch (Editor, Daily Report: People's Republic of China): Then it would be presumptuous for me to say I am saved.

Ray Whitehead: Well, you could say you're saved--there's an element of faith there, to be sure, or trust. You can be very confident, but you can't be absolutely sure. Now what I would say is, a lot of people are living better, acting better (in China); we can learn from that. At the same time, a lot of people have suffered more because of it, and so on. So I would just suggest that the point at which the salvation question will become real is the point at which China opens up, if it does. Then it becomes not a speculative question only, but a practical question.

Charles West: Can I come in on that? As I understand the use of the word "save" and "being saved" in the Bible, it has several levels of meaning. In the Old Testament it means exactly what Ray (Whitehead) said it meant in the paper: you're rescued. You're rescued from your enemies, saved from your enemies. So it is throughout the Pentateuch--a very simple, very external meaning. In the Psalms there is a deeper meaning because at one and the same time the Psalmist pleads for salvation from his enemies, rescue from his enemies, victory over them, and he will ask to be saved from his own unrighteousness, his own sinfulness, and therefore to be cleansed. So you have that ambiguity there also.

In the New Testament the word saved is really not as prominent as many of our evangelical friends have made it in their preaching. Justification is a more important concept and justification means you are made right and just by God's intervention turning you around and putting you into a proper relationship with him and with your neighbor. And then sanctification--growth and holiness--comes on top of this.

Now in theology, salvation has usually been what happens at the end of the whole process of one's life--a life of being sanctified by the God who is holy, by no power of one's own, but by responding to him. Now if you talk that way, then it seems to me it is inappropriate to talk about the building of social justice and the achievement of good things in this world by any social movement or even by an individual as salvation. It's good in itself, but salvation is coming into that ultimate relationship with God, and when we say that those outside the Church can be saved and that God's saving power is far beyond anything we can control, we're talking about God's concern, of how God will work with the whole lives of people, and it doesn't undercut in any sense the urgency with which we want to bring people into a positive relationship with God in Jesus Christ here in this world, in order that they may be fruitful and creative in expressing that relationship for the help of their neighbors.

Ray Whitehead: I think what we get down to, what you're raising, is the question of the individual being brought into this understanding of the right relationship with God. This gets down to the very question, then, that I raised-- of what it is we hope for in China. And the question on my mind then is: what is the next step on the basis of the definition of salvation? Is the fullness of life possible for people in China today only if by some means they can be confronted with the Christian Gospel in some explicit way? And if so, then does that justify the electronic evangelism and the bringing of Bibles and balloons into China, and so on, that is being attempted? What I suggested in my paper is that there can be a time for silence; in other words, we cannot honestly evangelize the Chinese people today, and does that mean they can't be saved because we can't do it? I start out with how one agonizes in the situation and then try to find the theological answers to those problems. And I just cannot justify this--what seems to me dishonest techniques of evangelism in China, nor can I decide that the people of China are somehow deprived because of this.

(At this juncture Langdon Gilkey shifted the focus of the discussion on China and salvation to the larger question of the relation of culture and religion:)
I like the phrasing of our agenda, "The purposes of God in human history," rather than the word salvation, though I don't want to separate the two because it seems to me that the debate we're carrying on here concerns the relationship of God's purposes and action to history. This is history in culture and this has been the substance of, I think, the most important debate, at least in Protestant and I think probably now in Catholic theology (considering Liberation Theology) in the last 200 years, and we've flipped back and forth on this. The nineteenth century was devoted to the realization that people had to be saved culturally, socially, historically in order to be saved. This was Rauschenbush's great insight and we've all learned from it and I don't think any of us in this room would want for a minute to relax that wonderful point, that people in Hell's kitchen who were driven to poverty, to prostitution, can't be called to be saved because something has happened inside. It's this, I take it, that Ray is witnessing to.

I think what the twentieth century has discovered and reacted too much against was that--as I think Niebuhr was the man who put this so marvelously--you can have indeterminate possibilities of justice, but the problem of sin remains. Our own experience with the Enlightenment seems to me to illustrate the ambiguity of even the greatest cultural achievements and to illustrate to us that (I'm speaking about our own culture) here was a culture with this tremendous hope of bringing this historical salvation to mankind, and we can feel the depth of the ambiguity of it and how much more each one of us individually needs and how much more is necessary for human life to be full

even when you have levels of justice that you never dreamed
of, which we do have. But, heavens, we're still all--I
won't even use the verb that comes to mind--messed up.
And I suspect I get uneasy about salvation in China because my own somewhat gloomy view of history leaves me to
feel that what happened to the Enlightenment culture may--
you can never tell--may happen there and that there may be
depths of estrangement and of grace that are needed for
humans to be human in that situation.

I tried in my opening remarks to make a distinction among
the three great enemies: fate, sin, and death--I think
they're all very real, and they must be distinguished. I
tried to interpret fate as the kind of historical oppression that institutions bear, which is the Church's responsibility. This was the discovery of the Enlightenment and
of the social gospel. But this does not eradicate the
problem of sin, and certainly doesn't eradicate the problem
of death. There is every reason to bring the gospel, but
there's every reason to say God's providence is at work in
China and to welcome that, it seems to me. God's providence was at work in the Enlightenment, and we should
welcome this. I feel uneasy using the word "salvation"
(which includes fate, sin, and death to me) about any of
this and therefore I'm a little hesitant about it; but
heavens, let's say God's providence is at work there. God
is at work wherever justice is found, wherever there are
new levels of human community. We all know that even
though this happens, humans are still estranged, and that
there can be a message, as Charles put it, of justification
even in that estrangement, of the need for acceptance even
when there are high levels of these things. So I would be
inclined to say that we urge the whole richness of Christian symbolism, of creation, providence, revelation, atone-
ment, eschatology, and not get them too much mixed up
because then you've got, well, salvation, as I remarked,
as sort of the big bang at the end, but it is not very
clarifying at that point.

(The panelists then turned to a reflection on God's work in
history in terms of the Christian vocabulary of providence,
judgment and grace.)
Charles West: I think maybe the issue may be sharpened if
we use those words, judgment and grace, as an explication
of providence.

Langdon Gilkey: From the Old Testament it seems to me that
providence and new possibility, judgment and new possibility,

is a way of looking at the way God works in history. I
think one can find this in II Isaiah; one can find it very
beautifully also in Whitehead, in Tillich, in Ernst Bloch,
in the fact that history does produce new possibilities,
and China, heaven knows, is one. Now this is not exactly
the New Covenant, but it's an analogue in history of what
God is doing.

Joseph Spae: I think that what Langdon has said is that
once one has evolved a certain methodology to speak to this
question, then we can say that God is definitely at work
in China. I would call this the deductive method. You
got your information from the Bible; you got the information from Revelation. God wants every Chinese to be saved;
He wants it practically, existentially, and He makes no
exceptions for whoever the person is, wherever the person
was born, including Mao Tse Tung himself. This is the
deductive principle and is important in our effort to
understand God's salvific action in China. Now, at the
same time, when you say He is at work and He wants them to
eat--that is what I would call an inductive principle which
I bring into the question. Namely, without first of all
wanting to penetrate the mystery of salvation which is
beyond us and therefore giving God credit for also the
crooked ways to get to His final point, I would say that
somehow inductively we could find Him at work if the degree of humaneness, of humanity, the possibility of being
a fulfilled human being is being given by the particular
society in which He is at work, and to the degree that
this society calls salvation--here I think initially we'd
make a little distinction between the private salvation--
whether you are saved or he is saved--but salvation in the
Bible is really a community affair. To what extent is
present-day modern society amenable, conducive to, the
formation of a full human being, fully alive, which would
then be _ad gloriam Dei_, to the glory of God, as St. Gregory
of Nicea says?

Now, in this inductive affair, I think that many of us here
would want to have different opinions. In other words,
we might say not very much. It's a very oppressive society. Solzhenitsyn, a few weeks ago in Paris, when they
asked him about China, said, "I wouldn't be surprised that
the whole of China is one Gulag Archipelago." However, it
will take a Solzhenitsyn to bring that to the attention of
the West. In other words, regarding the quality of this
salvific action as it is inductively being seen within the
given existential situation of China, I think on this point,

as many of us have said, we ought to be awfully modest because we know so little about the real inner workings of the human mind within the possibilities that are given.

Ray Whitehead: We have to ask where Solzhenitsyn gets his information on China. Does he have clear information on that? He may have got it while he was in Russia and it might not be too dependable.

But what I would ask on the basis of Father Spae's earlier statement is why we are trying to make this inductive judgment or discernment? I think it leads us into some of the other questions that we listed. I mean, what are we going to do with this? If God's action is taking place there, it really doesn't bother us too much. I mean, it is there or it isn't there--that's something we don't have any control over or responsibility for. But I think there's another level of the discussion. If we discern demonic forces at work, then are we somehow responsible to react to them, to deal with them? Or how are judgment and grace expressed as these questions are raised within that context? And I would be very hesitant to say that either the judgment or the grace is mediated through the Church in that context. So maybe Charles (West) can tell us how he would see the judgment of God at work in China today.

Langdon Gilkey: Well, I would think that if one takes the prophetic word, and I think a great number of theologians--I think of Augustine particularly--have interpreted this correctly, the judgment of God is certainly warned by the prophet, but it's history that enacts the judgment of God. Now I would say the judgment of God on Western culture for its imperialism, for its technology at the present is being enacted, unfortunately, not by the poor little Church--then it wouldn't hurt us at all--it's being enacted by the forces of history.

It's very important, it seems to me, because of reactions to this kind of thing, as I tried to indicate, that there be a witness to one's own responsibility to a community in this judgment which the forces--the inexorable forces of history which I think the prophet meant by the judgment of God (and I would too)--are enacting. But it wouldn't be the Church that would bring the judgment of God on history. It would witness to it, but it jolly well better not be a mission Church; it better be a Chinese church if they're talking to the Chinese. I think it's very important for

the Church here to witness to the judgment of God on the
United States in terms of the destructive elements in world
order and so forth that we perpetuate. But it's a witness
to it--it isn't that we are bringing it there.

Ray Whitehead: Would you say the same thing about grace
also?

Langdon Gilkey: Yes, yes, right, absolutely. If it were
left up to the Church, the show would have stopped long
ago.

(The discussion now turned to the second major question before the panel: the mission of the Church, if any, in China.)
Charles West: The practical question, the question because
of which we are interested in all of this is: is there a
calling to the Church to do or say something about that
Chinese reality? That's really the second question here:
what is the importance, if any, of the mission of the
Church in China today?

Taking up your point about witness, I would say that it is
of critical importance. Without making any negative
statement about what God could not do if there were no
Church, it is nevertheless of critical importance that
there be a positive and definite witness to the Christian
message, to God and to His activity, which is trying to
be faithful to the actions of God in judgment and grace
in this society which lives in the presence of God, which
celebrates His presence in Christ and is nourished thereby
and is a community gathered around that center. It is of
critical importance for Maoist China that there be such a
witness in order to add a dimension, perhaps to sharpen
the conflicts or to add a dimension of understanding to
what is going on there. In other words, God calls His
Church--He calls it also in China, and that is a part of
His purposes in history also with relation to this communist society.

One other point: I think He calls the Church ecumenical.
Now, He calls not the American Church to go over there,
and not only the Chinese Church to arise from within, but
the Church ecumenical in the presence of this ecumenical
reality which is Chinese communism. I think that has to
be kept in mind as the point which transcends the nationalism of which we have to be so careful.

Joseph Spae: I think that what you say now, Charles, is

extremely valuable because the whole conference has been
dealing with the Church's role toward China. Subcon-
sciously, we want to do everything we can for the Chinese
people. We would like to bring them salvation--whatever
that means. And then the question can be turned around,
and it is an equally difficult question to answer--what
is the salvific role of China in regard to the Church?
Let me speak for the Roman Catholic Church, if you don't
mind, and a little bit for the Vatican where, after all,
I was working for four years. I tell you frankly, China
is weighing very heavily on our liver as we say in Flemish--
on our heart, you know--totally undigestible, totally unacceptable that one-quarter of mankind behaves that way it
behaves, and God forbid the Holy Spirit may be at work
there while they do not seem to need, as of now, the witnessing which we should legitimately and on the basis of
our very mission of the Church have brought to them.

So my question would be, can this meeting here come to
grips with that particular question? What is the salvific
role of China towards the Church? I have myself tried to
give an answer, so if you don't mind, the way I see it, I
would think that in China, there are millions of people
through whom the Holy Spirit invites us to a rethinking
of our faith. It is evident that historically speaking--
I'm not speaking about the past 25-35 years--but historically speaking, we have failed convincingly to appeal to
the Chinese to the point where they could really take us,
in the best sense of the word, as the disciples of Christ.
They missed us somehow in history, and if they brush us
off now, and it was so difficult for the intellectuals to
see what Christianity stood for, well, it's not only because they were too dumb to see what we were, it was simply
because we were not to be seen as indeed witnessing to the
benignity and the humanity of Lord Jesus. Therefore, the
first conclusion to be drawn in this role of China is that
our own witnessing to Christ was too feeble in history to
be understood by them. I will put the blame on us rather
than on them. They can take their share in history before
the eyes of God Himself.

Secondly, and this is a point to which I am very much committed, as many of you know, I do think that in our witnessing, the weakness of our witnessing has largely been
due to the fact that we as churches stood before the world
racked and riddled in our divisions. Charles brings up the
ecumenical meaning of the problem, but this is an extremely
important meaning which I have felt to the quick,

particularly in my work in Japan, and it must have been like this in China, too.

And therefore, could it not be said that at present the Chinese people are addressing to us what in Greek theology we call the Logos Paraclesios--a certain silent exhortation--they sit there and they watch you? And they watch you already for centuries and you never come through somehow. And it is not that they are judging us or anything like that. You might say there is a tremendous yearning, of "you have it; well, damn it, why don't you show it if you have it?" Excuse my language.

There's a silent "word of exhortation"; this is a term which occurs in Hebrews, 13:22. And then there's a kind of a speechless appeal which, to my mind, should contribute very much to the consolidation of our own faith because it warns us (Colossians, 2:7-8) not to be trapped and deprived of our freedom as Christians by some second-hand, empty, rational philosophy based on the principles of this world rather than on Christ. And finally, I would hope that this meeting at least says one word about the necessity of expressing ourselves, that is, our Christian faith, in a language which will be acceptable and understandable to the new Chinese; I fear that my Chinese is not only too rusty, the vocabulary is not of such a nature that I could possibly put anything over at all. While I am all for Mother Teresa, all for silent witnessing, I still do think that within the mission of the Church a vocal rendering of what we intimately believe to be true is necessary and that presupposes a verbal expression to those who listen to you.

Ray Whitehead: I think on that point, though, it would be wrong to jump too quickly into techniques. I mean that sounds like now we're going to language study and get ready again, and I want to avoid that. The point I raised in my paper is that if our activity as Christians made the Chinese and China curious, then we would have the starting point, and I think that's why I would agree with what you were saying. And what kind of activity would make them curious about our Christian faith? It has something to do with how we live within the social structures, the economic structures of the society. And so that in a sense, our mission in China, if you want to use that terminology at all, is really how we are acting and living in relationship to Apartheid and to economic repression in Latin America and to this whole range of problems, and unless there's some clear line of activity there that makes people in China curious about what Christians are, then we don't have the option of a verbal communication; in a sense the judgment is there on us.

Richard Sorich (Consultant to the China Program of the National Council of Churches):
I'd just like to put in a thing here, Ray, on what you were saying about the Chinese watching us. Maybe they'll watch us; we hope that they'll watch us. The ways that I'd like us to communicate to China, and I feel we should be thinking seriously about that and I don't think we are, is to relate not only to questions like Apartheid, but relate to Chinese elsewhere in the world, and not be quite as selective as we may have been in the past in that relationship.

For example, I think there are a whole lot of people in Hong Kong that we should have been relating with long ago, with whom we should have gotten into a dialogue, an interaction, and I think that's true of Chinese elsewhere in the world. I think perhaps, as I mentioned earlier today, there's a diversity in China that we don't perceive or understand, and I think some of that diversity is expressed by Chinese outside of China.

Ray Whitehead: Could you be more specific on that?

Richard Sorich: Well, for example, I think that the people who are in the group that publishes the journal called Yellow River in Hong Kong are people who are worth relating to seriously--listening with humility and seriousness to the things they say. They published a book that you may be aware of, The Story That Moved the Earth to Tears, a series of essays, short stories and poems by former Red guards and others still inside China, which expresses their romantic feelings and shows that at least these people are still very much like other Chinese elsewhere. And I think such activities would expose us to a wider range of understanding about the big China, and I think it would be kind of a training ground for us, a way of starting dialogue that hopefully can eventually take place with the people on the Mainland of China. And I think that they would take an interest in our interactions with Chinese elsewhere.

Jonathan Chao (Dean, China Graduate School of Theology, Hong Kong):
I appreciate the panel's definition of Salvation and the second point of the witness of the Church. I also

appreciate Father Spae's analysis, but I still have an argument with Ray (Whitehead). Father Spae speaks of our witness in the past, in Chinese history, being so weak that the Chinese tended to by-pass us. Still we must communicate Christ to the Chinese people so that they can recognize the content of our communication being of the Spirit, being of Christ. Otherwise we are not going to communicate. From Sister Teresa in India or the Christians in Chinese regions today, by their work and by their words they do manifest that the Spirit of God is in their midst, as individual persons, as communities, so that the sign of the Kingdom is recognizable as of God. Now Ray would suggest that we communicate through participating in liberation or social reform, in Apartheid in South Africa and the like. Now if, as according to your earlier statement, wherever there is liberation and justice, there is the Kingdom of God, I, as a Chinese Christian, cannot recognize your social involvement as being Christian, because any good Confucian can also be involved in social justice. So it does not matter whether the communication stands in act or in word. It must be recognizable as the work of the Spirit to be authentically Christian.

Charles West: What is the characteristic of the work of the Spirit?

Jonathan Chao: Well, there arises from the Christian churches in China this sign of love in the community. And there is the actual experience of Christ and the Holy Spirit in their lives in overcoming difficulties in life, the religious dimension that Tom spoke about last night, and the ability to forgive and to even participate in social reconstruction under its communist government. But still, it is a motive of obedience to Christ.

Charles West: I would add just one point to that: the ability to participate in social reconstruction along with those of another ideology without however conforming one hundred per cent to the demands of that other ideology. In other words, Christians, in the character of their repentance and their witness, are always uncomfortable partners with others because they have another dimension and another Lord.

(Later in the discussion, which had by now been opened to the entire group, Ray Whitehead was asked about the third question before the panel--a theological evaluation of Chinese Marxism or Maoism.)

Ray Whitehead: It seems to me that it is not a question
of a lack of confidence or a lack of faith when one looks
at China with some openness to accomplishments there
under Maoism, but it's the opposite. I think it's a lack
of faith that leads us to deny that something good could
come out of Peking. I mean, if we have the faith and confidence, then we can deal with the realities in a different
way.

I think there's the problem of assessment that I raised
earlier on. What was the cost? I don't think there's
such an easy answer to that--there's a great cost in human
life, a great cost in human freedom if one looks at the
total picture in this regard. If you talked about self-
sacrifice, there were a lot of Maoists who sacrificed
their lives in the struggle for the revolution. I think
that was a factor there. It doesn't seem to me, though,
it's a matter of praising Maoism or seeing this as some
final culmination. It's really a question of whether or
not we can look at what has taken place in China in this
movement, not that this replaces Christianity for us or
that this becomes some kind of Utopian ideal, but to be
able to look honestly at this and discern the power of God
and the movement of the Spirit in things outside of our
realm, that we don't control as Christians, that are outside of our own purview.

I think if we look at the question of social transformation
and individual transformation, it's not a simple process
that works from the outside in. It seems to me it's dialectical; the relationship of self-revolutionization in
China and social revolution is always in a dialectical
tension or dialectical process, so that when you change
the objective you also have to change the subjective world,
and when you change the subjective world you have to change
the objective world. And I think there's something in
that process that's instructive to us as Christians because we tend sometimes to assume that we can change our
subjective world and that that's going to change the
objective world. In other words, if we make everybody
Christian, there won't be any more oppression or problems
of exploitation. That's oversimplifying it, but that is
a theology we've lived with up to this point. There is a
question, there is something to be learned in dialogue--
not that that's the answer, but it certainly will lead to
mutual benefit.

Franklin Woo (Director, China Program, National Council of

Churches):
I would like to address my remarks to Father Spae. The
lesson China is teaching the West is something I hear
echoed both in India and also in the Liberation Theology
of Latin America, and I think it's just the logical next
step to what you're saying which is something like this:
that our theology, as we currently have it, is woefully
inadequate. In basic terms, we've talked here about the
inadequacy of our theology of the Kingdom, of salvation,
God, and person. I hear these other cultures calling upon
us for a radical reassessment of our most basic beliefs,
not simply as a means or a strategy for expressing these
beliefs more accurately, but rather towards a deeper self-
understanding, and then perhaps to begin to share.

Joseph Spae: Well, the last thing I said about the need
for a new Chinese language to express the truths we hold,
that was exactly what I wanted to say. In other words,
language is not simply a grammatical affair; it is the
total content of what we believe presented so that it
could be understood by the people to whom we are talking.
I doubt very much, for instance, whether the Western type
of theological expression with which we have grown up,
which may be legitimate for our own purposes--whether
this is the type we can legitimately bring into India,
China and Japan. It involves major problems of translation into an entirely new language for it to be understood
by them.

Franklin Woo: Do you see this type of theologizing
beginning?

Joseph Spae: Yes. However, I would think (and here, perhaps I would join Ray) even the best possible expression
of what we have to say is only, perhaps, half of the message or even less than half of the total message. By this
I mean that no matter how good our expression is, what we
need most of all is the implementation of the evangelical
values with the view of producing a new human society.
What we say will not be judged on the strength of how
cleverly we say it, but on how cleverly, that is, how
divinely we do it, and I think that at present the challenge of China is simply this: we need to confront the
idea of moral transcendence and moral excellency that has
to become incarnated in, let us say, the new Chinese about
whom you are speaking. We ought to confront this with the
ideal implied in the new life of a Christian. And if,
everything else being equal, the fruits of the tree seem
to be less noble on the Christian side, it is not because

Christianity has not produced them; it is because we are
not good enough Christians. That will be the acid test
for our new Theology.

(The discussion concluded with Theresa Chu (Pro Mundi Vita)
reminding the participants of the special view of change
and revolution in Maoist thought;)
The question of struggle is a very important one, and I
think that it has to be seen in the context of the Chinese
society and Chinese history at the moment when the revolution probably concluded. In other words, even a psychologist would grant a neurotic patient the right to understand
the patient from within, the patient himself. We owe it to
Mao's ideology to look at it from within and in the context of Chinese society. And in that sense, or from Mao's
viewpoint, he shifted his position from gradualism in reform to a revolutionist stance because he felt that the
evil within the structure of Chinese society was big
enough to call for this revolution. In other words,
struggle is in variance with evils which we as Christians
may not see in the social structures of our society or of
Chinese society. In Mao's analysis of the situation at
that time, he saw its evil as such that it drove him
towards the struggle. And concerning Jonathan's example
of Mother Teresa (you know I admire Mother Teresa very
deeply) I think I must caution the good Christians here
that that type of charity is not sufficient from the viewpoint of the Maoist. It is a one-to-one individual
charity, and it is a dispensing of good things from above,
or a partial remedy brought to individuals from outside
themselves. And what the Maoist would appreciate is precisely the transformation of society from within, and
therefore the people themselves have to help themselves
to change.

V – THE NOTRE DAME CHINA CONFERENCE: A PROSPECTIVE EVALUATION

Joseph J. Spae

The Notre Dame Conference on China was a successful venture in more than one respect: (a) It brought some of the finest North American experts on China together for the first time; (b) it revealed, sometimes painfully, the ceiling of our present information and of our theological grasp on the China situation; (c) it reminded us of a plurality of theological views bearing upon our ecumenical togetherness related to China; (d) it called for some practical decisions which would assure the continuity of our work.

In what follows I will summarize some of the important topics discussed and point to some areas in which the thrust generated at Notre Dame could be pursued.

I.   In the theological field.

One of the questions arising in the discussions concerns our recent missionary experience. How do we explain that

    our missionaries, living in the midst of the
    greatest revolutionary upheaval in modern his-
    tory, nowhere refer to that cataclysmic event,

or to the social forces that brought it about;
nor do they point to the need to understand and
relate to such events in the future.[1]

What lessons do we draw from this fact?

The Chinese Christians--and those of the West--
if they are going to serve as the salt and leaven
of society, must practice that kind of self-
giving and responsiveness to divine grace that
will lead to the rediscovery of the Church's
"ultimate identity precisely in that divine self-
emptying through which it first came into existence. It is only in such a perspective, in such
a Church, in such a world--all three being still
in the making--that the legacy of Christendom
and the century of Mao can ever come to be seen
as reconcilable."[2]

What does the above statement imply for the aggiornamento
of the Church in relation to China? In other words, what
is China's role vis-a-vis Christianity at large? I submit that one answer to this question could be this:
Through millions of good, long-suffering people, the Holy
Spirit invited us to a rethinking and restating of our
faith. The Chinese people serve us with a solemn warning
that the tone of our proclamation, past and present, is
too low, and that the force of our witnessing is too
feeble for them to be impressed. Our Christian churches
stand racked and riddled in their divisions. It is
difficult to see them as the community of Christ's disciples. Hence their claim to relevance in Chinese
nation-building is refuted and refused.

Meanwhile, both China and the Church go through a stage
of suffering and purification, the redemptive value of
which the Conference has stressed. For Christianity,
this means that the Chinese people address to us their
logos parakleseos, their silent exhortation which should
contribute to the consolidation of our faith and invites
us not to be entrapped and deprived of our freedom by
some secondhand, empty, rational philosophy based on the
principle of this world rather than on Christ. (See
Colossians 2:7-8.) Maoism is part of God's judgment on
the Church (Isaiah, 10).

One aspect of this judgment leaves Christians no rest.
It is this: the basic reason for China's impermeability

to Christianity may very well be the striking imbalance
between the historical image of the Church and the implementation of the evangelical values in the West with a
view to producing a new and more human society. In the
final instance, China forces us to a confrontation between the ideal of moral excellence as incarnated, at
least theoretically, in "the new Chinese man" and the
same ideal in "the new life of a Christian." In this
context, China plays a prophetic role in regard to the
Church, a role which we humbly record and accept.

The Notre Dame Conference raised a number of theological
questions which rate priority in our China study:

> If Maoism is a complete "ideology" and hence a
> quasi-religion, what does this mean when we com-
> pare it with Christianity, which is both an
> ideology and a religion?

> How do we discern the "redeeming word of God" in
> an avowedly non-theistic culture?

> How do we define private and communal freedom, or
> the lack thereof, as a minimum requirement for
> humane living and, hence, for religious behavior?

> What "freedom" should legitimately be hoped for
> by Christians in a society whose direct concern
> is not with the quality of life but with sheer
> survival?

> To what extent could the Catholic Church practice
> a kenotic attitude towards China as advocated by
> Vatican II in relation to the non-Christian
> religions?

> What is required of Christians, in the light of
> the China situation, by way of rethinking some
> basic theological categories, such as God, Church,
> community, revelation, grace, etc.?

> Granted that a renewal of institutional contact
> with China may become a possibility, what kind of
> pastoral preparation would we wish the Church to
> make so that this contact be orderly and accept-
> able, also from the point of view of the local
> Chinese churches in Taiwan and the diaspora, not
> to mention the remnants of Christianity in

continental China?

How must the present situation in China theologically be seen? Can we speak, not so much
of the "gesta Dei per Sinenses", as of the
"praeambula fidei Sinica?" How do we view these
praeambula in light of God's salvific will for
all mankind?

Domenico Grasso writes: "We believe that Communism, precisely because it has created a more
just society in China, will have prepared the
way of Christianity."[3] How can this statement
be verified from observable facts?

What is meant by the universal relevance of the
Christian faith, as defined by Vatican II, when
one-fifth of all mankind has been barred for
centuries from its proclamation? How is "salvation through Christ" obtained for those who do
not know Him? What do we mean by transcendental
experiences in the Chinese context?

The Conference made frequent reference to "the
signs of the Kingdom," and to "the fruits of the
Spirit." How does one distinguish the existence
of those signs and fruits within the limits of
actual observation in China? With the inbuilt
ambiguity of what they see and hear, how do
theologians discover God's saving action?

The Conference insisted on integration of orthodoxy and orthopraxis. How does theology define
the necessary and acceptable degree of such an
integration?

The Conference stressed the willingness of the
churches to give their help to China whenever
possible. What then are the needs of Maoist
China which the Church feels she could help re-
lieve? Has Maoism perhaps introduced Christian
answers to China's needs by the back door? The
Maoist disregard of Christianity--is it based
on reasons true or false?

If we assume a prophetic role of China vis-a-vis
the Church, which is the prophetic role of the
Church vis-a-vis China?

In what sense could Maoism prepare the Chinese people for an understanding of man which could serve as an introduction to that "veritable humanism" which Paul VI has claimed for Christianity? Is such a humanism possible without a fair degree of personal renewal and liberty of conscience? What do these ideals mean within the Chinese context?

Finally, what would be an ecumenical expression of the basic Christian faith and practice understandable to Maoist-educated people? What are our means of writing it, of bringing it to their attention?

The previous Conferences, and particularly that of Brugge, October 1976, had debated some of these themes or singled them out for further study, and they will be with us for a long time to come. In working them out, care ought to be taken to "do theology" with due regard of what is uniquely Chinese in Chinese Communism. We should also heed the Lutheran criticism of Bastad and Louvain voiced at their Columbus meeting and not deduce a concrete possibility from a hypothesis which is then transformed into a reality.[4]

The Conference repeatedly stressed the need for modesty in our conclusions and remained aware of the monumental ignorance under which we labor. The questions were raised: What would be the real feelings of the Chinese people if they could express them freely? Would these feelings be uniformly anti-Christian and anti-religious as they now are officially said to be? Many participants at Notre Dame would doubt it.

II. In the ecumenical field.

My specific interest in suggesting the Notre Dame Conference was the ecumenical aspect of the China problem. While I am highly appreciative of what the Conference did in the theological field and remain grateful for the ecumenical progress registered at Notre Dame by way of friendship and mutual understanding among the Churches through their participants, I had hoped that more concrete "ecumenical conclusions" might have been reached. Obviously, ecumenism takes time. The following suggestions were voiced at the Conference:

The conscientization of our churches to China should
be carried out, as much as possible, in an ecumenical
way by an interconfessional team.

Fairbank claims that China's repudiation of the
missionary gift worked like a disease in the consciousness of many Americans, infecting the relationship between the countries more than has yet
been assessed. If this be so, there is a common
task for churches in the USA to discuss and remedy
the situation.

We feel the need for an ecumenical in-depth study
of Christianity's approach to China, past, present
and future. Such an approach, in the future, will
require new pastoral, cultural and linguistic
skills.

Better liaison between the Hong Kong, Taiwan,
American and European groups is needed.

The preparation, under the auspices of Christians
in East Asia, of an International Conference which
would bring all China study groups together for
mutual enrichment is of great importance for the
updating of our information, for the ironing out
of our differences, for our future planning, and
for the sake of our ecumenical togetherness.

In line with the above suggestion, it was hoped
that Peter Lee (whose absence from the Conference
was much deplored) could be prevailed upon to report on the feasibility of setting up facilities
at Tao Fong-Shan (Hong Kong) for a small revolving
group of scholars-in-residence, allowing them to
spend some time together at quarters close to the
mainland, and collaborate with him in the preparation of the International Conference mentioned
above.

III.   In the field of continuity.

The real success of the Notre Dame Conference depends on
its search for continuity. It was the wish of all participants that a way be found to continue the ecumenical
venture begun here. To that effect it was suggested:

That an American Catholic university with

theological as well as China studies resources
would be a good base for such continuity. Such
a place could function both as a locale of research and as liaison with other China groups
outside the United States.

That regular meetings be organized between representatives of the China groups to discuss work,
strategy and information.

That we all make an effort to conscientize our
churches to the magnitude of the China problem
and to the ecumenical opportunities which it
offers. Within the Catholic Church, this
effort would certainly be welcomed by the many
religious societies which formerly sent person-
nel to China.

The Notre Dame China Conference, like its predecessors,
has impressed us with what remains to be done. The
Church, before asking China to welcome Christianity
again, must change and purify itself so as to be capable
and worthy of serving this great nation.

NOTES

1. Donald MacInnis, "The People's Republic of China--Challenge to Contemporary Missiology," unpublished manuscript, p. 162.

2. Ibid., p. 170; the quotation is from Fides, April 4, 1974.

3. Michael Chu, ed., The New China, A Catholic Response (New York: Paulist, 1977), p. 113.

4. See the Lutheran World Federation's Marxism and China Information Letter, No. 15.

NOTES ON CONTRIBUTORS

Lawrence J. Burkholder was Director of Church World Service and Director of the National Clearing Committee of the United Nation's Relief and Rehabilitation Administration in China from 1944 to 1948. Victor S. Thomas Professor of Divinity at Harvard University from 1961 to 1970, he is now President of Goshen College, Goshen, Indiana.

Richard C. Bush has served as Director of the Christian Study Centre on Chinese Religion and Culture in Hong Kong and as Professor of Religion and Philosophy at Tunghai University. Currently the Director of the School of Fine Arts and Humanistic Studies at Oklahoma State University, he is the author of Religion in Communist China and Religion in China.

Julia Ching was born in China and has taught at the Australian National University, Columbia University and Yale University. The author of To Acquire Wisdom: The Way of Wang Yang-ming and Confucianism and Christianity, she now teaches at the University of Toronto.

Langdon Gilkey taught at Yenching University before being interned as a prisoner in Shantung from 1943 to 1945. He is presently Shailer Mathews Professor of Theology at the

University of Chicago and among his writings are included
Catholicism Confronts Modernity and Reaping The Whirlwind:
A Christian Interpretation of History.

N. J. Girardot is Assistant Professor of the History of
Religions in the Theology Department at the University of
Notre Dame. The editor and co-editor of two symposia and
several books on the History of Religions and Chinese religion, he has also published articles on the Taoist tradition and other related fields in the History of Religions.

Eric O. Hanson is Assistant Professor of Political Science
at the University of Santa Clara. He has studied at Fu
Jen and National Taiwan Universities and received his
doctorate from Stanford University. He is currently doing
research on Catholic Church policy in Asia under a Walsh-
Price Fellowship.

Yu-ming Shaw was born in China and received his doctorate
from the University of Chicago. Assistant Professor of
History at the University of Notre Dame, he has authored
many articles on Chinese intellectual history and is
presently completing a biography of Rev. John Leighton
Stuart.

Joseph J. Spae is the founder of Oriens Institute for
Religious Research in Tokyo and former General Secretary
of Sodepax (the ecumenical Committee on Society, Development and Peace) in Rome and Geneva. The author of several
books on Japan and Christianity, he is actively engaged
in the Buddhist-Christian encounter.

Laurence J. Thompson was born and raised in China and has
spent many years in Asia with the Foreign Service, the Asia
Foundation and Taiwan National University. The author of
a number of works on Chinese religion and thought and on
the early history of Taiwan, he is Professor of East Asian
Languages and Cultures at the University of Southern
California.

Donald W. Treadgold is chairman of the Department of History
at the University of Washington and President of the
American Association for the Advancement of Slavic Studies.
He is the author of a two volume work, The West in Russia
and China and has also edited Soviet and Chinese Communism:
Similarities and Differences.

Charles C. West, a missionary in China from 1947 to 1950,

is Stephen Colwell Professor of Christian Ethics at Princeton Theological Seminary. He has written many books, among
them <u>Christian Witness in Communist China</u>.

James D. Whitehead is a pastoral theologian who worked in
Korea from 1964 to 1967 and is currently involved in research on Chinese Buddhism. A consultant in education and
ministry, he has authored, with Evelyn Eaton Whitehead,
<u>Christian Life Patterns: Psychological Challenges and
Religious Invitations in Adult Life</u>.

Raymond L. Whitehead lived and worked in Hong Kong from
1961 to 1976. He is Director of the Canada China Programme
of the Canadian Council of Churches and teaches social
ethics in the Toronto School of Theology. He is the author
of <u>Love and Struggle in Mao's Thought</u>.